Boys and Girls

Learn Differently!

Boys and Girls Learn Differently!

A GUIDE FOR TEACHERS AND PARENTS

Michael Gurian

and

Patricia Henley

with Terry Trueman

JOSSEY-BASS
A Wiley Company
San Francisco

Jossey-Bass books and products are available through most bookstores. To contact Jossey-Bass directly, call (888) 378-2537, fax to (800) 605-2665, or visit our website at www.josseybass.com.

Substantial discounts on bulk quantities of Jossey-Bass books are available to corporations, professional associations, and other organizations. For details and discount information, contact the special sales department at Jossey-Bass.

Printed in the United States of America.
Book design by Ralph L. Fowler.

Library of Congress Cataloging-in-Publication Data

Gurian, Michael.
    Boys and girls learn differently : A Guide for Teachers and Parents / Michael Gurian and Patricia Henley with Terry Trueman. —1st ed.
        p. cm.
    Includes bibliographical references and index.
    ISBN 0-7879-5343-1 (alk. paper)
        1. Sex differences in education —United States Case studies. 2. Educational change — United States —Case studies. I. Henley, Patricia, date. II. Trueman, Terry. III. Title.
    LC212.92 .G87 2000
    370.15'1 —dc21   00-011519

FIRST EDITION
HB Printing   10 9 8 7 6 5 4 3 2 1

To Gail, Gabrielle, and Davita Gurian

*To the boys and girls in preschool through twelfth grade,
and to Bob Henley*

To Patty Nasburg and Jesse Trueman

*and to the students who have kept us young and interested and
truly involved in learning and teaching*

ACKNOWLEDGMENTS

The authors wish to gratefully acknowledge both the editing and production staff at Jossey-Bass. First and foremost, thanks are due Alan Rinzler, one of the finest editors in the business. It is an honor to work with a person of his caliber, and to work also with his colleagues, Leslie Iura, Amy Scott, Lasell Whipple, Alison Wong, and so many others. Special thanks are also extended to Debra Hunter, whose confidence in this work has made it possible. Without Susan Schulman, our literary agent, this book would not have found a smooth course. Thanks to her and her staff as well.

Many thanks to all the teachers around the world who have made this project possible. Special thanks go to the teachers and administrators of these school districts in Missouri and Kansas:

Grandview, Missouri

Hickman Mills, Missouri

Independence, Missouri

Kansas City, Kansas

Park Hill, Missouri

St. Joseph, Missouri

Special thanks to the superintendents of these districts, who adjusted their own and their district's busy schedules to plan and implement the Michael Gurian Institute in Kansas City, Missouri: Gayden

Carruth, Dan Colgan, Jerry Cooper, Ray Daniels, John Martin, David Rock, and Robert Watkins.

This book simply could not have been written without the leadership of these individuals and their staff, and the participation of the teachers in the actual daily occupations of the institute. Unfortunately, the teachers are too many to name, but each has our thanks, and many appear in the pages of this book.

Deepest thanks go also to Russell Thompson, Susan Anderson, Rita Shapiro, Jerry Cooper, and Michael Boothe, the staff of the Missouri Center for Safe Schools, who gave their consistent support and leadership. Administrative assistant Rose Ford went beyond expectations to complete this project—thank you, Rose!

Among the Spokane, Washington, staff, we give special thanks to Stacie Wachholz, who is administrative assistant extraordinaire. Her contributions have been enormous. Many thanks also to Sister Mary Eucharista, Abe Wenning, Sara Stoker, Kristi Harju, and Marie Graham, as well as Nate and Katherine and the other student assistants and research assistants who contributed so wisely to this book.

CONTENTS

PART TWO
CREATING THE ULTIMATE CLASSROOM
FOR BOTH BOYS AND GIRLS
69

Boys and Girls
Learn Differently!

INTRODUCTION

Almost twenty years ago, I went with two friends, whose first child was three, to a preschool–day care center. Jennifer's mom, Emily, wanted to return to work part-time. There was a preschool about two miles from the house. I had no children yet and was not married, but I certainly was curious—a young man in graduate school who had been, over the preceding three years, both delighted and confused by this new little person in my good friends' lives. At times, of course, I had even been jealous of the girl. I had lost my friends to her and was too young to realize that soon my own children and I would become lost to others as well.

Truthfully, I knew almost nothing about kids at that time—twenty-four years old—except what I'd picked up from being one, and what I had learned about human development in college and graduate school. I had never set foot in a preschool (except perhaps as a small child). I was only going along because of the coincidence of Frank and Emily's car being out of commission; they needed me to drive them to the preschool in my beat-up red Opel.

We arrived that morning just after ten, at a front door painted blue with a red clown face staring out. Beyond the door were the squeals of many children, a few cries, the sound of adult voices. It was a sunny spring day. In the backyard were calls and squeals as well—all sounding alike as young boys' and girls' voices do—of children having a great time.

Once we got inside the foyer and then the large living room play area, the sounds of the children were still all the same, but what we saw was amazingly different. The boys were mainly congregated around an area of plastic blocks with a raised plastic climbing contraption in many colors. They were building something, climbing, and throwing. The girls, on the other hand, were congregated near a doorway to another room, most of them holding a doll or stuffed animal under an arm, telling each other something about how the veterinary hospital would work, who would be the doctor, the nurse, which animals would come in first. The great contrast between these two groups of children startled me—not just because it was inherently intriguing, but because it seemed so "natural."

As we toured the place, we went to the backyard, in which again we saw the boys doing one thing and the girls another. The girls congregated in one section of play equipment talking to each other, a few of the girls still holding a stuffed animal, while the boys were throwing and kicking a somewhat flat basketball.

We continued our tour of the preschool, Frank and Emily asked questions, the teacher guiding them asked questions. One of the girls came up to Jennifer, staring at her, smiling, then walked past.

When we left the preschool, Frank and Emily debriefed each other while I drove. Back at their house, Frank, who had just finished his M.Ed. program, said, "Fits the research, those kids, did you notice? Different gender groups. Socialized already to separate from each other. Amazing. Getting an androgynous classroom is going to take a while, given all the cultural pressure on boys and girls to be so different from each other."

Emily, who had been a teacher and would soon return to that world, agreed: "The power of the society to shape our children is truly something. Every class I have it's like that. It was like that in all the European countries we lived in." (She was raised a military brat, her father posted all over the world.)

A wonderful and rousing discussion ensued in which, in the end, we all agreed that our intense cultural socialization was ruining our kids, ultimately creating war and distress, oppressing women and repressing men, and potentially ruining Jennifer. For a number of reasons that included the starkness of boy-girl difference at the preschool, Emily and Frank decided to look at other options for their daughter.

For my part, I walked away from the experience having stumbled onto something that, over the next two decades, would change my life: a strange, hidden sense that what was going on with those children needed further exploration—a compulsion to push myself beyond where our academic thinking was in regard to nature and nurture. Frank's M.Ed. program and my own graduate school taught almost nothing about nature, the brain, hormones. This did not satisfy me. I had lived overseas as a child, including two years in India. Whether on the Asian continent, in the Middle East, in Europe, or in the Americas, I felt the tug of nature in human relations, a tug that seemed to me far more essential in shaping me and everyone around me than contemporary Western culture wanted to admit.

That morning with Frank and Emily was a watershed moment of personal and professional consciousness. It needed many years of thought, research, and study. For the last two decades, I have been researching and applying information and material from around the world, first to learn why in Jennifer's potential preschool there was such glaring contrast between the boys and the girls, and second to find out how learning the answer to that question could help me and others shape the lives of children.

Frank and Emily and I are no longer in touch, but my morning with them now comes fully to fruition in this book. Without denying the profound influence of culture on a child, *Boys and Girls Learn Differently!* presents the even deeper *natural* layer of why boys and girls learn differently and how educators, parents, and all concerned can use that information to create the ultimate classroom for *both* boys and girls. It is by expanding our understanding of male-female difference that we can show all children the vast potential of their lives in the educational world.

Brain-Based Research

In the 1990s, brain-based research came into its own. We've learned so much about the brain it is dizzying. There's a great deal we don't know about this organ—the only physical organ in the known universe that can contemplate itself—but we know so much that now, to walk into a classroom or home without knowledge of both how the brain works and how the male and female brains learn differently is to be many steps behind where we can and should be as teachers, parents, and caregivers of children. This book is dedicated to bringing the crucial sciences of this research to educators and parents in a way that will inspire our schools, homes, and culture to do the best for our kids.

Although children are shaped by our cultural environment, this culture did not arise in a vacuum. It is the result of a history of neural responses to natural surroundings and processes. Culture is the result of the strivings, both timorous and excessive, of nature, especially "neural nature": the human brain, about which teachers and parents want to know so much more. My coauthors and I have a passion to integrate understanding of culture and nature in the lives of children.

As you read, much of what we know about the brain itself—the subject of Part One of this book—will match your grandparents' intuitions, but some will not. All of it is intriguing; most of all, each new piece of knowledge generated by brain-based research inspires new innovations in the care and education of our children. In this book, we have brought together three primary points of view on brain-based research:

1. Neurological and endocrinological (hormonal) effects on learning and behavior
2. Developmental psychology, especially the effects of natural human development cycles on learning and behavior
3. Gender-difference research, that is, research comparing both environmental and neurobiological areas of differences (and similarities) between boys and girls

Whenever we refer to *brain-based research* in this book, we are referring to the coalescence of these three fields.

In addition, I've studied thirty cultures to make sure the conclusions presented in this book have sound validity around the world. Nothing is included here that has not been corroborated multiculturally.

Because our children need us to know their minds so we can be better teachers and caregivers for them, I've focused attention in Chapters One and Two on knowledge that can be easily applied to classrooms, day cares, homes, and other child learning environments. My experience has led me to believe that the early part of the new millennium is truly going to be the Age of Innovation. We have available to us far more freedom to innovate, and much more capacity to follow through, than human beings have ever had.

Teachers, parents, and caregivers all around us are making innovations every day that each of us can use, if only we know about them. We have available to us far more biological and neurological information about how our children actually learn—and learn best—than ever before. Part One lays out the brain-based foundation, so to speak, for innovations that teachers and caregivers are already applying around the world. Many of these innovations are then offered for your use in Part Two, where we watch how brain-based research can be practically applied and innovatively used to create the ultimate classroom for both boys and girls.

Creating the "Ultimate Classroom"

A teacher at a training I was doing a few years ago raised her hand. "These brain-based innovations and this vision you're laying out to us here," she said, "is really interesting material, but in a few hours we're just getting fragments. Would you please write a *practical* book that gives these details for all grades in a student's school life? Many of us will teach different years of kids. It's time someone brought it all together to help us, from preschool until the student graduates." I felt she was right, and I hope Part Two of this book fulfills that request.

Part Two is grounded in real and usable teacher innovations. Based on information about brain itself, as well as biological and cultural similarities and differences in boys' and girls' learning, Chapters Three through Six show how to set up and alter learning environments, at school and at home, to fit both the similar and dissimilar needs of boys and girls.

Part Two of the book is not a general or theoretical statement on educational reform; there are more than enough of those in print. Part Two is a *practical blueprint* you can use to make not just an effective classroom but "the ultimate classroom." The blueprint helps teachers, parents, and caregivers identify their strengths and weaknesses as teachers of boys and girls, as well as recognize the successful and unsuccessful elements of a learning environment. It is based in *actual teachers' experiences.* Although the bulk of the book directly applies to classrooms in school environments, parents, grandparents, and other caregivers will discover that much, if not most, of it applies to their lives as "teachers" of children. I hope parents and others substitute themselves for the word *teacher* when reading this, for parents and other caregivers are teachers too. To help in this effort, at the end of each chapter in Part Two we've also included tips specifically for non-professional educators, under the general-purpose list heading "Tips for Parents."

The blueprint this book offers does not generally call for major upheaval in teaching practices, but rather, innovation at intricate levels that end up changing the life of a teacher (again, broadly understood) and, ultimately, a child. When it *does* call for major upheaval, I hope it will be one with which you'll ultimately agree.

The Gurian Institute at the University of Missouri-Kansas City

The biological and neurological information in this book comes from a number of sources listed in the Notes and the Additional Resources that end the book. This material, however, would be dry science if it were not immediately put to work in classrooms. At the University of Missouri-Kansas City, we have been doing just that.

The Michael Gurian Institute has been a learning environment in which teachers from Missouri school districts, from preschool educators through high school, apply the best of the new science in their everyday classrooms and share results with other teachers. These teachers have been trained in how boys and girls learn differently and have developed innovations to fit their new knowledge. (The Michael Gurian Institute, www.gurianinstitute.com, now provides these trainings internationally.)

These teachers have helped develop the blueprint for "ultimate education" in this book. The blueprint we provide has already had success in their schools and school districts. It is for that reason that we have had the confidence to report it in this book. In the Hickman Mills School District in Kansas City, discipline problems were cut by 35 percent within six months of teacher training in how boys and girls learn differently. In the St. Joseph School District in St. Joseph, Missouri, results of the training astounded Superintendent of Schools Dan Colgan.

> We focused the Gurian Institute training on one school, Edison Elementary, headed by Principal Debbie Murphy, who took the helm at Edison in 1993 with the difficult job of improving an elementary school that had consistently tested at the lowest ends of the academic spectrum. Debbie applied a number of core training models, culminating in an immersion of her key staff in the Gurian Institute in the 1999–2000 school year.
>
> Something amazing happened as a result of this training.
>
> Edison, which had previously tested at the bottom of eighteen District elementary schools, now tested in the top five slots, sometimes in first and second. Statewide, Edison outscored state data in every subject area, sometimes doubling or tripling the number of students in the top achievement levels. Instead of the usual large number of children at the bottom end of achievement testing at Edison, there were now only two who would require state-mandated retesting. Two failing students out of 400 total students in the school is the best number we've yet achieved. We've also seen a drastic drop in discipline problems.
>
> Principal Murphy told me, "I used to have pages and pages of failure and discipline reports on my desk. That has changed." She was also amazed to notice that the difference in gender-specific discipline and academic failure reports—boys generally make up the larger

number of discipline and academic failures than girls—.
Discipline problems had dramatically declined, the disci
not as wide between the genders, and now both boys and &
performing at the top academic levels in our state.

   We believe the Gurian Institute training in the specific lear
styles of boys and girls, and in gender-specific teacher, student, &
parent bonding strategies, were so effective that we now have tool
educators to fully educate all our students. This training has change
the way we do the business of education in St. Joseph.

This book could not have been written if not for the hundreds of teachers who have been involved in this pilot process. Most of the innovations, anecdotes, and classroom blueprints we share with you in this book were given to us by people doing the very teaching work you are doing, in whatever form you do it. Our acknowledgment of them and thanks to them cannot be overdone. Because of them, you are not reading a book of secondary research; you are reading and applying a resource for real innovation that works!

   The ultimate classroom is generally thought of as taking place in a school setting, so most of the innovations in this book apply to teachers. Often my coauthors and I speak directly to teachers in order to help them. At the same time, anyone giving care to a child—whether a parent, a grandparent, a day care provider, or a policy maker—will find a wealth of material here to help make any environment the ultimate classroom. Brain-based research and our own Missouri study have taught us that the child's classroom exists *in every setting the child steps foot in;* thus, we are all teachers.

Boys and Girls Learn Differently

A primary area of concern for nearly every teacher is the differences we each intuit in the males and females we teach. We all know that there is immense overlap between the genders, and that each child is an inherently sacrosanct individual not to be limited by a gender stereotype, but we also know that *boys and girls learn differently right before our eyes.*

As teachers, we are the leaders of classrooms filled not just with students or kids but with boys and girls. When we were in graduate school, or in teacher certification programs, or wherever it is that we learned how to teach, we did so on the premise that each student is an individual. This was good learning, and to a great extent it makes us the good teachers we are today. But it lacked a component that we sorely miss the longer we actually teach in the classroom: it lacked sensitivity and clarity about what individual *girls* need and what individual *boys* need.

Boys and Girls Learn Differently! is rich in insight and the particulars of practical innovation for teaching girls and boys in areas where each is weak and each is strong, each is vulnerable and each is dominant. I could not have written it without the help of my coauthors. I cannot thank them enough.

Patricia Henley and Terry Trueman

Each of the three authors contributing to this book has a passion for the learning process and the care of children. I have been blessed to know Patricia Henley, an assistant research professor at the University of Missouri-Kansas City; she has been a school superintendent, principal, vice principal, and classroom teacher for over twenty years. She is a professor at UMKC, a former director of the Missouri Center for Safe Schools, and also the director of the University Academy in Kansas City. Without Patricia, this book could not have been written. Though I actually wrote the book, Pat provided stewardship of the classroom research process for the Gurian Institute study that made Part Two possible.

Patricia brings a wealth of professional expertise and wisdom, as well as clarity about the specific needs of girls; she has paid special attention to them in her decades of research and teaching. I am the father of two daughters, and thus instinctively attentive to girls' issues; but I am also the author of nine books in male development. Thus my research has focused more on boys than girls. Patricia makes sure our work is gender-balanced.

I have also been privileged to know Terry Trueman, who has taught for nearly thirty years in mainstream and special education in Washington state and overseas. His help in culling through material, creating tables and graphs for brain-based research, and understanding special education has been invaluable.

Patricia, Terry, and I have committed ourselves to bringing you a preschool-to-college blueprint of innovations that constitute the ultimate classroom. We hope you find the blueprint useful and a spur to new dialogue; and we hope you'll write us with your comments, your questions, and your innovations.

January 2001   Michael Gurian
Spokane, Washington

How Boys and Girls
Learn Differently

Our brain has always defined the education profession, yet educators haven't really understood it or paid much attention to it. . . . Our brain is at the edge of understanding itself!

—ROBERT SYLWESTER, *A Celebration of Neurons*

Males and females are equal in their common membership of the same species, humankind, but to maintain that they are the same in aptitude, skill or behavior is to build a society based on a biological and scientific lie.

—ANNE MOIR AND DAVID JESSEL, *Brain Sex*

How the Brain Learns

Inherent Differences Between Boys and Girls

> Boys and girls are different, and that's the truth. When I was a young teacher this thing started of saying they weren't different, and I kept my mouth shut, but I raised three kids of my own and I taught hundreds and I just didn't believe what I was hearing. Now I'm so glad we're all talking about the differences between boys and girls again.
>
> —NANCY LYNN, TEACHER FOR ALMOST FORTY YEARS

NANCY LYNN TAUGHT NEARLY EVERY GRADE IN HER THIRTY-EIGHT-YEAR career. We met her when she was a "retired" volunteer ("I'm retired but busier at school than ever!"), providing reading tutorials and coteaching learning disability classes. She was a small, thin woman of sixty-nine whom the kids called "Mrs. Lynn," never "Nancy." Though tiny in stature, she commanded respect, and she moved among her students with grace and confidence.

She spoke the words with which this chapter begins at a teacher training. "I'm not too old to keep learning," she told us. Nancy was a kind of leader at the training. She told us some poignant stories.

She told us about a boy who just couldn't sit still. To help him stop getting in trouble constantly for his fidgeting, she decided to ask him to run errands for her. This gave him something to do. She told us about another boy whom she could barely manage in fourth grade. He was overly aggressive and often angry. One day on the playground, the class discovered a dead squirrel. This boy bent to the squirrel, held it a moment, and looked (untypical for him) very tender. Nancy let him hold it; she talked to him and asked him to lead the burial service.

"He was so different after that day," she recalled. "He felt so bad for the squirrel. I think he understood life better after that and became a better boy. He just needed to see how things really were in the world around him. He needed to see what that aggression, which he sure had a lot of, really does in the world. My role was not just to teach him reading, writing, and 'rithmetic. My job was to help teach the boy in him how to be a good young man."

She told us about a seventh-grade girl whose father had died during the summer. The girl, very bright, was underachieving. In Nancy's words: "She was just sort of disappearing into herself, not participating anymore, letting her grades fall." Nancy decided one day to drive her home from school herself and try to become close. Nancy ended up becoming a friend of the family and helping the girl not only achieve again but also work through her grief. Nancy was practicing an intuitive, early version of what we now refer to as raising a child's self-esteem and making sure a girl doesn't lose her voice. In Nancy's words, "Sometimes girls are very fragile and need a special kind of attention. Girl attention."

Coming from someone of so much experience, these stories opened the door to other comments at the training. Some of the parents and teachers who had not wanted to talk strenuously about male-female difference felt more courage to do so.

"Boys and girls are so different," said a parent of four. "They just come out of the womb that way. I had two of each, and I started out thinking they'd be the same. They weren't."

"I've taught twenty years," said another teacher, "and if I've learned anything it's that while boys and girls are the same in lots of ways, they are definitely different. Every year I change the way I teach just to accommodate that one fact."

Parents and teachers like these have seen the whole gamut of changing theories in education. Teachers like Nancy Lynn are a joy to talk to, for many reasons. They carry the very energy and history of our culture in their hearts, minds, and memories, reminding us that education has always held out to us a vast banquet of possibilities. Nancy inspired the workshop by reminding us that educators do not have to limit their thinking to be effective.

For more than a decade, I have been asking these two questions at teacher trainings and seminars: "When you were being trained to be a teacher, how many of you were offered a class in the *actual development of the student's brain?*" and "How many of you were offered a class in the *developmental differences* between the way a *boy's brain* works and a *girl's brain* works?"

Generally, about 10–20 percent of the attendees raise their hands in answer to the first question. To the second, usually no hands go up. As the day of training proceeds, all of us come to agreement that for too many decades, biological information about the development of a child's brain, as well as the crucial differences between male and female brain development, has been fragmentary, incomplete, and sometimes nonexistent. This state of educational training has brought real harm to our educational culture. We are walking into classrooms unprepared to do our jobs. We are putting boys and girls together in classrooms and a system of education that is unprepared to deal with who these children really are.

In this chapter, we present some of the newest and freshest research into the brain, brain similarities, and male-female brain differences. As you read much of this information, you will probably say to yourself, "Oh yeah, I guess I knew that." But a lot of it will startle you; then, when you sit back and notice the ideas and facts at work among your students, we hope you will say, "A-ha, so that's why such-and-such happens," or "OK, so now I see how to make my classroom even better."

The Wide Spectrum of Gender in the Brain

As you master this material, we hope you will check the research by keeping your own journal of observations. For a month or so, mark down "gender experiences" you see in your classroom, or home, or wherever it is that you are a teacher of children ("Today Jimmy did such-and-such." "Today Heather said something that . . ."). A detailed journal generally corroborates most of the brain-based research we lay out in this chapter, and it leads to new insight into how you can interact with these male and female brains.

At the same time, you will discover many exceptions to what we say. Brain development is best understood as a spectrum of development rather than two poles, female and male. Many of the children you have contact with lean toward the female extreme on their brain development spectrum, many others toward the male. Mainly, your girls lean toward the female and boys toward the male, but you will notice some boys at the female end and some girls at the male. You will also notice a number of "bridge brains." These are boys and girls who possess nearly equal qualities of both the male and female brains. They are, in a sense, the bridge between male and female cultures because their brains are the most "bi-gender."

The material of this chapter should not be used to stereotype or limit males and females, because each child is an individual. Rather, it should be used to *add* wisdom to the individuality already assumed in every human. Of course, difference is not evidence of gender superiority or inferiority in general. There are some things boys tend to be better at than girls, and vice versa. There is a skill superiority already built into general male and female brain development. But this in no way means there is an inherent male or female superiority in moral or social terms. Unfortunately, when it was discovered, a hundred years ago, that the male brain was 10 percent larger physically than the female, some neuroscientists of that time proclaimed, "You see, this corroborates what we've said all along: men are smarter than women." Interpretations like this can make all of us a little afraid of saying that boys and girls learn differently because their brains are different.

Nonetheless, we certainly hope this chapter helps you become fearless in pursuit of the wisdom inherent in brain difference. Camilla Benbow, a researcher at the University of Iowa, has studied more than a million schoolchildren to discover how reliable the early findings on the reality of brain differences really were. She discovered marked, sex-different approaches and attitudes to learning and living between boys and girls for which she initially sought explanation in one or more overriding cultural events or social experiences. Benbow, and most researchers like her, started doing their research twenty years ago, when searching for sociological reasons for male-female difference was the accepted practice. Benbow ended up with this result: "After fifteen years of looking for an environmental explanation and getting zero results, I gave up." The differences, she discovered, were in the brain, with culture playing an important part but not the defining role that many people have wished to believe.

Other researchers, notably Laurie Allen at UCLA, have discovered actual structural differences in the brain. Still others, such as Ruben Gur at the University of Pennsylvania, have discovered functional differences using positronic emission tomography (PET) scans. Their research has been corroborated all over the world. The best primary text we know of for getting a whole picture (on a worldwide scale) of brain-based gender differences is *Brain Sex*, by Anne Moir and David Jessel.

In the end, what all of us in this field have discovered is that once brain difference becomes real for those who teach children, a number of doors to better education open. Let's open some of them now and walk through. True equality of education occurs, we will discover, as each teacher embraces the fact that we need to know more about how the brain in general learns, and how boys' and girls' brains learn differently.

How the Brain Works

How does the brain actually work? Our answer to this question is far more complete than it was two decades ago, but it is a long way from finished. One might just as well attempt to fully describe how the planet works, how our solar system works, or how the universe works, for the brain is no less complex, fascinating, and mysterious than these other things are. In describing and graphically illustrating the workings of the brain, we must leave out more than we put in. For the purposes of this book, we strive to include all the areas where there is, ultimately, some difference between male and female brains.

Every human brain has one hundred billion neurons (as many cells as there are stars in the Milky Way), and one hundred trillion glial, or connecting, cells. An adult human brain is eight pounds of dense matter in three major layers: the cerebrae cortex at the top; the limbic system in the middle; and the brain stem at the bottom, connecting with the spinal cord. Historically, for more than two million years, the brain has grown from the bottom up, the upper limbic system and the four lobes of the cerebrae cortex (neocortex for short) developing later than the lower limbic and the brain stem.

In general, the three layers of the brain are known for distinct functions (though all functioning areas of the brain constantly interact). The brain stem is where fight-or-flight responses are harbored. When we're in an immediate crisis, we often feel our instincts take over. It happens in the brain stem. This most primitive part of our brain is essential for our survival.

Our limbic system is generally where emotion is processed. A sensory stimulant comes into the brain through our eyes, ears, skin, or other organs, and we experience an emotive response to it; the immediate sensual and emotive response resides, to a great extent, in the limbic system in the middle of the brain. Although some aggressive responses are brain-stem responses, others come from the limbic system as well—specifically from the amygdala, which lies at the bottom of the limbic system, just above the brain stem.

The four lobes at the top of the brain are generally where thinking occur. In each lobe, different sensory stimulants are also processed. Certain cortices in the top of the brain (for instance, the prefrontal cortex) handle the majority of our moral and other decision making. The top of the brain is divided between the left and the right hemisphere. The left is primarily associated with verbal skills—speaking, reading, and writing—and the right is primarily associated with spatial skills, such as measuring, perceiving direction, and working with blocks or other objects.

When we are teaching a child the higher-order content of a novel, or how to do math, we are generally speaking to the top of the brain, though emotional responses often mix in, especially if the student has an emotional reaction to the content of a book or lesson. In this way, the neocortex and the limbic system work together.

An example of an emotional reaction is "I feel sympathy for Hester Prynne" or, less obviously, "I can't do this, it's too hard." Either way, the emotive response in the limbic system can slow down or shut off most thinking in the top of the brain, depending on how tough the emotional moment is. In neurological terms, a child who thinks she can't do it might fulfill her own thinking: during the crisis of esteem her blood flow remains heavily in the middle of the brain, not moving up to the thinking centers. When we tell a child to "think before you act," we are actually saying, "Redirect your blood flow from the limbic system, and even from the brain stem, to the top of the brain before you act."

We may never understand all of the machinations, functions, and potentials of our brain. It is not our purpose here to try. Our goal should be to look at what we *do* know about how the brain learns and what we are discovering about the important differences in how male and female brains operate. By taking these first, tentative steps toward understanding, we can help our children become comfortably and fully themselves—accepting their differences, celebrating their natural strengths, and aiding them in compensating for their natural weaknesses. Table 1.1 shows the similarities and differences between the male and female brain.

How Boys' and Girls' Minds Are Different

There are a number of categories of male-female difference to consider. We present some of these expositionally, while including two tables by which to make an even deeper comparison. There are many differences we could present, but we have preselected those that seem most essential to learning strategies. You'll find that each category contains mainly highlights of what appears in the tables.

Developmental and Structural Differences

In most cases, and in most aspects of developmental chronology, girls' brains mature earlier than boys'. An example is in the myelination of the brain. One of the last steps in the brain's growth to adulthood occurs as

TABLE 1.1

BRAIN GENDER DIFFERENCES

PART OF BRAIN	FUNCTION	SIMILARITIES AND DIFFERENCES	IMPACT
Amygdala	Part of limbic system involved in emotional processing	Larger in males	Helps make males more aggressive
Arcuate fasciculus	Curving bundle of nerve fibers in the central nervous system	Likely develops earlier in girls as evidenced by their earlier speech capabilities	Females speak in sentences earlier than males do
Basal ganglia	Control movement sequences when necessary, e.g., walking	Likely to engage more quickly in male brain—when required	Males generally quicker to respond to attention demands in physical environment
Brain stem	Connects brain to spinal cord; handles primitive drives	Male brain at rest here to greater extent	Faster, immediate, and physical crisis response moves data to brain stem more quickly
Broca's area	Motor area for speech; processes grammatical structures and word production	More highly active in females	Improved verbal communication skills in females
Cerebellum	Contains neurons that connect to other parts of the brain and spinal cord and facilitate smooth, precise movement; balance; and speech	Stronger connecting pathways in female brain between brain parts	Females have superior language and fine-motor skills; males less intuitive, as fewer parts of brain involved in tasking

PART OF BRAIN	FUNCTION	SIMILARITIES AND DIFFERENCES	IMPACT
Cerebral cortex	Contains neurons that promote higher intellectual functions and memory, and interprets sensory impulses	Thicker in males on the right side of brain; thicker in females on the left side	Males tend to be right-brain dominant; females tend to be left-brain dominant
Cerebrum	Upper or main part of the brain, largest part of human brain, controls conscious and voluntary processes; the thinking center	Females use more volume and particular areas to do same tasks	Greater capacity to multitask in females; female cerebrum always active
Corpus callosum	Connects two hemispheres of the brain	Larger in females	Helps females coordinate two sides of brain better
Dopamine	An intermediate biochemical product in the synthesis of norepinephrine, epinephrine, and melanin; neurotransmitter	In healthy brains, few differences known between male and female patterns	Problems in dopamine and other select neurotransmitters a likely cause of brain disorders more prevalent in males, such as schizophrenia and autism
Estrogen	Several female sex hormones that cause estrus; shapes female brain	Much more present in females than males	In females lowers aggression, competition, self-assertion, self-reliance
Frontal lobe	Facilitates speech, thought, and emotion; produces neurons for skilled movement	Likely more highly active in females	Improved verbal communication skills in females

(continued)

PART OF BRAIN	FUNCTION	SIMILARITIES AND DIFFERENCES	IMPACT
Hippocampus	Ridge along the lower section of each lateral ventricle of the brain; memory storage	Significant difference in size; larger in females; number and speed of neuron transmissions higher in females	Increased memory storage in females
Hypothalamus	Controls automatic body processes (heart beat, breathing, temperature); also controls sexuality differences	Female and male cell structures and patterns significantly different; denser in males, less dense in females	Males greater and more constant sex drive
Left hemisphere	Processes language in most people; reading, writing, math, verbal thoughts and memory, temporal, sequential language, linguistic consciousness, conscious self-image, defense mechanisms, projection, self-deception, denial	Usually better developed in the female brain; creates superiority at language tasks	Females superior at listening, communicating, all language-based learning
Limbic system	Amygdala, septal nucleus, hypothalamus, pleasure principle, hippocampus, memory, emotions	Female brain at rest here to greater extent	Moves sensory data up the neocortex more rapidly
Medulla Oblongata	Widening continuation of the spinal cord, forming the lowest part of the brain and containing nerve centers that control breathing and circulation	Likely increase in male brain-stem functioning implies stronger relationship to connections between medulla oblongata and resting male brain	Possible increase in SIDS death in males could be explained by this relationship; increased male aggression

PART OF BRAIN	FUNCTION	SIMILARITIES AND DIFFERENCES	IMPACT
Melatonin	Hormone produced by the pineal body; lightens skin pigmentation, inhibits estrus; secretion inhibited by sunlight	Likely higher concentration, at times, in females	May be partial explanation of females' increased sensitivity to bright light
Neocortex	Thin, gray outer layer of the brain's cortex; associated with human thought and higher intelligence	Difference in basic size of brain affects amount of brain material (male brains have greater mass)	Basic kinds of intelligence likely influenced by these differences
Neurotransmitters	Biochemical substances that transmit or inhibit nerve impulses at a synapse; deliver messages from one neuron to the next; vitally important in brain functioning	Some neurotransmitters more prevalent in males, some in females	Clearly affect differences in how male and female brains process data
Occipital lobe	Detects and interprets visual images	Differences evident in divergent responses to light sensitivity	Females see better in lower light; males see better in brighter light
Oxytocin	Hormone of the posterior pituitary gland; increases contractions of the smooth muscle of the uterus and facilitates secretion of milk	Much more functionally present in females than males	Likely involved in mother-child bonding capacity being increased at birth

(continued)

PART OF BRAIN	FUNCTION	SIMILARITIES AND DIFFERENCES	IMPACT
Parietal lobe	Perceives and interprets bodily sensations such as touch, pressure, pain, and temperature	In females, more data move through than in males; male brain better at "zoning out"	Females have more tactile sensitivity
Peptids	Brain chemicals; group of compounds formed from two or more amino acids; cortisol and endorphins	Same compounds exist in male and female, but significantly different levels among peptides	Low cortisol levels lead to feelings of euphoria; high cortisol levels can lead to despair
Pituitary gland	Secretes hormones influencing growth, metabolism, and activity of other glands	Likely more strongly or directly relates fight-or-flight data from hypothalamus to endocrine gland system in males	Males' fight or flight more rapidly engaged
Progesterone	Steroid hormone of the corpus luteum, active in preparing the uterus for fertilized ovum	Much more functional and present in females	Primarily to promote conditions for healthy pregnancy
Right hemisphere	Interprets emotional contents; tone of voice; facial expressions; gestures; melodic speech; social, musical, visual, spatial, and environmental awareness; unconscious self-image, body image, emotional and visual memory	Boys use right side of brain to work on abstract problems; girls use both sides	Males superior at spatial relationships

PART OF BRAIN	FUNCTION	SIMILARITIES AND DIFFERENCES	IMPACT
Sensory system	Includes two parts: receptors, which receive sensory input, and transformers, which take separate pieces of information and process into integrated knowledge	Clear differences throughout entire sensory reactive system	Different sensory strengths and weaknesses consistent in common male and female patterns
Serotonin	Both neurotransmitter and hormone; regulates body temperature, sensory perception, and onset of sleep	Gender differences in these physiological states likely explained partially through differences in amount and distribution of this monoamine	Basic differences in male and female sensory perception styles likely affected by serotonin levels
Synapse	Minute space between one nerve cell and another through which nerve impulses are transmitted	Likely high level of similarity in male and female brains	Subtle differences (affected by hormones?) could be partial explanation of different responsiveness in genders
Temporal lobe	Part of memory storage; recognizes some tones and volume	Stronger neuron connections in females would explain superiority in language tasks	Female connections and neuron pathways produce superiority at communicative tasks

(continued)

PART OF BRAIN	FUNCTION	SIMILARITIES AND DIFFERENCES	IMPACT
Testosterone	Male steroid sex hormone	Much more present and functional in males	Increases aggression, competition, self-assertion, and self-reliance
Thalamus	Regulates emotional life and physical safety; processes incoming sensory information; tells us what's going on outside body	Processes data faster in females, especially at certain times in menstrual cycle	Greater stress and activity in female thalamus at varying times during menstruation
Vasopressin	Hormone secreted by posterior lobe of pituitary gland; increases blood pressure by constricting arterioles	Involved in water retention, blood pressure, and memory	Differences in males and females in all these areas suggest some differences in this peptide's involvement in males and females
Werencke's area	Links language and thought; word comprehension	Likely more highly active in females	Improved verbal communication skills in females

the nerves that spiral around the shaft of other nerves of the brain, like vines around a tree, are coated. This coating is myelin, which allows electrical impulses to travel down a nerve fast and efficiently. A ten-year-old is generally a more developed human than a toddler, and an adult more so than a ten-year-old, in large part because of myelination. Myelination continues in all brains into the early twenties, but in young women it is complete earlier than in young men.

This is a maturity difference at the tail end of childhood, but the differing maturity occurs at the beginning as well. Girls, for instance, can acquire their complex verbal skills as much as a year earlier than boys. Thus, quite often a preschool girl reads faster and with a larger vocabulary than a peer boy does, and she speaks with better grammar. In general, female brains develop quicker than male brains. Brain development in infants is often most pronounced in the right hemisphere and gradually moves to the left. In females, the movement to the left starts earlier than in males.

Perhaps the most familiar structural difference in the brain is the corpus callosum, the bundle of nerves that connects the right and left hemispheres. In females it is up to 20 percent larger than in males, giving girls better cross-talk between the hemispheres of the brain. There is more (and quicker) development in females than males in the prefrontal lobes, where affect regulation finds its executive decision making, and the occipital lobes, where sensory processing often occurs.

Girls take in more sensory data than boys. On average, they hear better, smell better, and take in more information through fingertips and skin. Females tend often to be better than males at controlling impulsive behavior. They tend to self-monitor high-risk and immoral conduct better than boys (on average)—especially if the boys and the girls are equally untrained in ethics or impulse control. In other words, girls are by nature less likely to take moral risks than boys. Boys are more likely to physically show natural aggression.

Girls tend to have better verbal abilities and rely heavily on verbal communication; boys tend to rely heavily on nonverbal communication, being innately less able on average to verbalize feelings and responses as quickly as girls. This has immense ramifications in our present culture, which relies so heavily on talk, conversation, words. We are all far better trained at listening to words than at watching silent cues, which often makes communication with a male difficult.

Males tend to have more development in certain areas of the right hemisphere, which provides them with better spatial abilities such as measuring, mechanical design, and geography and map reading. Lynn S. Liben, of Pennsylvania State University, recently reviewed data from the 1999 National Geography Bee, a geography-based contest hosted by Alex Trebek that has attracted five million participants. Of those millions, forty-five times more boys than girls are likely to be finalists.

Like many researchers, Liben and the coauthors of her study concluded that although to some extent the boy-girl gap can be accounted for by cultural factors, the lion's share of the gap stems from better cognitive spatials in the male brain. "There really are some differences biologically," she said; "I feel I have to say this as a woman."

Chemical Differences

Males and females have a differing amount of most of the brain chemicals. Perhaps the most telling difference is in how much serotonin each brain secretes. The male brain secretes less than the female, making males impulsive in general, as well as fidgety. Differences in vasopressin and oxytocin are also substantial. For instance, the crying of a child stimulates secretion of oxytocin in the female brain to a far greater degree than in the male brain. Oxytocin is just one of the brain chemicals that, being more constantly stimulated in females, make the female capable of quick and immediate empathic responses to others' pain and needs.

Hormonal Differences

Although males and females both possess all the human hormones, degree of dominance differs. Females are dominated by estrogen and progesterone, males by testosterone. These hormones are contrasting in their effects. Progesterone, for instance, is a female growth hormone and also the bonding hormone. Testosterone is the male growth hormone, and also the sex-drive and aggression hormone.

Whereas a girl may be likely to bond first and ask questions later, a boy might be aggressive first and asks questions later. A girl is likely to try to manage social bonds in a group situation through egalitarian alliances, but a boy tends to manage social energy through striving for dominance or pecking order.

Human behavior is far more driven by hormones than we have wanted to admit. Despite the plethora of research on testosterone and premenstrual syndrome, we tend to avoid acknowledging the importance of hormonal differences. Yet male and female mood are very dependent on the interplay of hormones and the brain. Males receive five to seven "spikes" or "surges" of testosterone every day, beginning in prepuberty (generally around ten years old). During the spiking, hormonal flow can make their moods vacillate between aggressive and withdrawn.

Female estrogen and progesterone rise and fall with their hormonal cycle, making their moods swing as well. These hormones affect in-class emotive functioning, of course, because of mood, but they also influence learning performance. For instance, when female estrogen is high, a girl scores higher on both standardized and in-class tests than when it is low. When male testosterone is high, the boy performs better on spatial exams, like math tests, but worse on verbal tests.

There is great variety among boys and girls in their own hormonal levels. Some boys are high-testosterone: very aggressive, socially ambitious, striving for dominance, heavy in muscle mass, or a combination of these conditions. Some boys are low-testosterone, more sensitive, softer in appearance and manner. By adulthood, males can end up with twenty times more testosterone than females, but possibly also only five or six times as much. Female hormone levels vary, of course, with the time of the month and other circumstances (such as hearing a child cry, seeing another person suffer, becoming pregnant, or even competing). When both males and females compete, their testosterone levels go up (females included), but males obviously have a much higher testosterone baseline; this makes males on average more aggressively competitive than females.

Functional Differences

How the brain uses its cell and blood activity differs considerably in males and females. Boys use the right hemisphere more, girls the left. Boys move more emotive material down from the limbic system to the brain stem (where fight-or-flight responses are stored); girls move more of it upward to the upper brain, where complex thought occurs. Ruben Gur, at the University of Pennsylvania, has used PET scans, magnetic resonance imaging (MRI), and other brain imaging techniques to show that the resting female brain is as active as the activated male brain. In his words, "There is more going on in the female brain." He is not saying it is necessarily superior, but he is showing that the female brain is using its resources, doing so quickly, and often, and in more places in the brain. The female brain, never at rest, has a true learning advantage.

Quite often a girl's response to a situation is more complex than a boy's. Males tend to manage stimulants with more of what is called "task focus." Because the male brain is not as activated in as many places, it becomes overwhelmed by stimulation more quickly than the female, causing it to decide on the importance of stimulants for their necessity to a task-at-hand. A lot goes untouched by the male brain because it does not attend to those things, preferring to manage stimulation by "sticking to a plan." The advantage in this is a quick, direct route to a goal. A disadvantage is that if the task goes badly or failure emerges, the male has fewer resources to redirect himself.

Two areas of greater functioning in the female are memory and sensory intake. Comparable greater functioning in the male is in spatial tasks and abstract reasoning. The male brain gives boys the edge in dealing with spatial relationships (such as objects and theorems); the female brain responds more quickly to greater quantities of sensory information, connecting it with the primacy of personal relationships and communication. Cultural factors certainly reinforce these tendencies, but the differences are innate, in brain functioning.

Some teachers, over the years, discover the power that comes from using their voices appropriately. Because girls and women are able to hear things better than boys and men, sometimes a loud voice is needed for boys. This fact makes an interesting basis for keeping boys near the front of the physical classroom.

Another intriguing difference applies to teaching music, especially choir. Six times as many girls can sing in tune as boys. Males and females even see things differently, with females generally far better at seeing in a darkened room. On the other hand, males see better than women in bright light. This suggests a biological rationale for how teachers should arrange their students in terms of distance or closeness to visual learning aids.

The differences between male and female students go beyond just hearing and seeing. Females react acutely and quickly to pain, although their overall resistance to long-term discomfort is stronger than in males. There is even rather strong evidence that males and females taste things differently. Generally, females are sensitive to bitter flavors and prefer high concentrations of sweet things. Males are attracted to salty flavors. The female nose and palate are more sensitive than the male. Interestingly, a superior olfactory sensitivity also increases in males just before females ovulate; and at a critical time of her menstrual cycle, the biology of a woman makes her even more sensitive to a male's biology.

Gender difference has been noted in the memory ability of males and females. Girls can store, for short periods, a greater quantity of seemingly random information; boys can do this more often if the information is organized into some coherent form or has specific importance to them. Boys can store trivia better than girls for a long period of time.

Whereas girls fare better at sensory data and varied memory, boys fare better at spatial skills in general. We heard a wonderful example of male-brain spatial development from Jeff Knight, of Balboa Elementary School, an elementary teacher who gave his students a stick figure grid to recopy in three-dimensional space. Nearly all the boys could do it, but many of the girls couldn't. The boys also mastered it more quickly.

Differences in Processing Emotion

Perhaps the least understood area of brain difference is emotive processing. We educators may give it too little credence because we have been taught to think of it as nonessential to learning. In fact, brain-based research shows us it is crucial.

This is an area where boys are generally more at risk for missed learning and processing opportunities. The female brain processes more emotive stimulants, through more senses, and more completely than does the male. It also verbalizes emotive information quickly. Boys can sometimes take hours to process emotively (and manage the same information as girls). This lessor emotive ability makes males more emotionally fragile than we tend to think. A boy who has had a crisis at home this morning may come to school with a higher cortisol (stress-hormone) level than, say, his sister because he has held in, or not processed, the emotional stress of the crisis at home. He may be unable to learn for much of the morning, whereas his sister may quickly process and even talk out the hard edges of the stress so that she can learn efficiently the very same morning. The male is often, thus, intrinsically fragile because he cannot

easily broken

guide his own emotions to processing and to words as quickly as a female does, and his fragility may extend to his ability to learn that day.

Both females and males must be equally understood and protected emotionally. So any brain research pointing out ways in which boys are more emotionally fragile than girls is not offered to take attention away from girls' emotional needs. It is offered to inspire us to a new vision of males. Males are simply not as tough as we think; often females are emotionally tougher (though it doesn't appear so when they overtly show distress in tears and in talk more than do boys). *discover a trait w/out*

tears + talk

Simultaneously, we have all intuited how girls often take things personally; this is a way in which they are fragile. Girls process more emotive information than boys; where male emotional fragility comes from having fewer brain functions available to process, girls' emotional fragility often comes from having so many emotive functions that they become overwhelmed by the emotional material.

reasoning

One brain difference related to emotive processing is potentially of great interest, and even startling. Present brain technologies such as PET scans and MRIs are just beginning to show us that when sensory information laden with emotive content (let us again use the example of the sibling students experiencing a crisis with a parent before school that day) comes into the female limbic system, brain activity may be moving quickly to the top of the female brain—into those four lobes where thinking occurs—more than in the male brain. The boy's brain, on the other hand, seems to have a tendency to move information quickly toward the bottom of the limbic system (that is, the amygdala) and the brain stem. In simple terms, this makes a female more likely to process the pain or hurt and get help from others to talk about it, since more of her activity moves up to the hemispheres that verbalize and reason over the crisis; by contrast, the male is likely to become physically aggressive (fight) or withdrawn (flight).

So a male's aggression-and-withdrawal response short-circuits intellectual and academic learning because his emotive processing is taking longer and involves less reasoning; in addition, less of his emotional crisis–response neural firing is in the top of the brain, where learning is occurring. He's more occupied in the lower brain.

It is important to say that there are many exceptions to this scenario. Many girls become aggressive and shut down after a crisis at home or a humiliation at school; many boys learn better during and after a crisis because they can shut off the emotions and get to work. Many things are going on in each brain and personality that can outweigh gender difference.

Even given these exceptions, however, it's essential for us to watch how the mind is coping with an emotional crisis or outburst. If we see a girl or boy moving the emotive information downward rather than upward (becoming violent or withdrawn rather than moving through the emotions verbally or with other strategies), we must intervene as needed to help it move up. In Part Two, we give you innovative ways to do so. Because many children can stay on their academic tasks even despite emotive pressure and pain, we come to notice that our innovations are generally directed to the girls and boys who cannot stay on task—those who are having trouble learning because they do not have the brain baseline emotive skills to process feelings quickly, or have not found in their schools and classrooms the structures they need to help them process emotions in healthy ways. Many of these structures end up not being just talk-oriented, since emotionality is only partially about "using words." More on this later.

The gender differences I have just outlined are the tip of the iceberg. We have collected more for you in Table 1.2.

Why the Brains Are Different

One of the intriguing things about brain-based research is our theoretical understanding of why the differences between female and male brains exist. We now have no problem proving they exist because MRIs and PET scans show us how certain structures in the brain differ, and how blood flow and neurotransmission varies with gender. But *why*? Why the differences that scientific technology has now taken out of the world of speculation and made fact?

We can answer the question in two ways: one involves human and natural history, and the other involves hormones in utero and at puberty.

TABLE 1.2

DEVELOPMENTAL GENDER DIFFERENCES

PREBIRTH

MALE	FEMALE
• Develops testosterone	• Develops estrogen
• Same structural brain first six weeks after conception	• Same structural brain first six weeks after conception
• "Set" *male* brain immune to *female* hormones	• "Set" *female* brain immune to *male* hormones
• Fetus generally more active, restless	• Fetus generally less active in womb
• *Male* cortex develops slower	• *Female* cortex develops faster
• At six weeks in utero sexual identity is determined, and brain changes	• Normal template of human brain appears to be female
• At six weeks colossal dose of male hormone changes brain permanently	• Lack of testosterone impact allows brain structure to remain female
• Brain is more lateral than female's	• Brain is less lateral than male's
• Less flexible	• More flexible
• Less internalized	• Less externalized
• Greater idling in brain stem (reptilian brain)	• Greater idling in cingulate gyrus (limbic system)
• Brain 10 percent larger (mass) than girl's	• Brain mass 10 percent smaller in girls
• Corpus callosum smaller	• Corpus callosum larger
• Produces less sarotonin (quieting agent)	• Produces more sarotonin (quieting agent)

INFANCY

MALE	FEMALE
• Prefers mechanical or structural toys	• Prefers soft, cuddly toys
• Looks at objects for shorter, but more active, periods	• Plays with objects for longer periods, but less actively
• Gazes at mother half as long as girl does	• Play is more sanguine
• Motor activity more vigorous than girl's	• At one week, able to distinguish another baby's cry from background noise
• At one week, cannot distinguish another baby's cry from background noise	• At four months of age able to recognize faces of people known in photos
• At four months of age cannot distinguish faces of people in photos	• Sensitive to bitter tastes; prefers sweets
• Sensitive to salty foods	• More sensitive to physical sensation on skin
• Less sensitive to physical sensation on skin	• More easily saddened
• More easily angered	• Better peripheral vision
• Better narrow vision and depth perception	• Superior perception at red end of color spectrum
• Superior perception at blue end of color spectrum	• More attuned to sensory input

INFANCY (continued)

MALE	FEMALE
• Take in less sensory "proximal" data	• Equal visual skill with either eye
• Left eye dominant	• Less tolerant of loud noises
• Less bothered by loud noises	• More comforted by soft, cooing words and singing
• Less interested in soft, cooing words and singing	• More able to recognize emotional nuance
• Less able to recognize emotional nuance	• 25 percent lower mortality rate than girls
• 25 percent higher mortality rate than girls	• Three times better at reading; reading as auditory activity (superior hearing)

TODDLERS

MALE	FEMALE
• Speaks first words later than girls	• Develops better vocabulary earlier than boys
• By age four and a half, 99 percent of speech is comprehensible	• By age three, 99 percent of speech is comprehensible
• Shows greater interest in exploring once standing is mastered	• Even after mastering standing, does not roam as freely as boys
• Greater muscle mass already evident by age three	• Greater concentration of fatty tissue still more evident than muscle at age three
• Less able to multitask	• Better ability to multitask
• Hears better in right ear	• Hears equally well with either ear
• Better auditory memory	• Better visual memory
• More likely to ignore voices—even parents	• Less likely to ignore voices—especially those familiar
• More physically impulsive	

PRESCHOOL AND KINDERGARTEN

MALE	FEMALE
• One-directional, less cross-talk between hemispheres, more focused	• More cross-talk between hemispheres of brain as shown by approach to activities
• Occupies larger space on playground than girls	• Congregates in groups of other girls in smaller spaces, often huddling together
• Playground activities involve more individual running	• Playground games are quieter and less active, more cooperative
• Playground games rough and vigorous, competitive and aggressive	• Playing with blocks, tends to build low and long structures
• Playing with blocks, builds high structures likely to topple over	• Newcomers greeted more warmly
• Newcomers to group ignored until they prove their worth and value	• Stories pay attention to human dynamics; particular concern with victim's feelings
• Stories filled with excitement and action, ignoring victims	

(continued)

PRESCHOOL AND KINDERGARTEN (continued)

MALE	FEMALE
• Games involve bodily contact, tumbling, continuous flow of action	• Games involve turn taking and indirect competition most of the time
• Primarily interested in objects and things	• Primarily interested in people and relationships
• Saying good-bye to mom takes approximately thirty seconds	• Saying good-bye to mom takes approximately ninety seconds
• Uses dolls for attack weapons and warfare	• Uses dolls for playing out domestic scenes
• More speech problems	• Fewer speech problems; seems to differentiate sounds better
• Picks same-gender peers for friends	• Picks same-gender peers for friends
• Expresses emotions through action	• Expresses emotions through words
• Less sensitive to social and personal context	• More sensitive to social and personal context
• Less attention span and empathy	• Greater attention span and empathy

GRADES 1–3

MALE	FEMALE
• Takes longer to attain reading mastery	• Reads better and sooner than boys
• Superior at certain visual tasks in bright light	• Superior at seeing in low light
	• Superior at hearing
• Better at test requiring circling of answers	• Better at test requiring listening to questions being read
• Hypothalamus functions to keep hormonal levels even	• Hypothalamus functions to fluctuate hormone levels
• Better general math	• Better verbal ability
• Better at three-dimensional reasoning	• Better at grammar and vocabulary
• More rule-bound than girls	• Less bound by arbitrary rules
• 95 percent of hyperactive children	• Only 5 percent of hyperactive children
• More able to separate emotion from reason	• Less able to separate emotion from reason

GRADES 4–6

MALE	FEMALE
• Hormones begin to increase at age ten	• Affected by hormone changes earlier than boys
• Primarily focused on action, exploration, and things	• Primarily focused on relationships and communication
• More likely than ever to use aggression to resolve differences	• Unlikely to settle differences with hitting
• Better at reading maps and deciphering directions	• Better at fine-motor skills and coordination for fine tasks
• Better at chess	• Better at learning a foreign language

GRADES 4–6 (continued)

MALE	FEMALE
• More likely to need remedial reading	• More likely to sing in tune
• Solves math problems without talking	• Solves math problems with language help
• Channel surfs on TV	• Watches one program for longer period

MIDDLE SCHOOL

MALE	FEMALE
• Testosterone develops body at ratio of 40 percent protein to 15 percent fat	• Estrogen develops body at ratio of 23 percent protein to 25 percent fat
• Testosterone indisputably an aggression-inducing chemical	• Estrogen generates greater activity in the brain (first phase of menstruation, increased concentration)
• When talkative in class, often attention-seeking	• When quiet in class, often confident
• 50 percent more likely to be held back a grade than eighth-grade girls	• 50 percent less likely to be held back a grade than eighth-grade boys
• Amount of male hormone relates directly to success at traditional male tasks	• Amount of female hormone relates directly to success at traditional female tasks
• More likely to be victim of physical abuse	• More likely to be victim of sexual abuse
	• Hypothalamus functions to fluctuate levels based on a twenty-eight-day cycle

HIGH SCHOOL

MALE	FEMALE
• Concentration on things directed at career considerations	• Concentration on more intimate personal relationships
• Focus on strength and muscularity for sexual attractiveness (fearing weakness)	• Focus on slender appearance for sexual attractiveness (fearing obesity)
• Social acceptance based on physical strength and athleticism	• Social acceptance based on peer relationships and beauty
• More likely to be involved in criminal behavior	• Less likely to be involved in criminal behavior
• In one study 69 percent of males suggested "fighting" as best way to resolve conflict	• In one study 69 percent of females suggested "walking away or talking things out as the best way to resolve conflict"
• Social hierarchies tend to be stable (boys "know their place")	• Social hierarchies tend to be fluid
• Pursuit of power a universal male trait	• Pursuit of comfortable environment a universal female trait
• Achieves far greater academic success after puberty	• Higher-than-normal estrogen level produces certain intellectual disadvantages
• IQ scores rise dramatically between fourteen and sixteen	

(continued)

HIGH SCHOOL (continued)

MALE	FEMALE
• Boys with XXY chromosomal pattern (an extra female chromosome) do less well at spatial reasoning	• IQ scores level off or drop during middle school but rise again at high school
• Bullies still popular among peers	• Girls with higher-than-normal level of testosterone better at spatial reasoning
• Jocks slightly more sexually active than male peers	• Bullies among girls unpopular
• If involved in high school athletics, more likely to get better grades and go to college (also more likely to drink and try drugs)	• Jocks less likely to be sexually active than girl peers
• More likely to succeed at suicide	• Less likely to become pregnant if involved in school activities
• 83 percent of students in advanced placement computer science classes	• More likely unsuccessful at suicide attempt
• Steroid use increasing among teenage boys	• 17 percent of students in advanced placement computer science classes female
• Matriculated (graduated) at lower levels than girls in high school and college	• Steroid use among girls up 100 percent since 1991
• Less likely than girls to suffer episode of clinical depression	• Outmatriculated boys in recent years in both high school and college
• Performance on writing examinations less affected by biological cycles	• Almost 50 percent of girls in one survey experienced at least one episode of clinical depression within five years of high school graduation
	• Performance on writing exams drops by as much as 14 percent during menstrual cycle
	• Outperform men in tests of verbal and communication skills

A Brief History of Brain Difference

Evolutionary biologists believe our brains differ by gender because it has been necessary in human evolution for humans to divide up tasks by gender. (If your personal religious convictions make evolution distasteful to you, then the evolutionary explanation can be changed to "God created us this way.")

From the evolutionary point of view, however, there was indeed some form of mysterious, even divine, inception to humanity, occurring some four million years ago, and gradual evolution of the human brain, beginning around two million years ago. As the brain evolved, its elements (amygdala, two hemispheres, brain stem, limbic system, and so on) diverged in development, to a degree, according to gender.

In order for the human species to survive, this divergence of sex roles *space* was necessary. Until about ten thousand years ago, when the agricultural age arose in many parts of the world, humans were hunter/gatherers, males responsible for hunting (a very spatial occupation) and periphery protection and war (very aggressive occupations); females were responsible for gathering roots and other vegetation and most child care (sensory and verbal occupations). Males built most of the large structures, forming large-group teams for their activities. Females did more of the inside work: arranging and managing internal home space, and working in dyads, triads, and smaller groups. Females verbalized in their intimate groups; males tended to carry out action in their larger groups.

Over millions of years, the brain both created and accommodated these circumstances. Females had to be better at verbal skills than males; males had to be better at spatials and more physically aggressive. Females had to care more about small-group consensus; males had to rely more on pecking-order hierarchies with dominant leadership. Females had to hear, see, and use all the senses and remember variety among things in order to provide the subtle brain development and care a child needs; males had to focus on the single task to provide for and protect communities of children.

Both the brain and its hormones—which are catalysts for brain activity—came to differ with gender. The differences existed (as they still do) even in utero; for instance, male babies tend to be aggressive, kicking the mother more). Human environmental socialization tended to enhance these tendencies in those cultures that required greater difference. Thus, in some small tribal cultures, where competition for resources within a community is not stiff, where everyone works together closely, and where there are few if any wars with other tribes, the gender differences are lessened. In cultures with larger populations (like ours) where there is immense competition for resources, where family and care units are increasingly independent from one another, and where conflict with other cultures is constant or imminent, the gender differences shine through more.

It is interesting to note that male and female hormones were not as far apart in their constitution a million years ago as they are now. We know this because testosterone level is directly related to bulking, or muscle mass, and fossil records show us that male and female bodies used to be closer in size than they are now.

Some evolutionary biologists argue that the most important determinant of hormonal gender difference is population growth. The larger the population, the more testosterone is required. Given present human social reality, males have little choice in increasing theirs; they are compelled to compete constantly for resources. Females have some choice; should they choose to attach to a bonding group (an extended family) or an alpha male (a competent male) during the child-raising years, they can avoid being increasingly competitive and thus not need to raise their own testosterone. Females can increase their testosterone by competing more (high-testosterone females will already do so) or by being injected with testosterone (and taking androgenic testosterone-based steroids). Some women have experimented with testosterone over the last few years; they become more independent, socially ambitious, and aggressive.

Given that both male and female testosterone levels are going up around the world today, the population argument seems valid. The more population we have, the more our brains (and therefore our hormones) anticipate the necessary increase in all the ways we can compete as individuals, communities, and a species, from testosterone-linked aggression to estrogen/progesterone-linked bonding and consensus building.

It is surely important for social theorists who strive to "androgynize" males and females to know this. Although in some ways boys and girls are definitely becoming more like each other (boys are learning to verbalize feelings better, and girls are learning to compete better on athletic and work teams), they are also becoming ever more different. More males are being born with high testosterone (for example, we are producing taller basketball players and larger athletes, and more males with better engineering and architectural spatial development). More females are being born with higher estrogen and progesterone; that is, we are producing more females who have better verbals and who in fact do not flourish well except in close attachments and relationships with mates and family. Brain-based research and its evolutionary perspective compel us to accept that *both* androgyny and separate-gender traits are increasing. The solution to the problems being experienced in the schools involves helping *both* the androgynous kids and the more gender-different.

The Role of Hormones in the Womb and at Puberty

The historical causation of gender differences in the brain probably goes back to hunter/gatherer society and continues in our high-population culture, but the logistical causation of brain difference lies in how male and female hormones influence development.

All fetuses start out female. In the first trimester of pregnancy, surges of testosterone from the mother's ovaries create the male. One set of surges compels the genitals to drop pelvically and become penis and testicles. Another series of surges wires the brain toward male structure and functioning. Thus, sex hormones change the brain's very architecture from female to male.

When the surges of testosterone, estrogen, progesterone, prolactin, and other hormones occur at puberty, we have a kind of second-womb or second-birth activity. The brain changes toward increased genderization yet again. For instance, in both sexes, surges of testosterone at puberty swell the amygdala (the part of the limbic system that generates feelings of fear and anger). This change is especially pronounced in boys, which explains the rise in aggressiveness seen in both sexes at adolescence, and especially in males who become high-risk. The increased level of estrogen at puberty causes sudden growth of the hippocampus, the part of the brain that focuses on memory. A larger hippocampus can mean a better memory. The hippocampus in girls grows larger than it does in boys—one reason girls and women are better than boys and men at remembering some things, such as names and faces in myriad social relationships. Women are also less likely than men, generally, to suffer from the memory loss that accompanies Alzheimer's.

Estrogen and testosterone seem to help flip on neurological switches at puberty, switches that were previously set by hormonal levels way back when we were still a fetus. Once flipped, these switches change a teenager's sex drive, along with a host of other attitudes and behaviors (irritability, aggressiveness, and moodiness, to list just a few).

Researchers have further found that a shift in prenatal hormones can affect us in ways that may not become clear until later in life. Testosterone shapes centers in the brain that process spatial information. In studies of girls with congenital adrenal hyperplasia (CAH), a condition that causes the adrenal glands to make excess androgen (a testosteronelike hormone) during prenatal development, their brains were found to be permanently changed. Sheri Berenbaum, a psychologist at Southern Illinois University Medical School, found that as teenagers, girls with CAH were more aggressive than their sisters and had better spatial skills (such as the ability to rotate objects in their minds, or to imagine how pieces of a puzzle fit together). These girls were also more interested than their sisters in becoming "engineers and pilots."

Why are male and female brains different? The best answer we have now is this: millions of years of human history are inherited in the neural systems of male and female children. This history is then imitated as the child's brain and hormones develop. Though of course with many exceptions, girls and boys develop their internal wiring differently, and the difference has profound effects on how boys and girls act, live, and learn.

In this chapter we've held up an X ray of the human brain, hormones, and development in order to discover the seat of the differences between boys and girls. Now let's look even more closely at how those natural differences directly relate to the learning process.

How Brain-Based Differences Affect Boys and Girls

Changing a child's mind is one thing, but changing my own is another. Recently in a human growth and development class I was teaching, we did a module for the kids on brain and gender differences. I'm not sure what I expected from the students—I think I expected them to be surprised that male and female brains were so different. What I got was a resounding "Duh!" That boys and girls brains are different came as no surprise to these kids, who are living the differences every day. It was me who was surprised. How humbling that was. The kids knew more than I did.

—ROSE ALDRICH, MIDDLE SCHOOL TEACHER

A MIDDLE SCHOOL TEACHER, DORIS, TOLD US THIS JOKE: "IF A MAN makes a decision and his wife is not around, is it still wrong?" A male teacher had another: "I just saw an ad on the Internet: 'Encyclopedias for sale, forty volumes. $1,000 or best offer. Am getting married. Wife knows everything. No longer need them.'"

We were together in a school district training that focused on how boys and girls are different, think differently, and talk differently. For just a few minutes, I suggested we focus on examples in male and female humor; we learn a lot about people from the jokes they tell! From this starting point, we would look at differences in how boys and girls got embarrassed, were emotionally sensitive, and handled their own learning weaknesses.

You can imagine the fun we had in this part of our training. We took time to get to know gender-relevant jokes not only to have a good laugh but also to ease teachers into exploring the very rich area of gender-oriented learning and emotional style even more fully. Just as boys and girls tell different jokes, just as men and women poke fun in different ways, so does gender difference affect nearly every area of learning in some nuanced way. In some cases, the nuance of difference is slight, like that in tonality between two people telling the very same joke. In some, however, the difference is major.

Let's look at ten nuances of learning that differ often profoundly between boys and girls, so much so that they themselves end up appearing in jokes.

Areas of Learning-Style Difference

Here are ten areas that brain-based research has been able to track around the world in the last two decades. I suspect that over the next few years, in school districts globally, more of these will be noticed and ultimately used for the good of classroom teaching.

Deductive and Inductive Reasoning

Boys tend to be *deductive* in their conceptualizations, starting their reasoning process frequently from a *general* principle and applying it, or ancillary principles, to individual cases. They also tend to do deductive reasoning more quickly than girls. This is a reason that boys, on average, do better on fast multiple-choice tests, for instance on the Scholastic Aptitude Tests. The better a person is at making a quick deduction, the better he or she does on the test that relies on this skill.

Girls, on the other hand, tend to favor *inductive* thinking, adding more and more to their base of conceptualization. They tend to begin with concrete examples; it is often easy to teach them concretion, especially in verbalization and writing. "Give me an example" is often easier to ask of girls than boys, especially early in the conceptualization process. More often than boys, girls begin from the specific examples and then build general theory.

Abstract and Concrete Reasoning

Boys tend to be better than girls at not seeing or touching the thing and yet still being able to calculate it. For example, when mathematics is taught on a blackboard boys often do better at it than girls. When it is taught using manipulatives and objects—that is, taken off the blackboard, out of the abstract world of signs and signifiers, and put into the concrete world of, say, physical number chains—the female brain often finds it easier.

Males like abstract arguments, philosophical conundrums, and moral debates about abstract principles. We must reiterate that there are many exceptions to all these rules. In general, however, the world of the abstract (including proclivity toward abstract design) is explored more by the male brain than the female. Architecture and engineering, which rely so much on abstract design principles, are worlds toward which (since the designing associated with hunting and the earliest edifices) the male brain has gravitated. We often recognize a bridge-brain female when we see a girl excelling in industrial design. We see that her spatial abilities surpass that of many boys.

Use of Language

During our joke session in our training, a female teacher told us this one: "My husband hasn't talked for three months. It's not that he's angry with me. It's just that he doesn't want to interrupt!" This area of male-female difference is one so well known, at least intuitively, to most of us that we generate wonderful jokes about it. On average, females do produce more words than males. During the learning process, we often find girls using words *as they learn,* and boys often working silently. Even when we study student group processes, we find females in a learning group using words more than males. We also find that word users in the male groups tend to be fewer—for example, one or two dominant or attention-seeking males use a lot of words, and the other males far fewer, whereas there is more parity in word use among the female group.

Girls also tend to prefer to have things conceptualized in usable, everyday language, replete with concrete details. Boys often find jargon and coded language more interesting. As one brain researcher told me years ago, "It's just not as much of interest to females to create the kind of verbal obfuscation legalese uses. If Western culture's founding lawyers and judges had been women, judicial language would be easier to understand."

Whether it's language from sports trivia, the law, or the military, boys tend to work out codes among themselves and within their own cognating process, and rely on coded language to communicate.

Logic and Evidence

Girls are generally better listeners than boys, hear more of what's said, and are more receptive to the plethora of details in a lesson or conversation. This gives them great security in the complex flow of conversation, and thus less need to control conversation with dominance behavior or logical rules.

Boys tend to hear less and more often ask for clear evidence to support a teacher's or other's claim. Girls seem to feel safe with less logical sequencing and more instructional meandering.

The Likelihood of Boredom

Boys get bored more easily than girls; this quite often requires more and varying stimulants to keep them attentive. Girls are better at self-managing boredom during instruction and all aspects of education. This has a profound impact on all aspects of learning. Once the child has become bored, he is likely not only to give up on learning but also to act out in such a way that class is disrupted and he is labeled a behavioral problem.

Use of Space

Boys tend to use up more space when they learn, especially at younger ages. When a girl and a boy are put together at a table, the boy generally ends up spreading his work into the girl's space, not vice versa. Boys tend to learn by using more physical space than girls do. This natural tendency can affect psychosocial dynamics. Unaware of how necessary it is for many boys to use space, teachers inadvertently consider the boys impolite, rude, or out of control. In fact, they are often just learning in the way their spatial brains learn.

Movement

Girls do not generally need to move around as much while learning. Movement seems to help boys not only stimulate their brains but also manage and relieve impulsive behavior. Movement is also natural to boys in a closed space, thanks to their lower serotonin and higher metabolism, which creates fidgeting behavior.

Many teachers find that the one or two boys who can't stop moving in class can be managed by putting them to work, as with letting them hand out papers or go sharpen pencils for the teacher. At all ages, stretch breaks and sixty-second movement breaks are very helpful. Teachers often find, too, that allowing a boy to play with something (silently) in his hand, such as a nerf ball, while he's learning can help. He's moving, his brain is being stimulated, he feels comfortable, and no one else is being bothered.

Sensitivity and Group Dynamics

Cooperative learning, which is good for all children, is often easier for girls to master in the early stages of its use. Girls learn while attending to a code of social interaction better than boys do. Boys tend to focus on performing the task well, without as much sensitivity to the emotions of others around them.

Pecking orders are flagrantly important to boys, and they are often fragile learners when they are low in the pecking order. By *pecking order* we mean where the kid fits in the group's social strata. Pecking order is established by physical size, verbal skills, personality, personal abilities, and many other social and personal factors. Over the many years of schooling, children generally find themselves at the top of a pecking order in one circumstance or era of childhood and at the bottom at another. Some children seem to gravitate toward the top of large-scale pecking orders, as in the phenomena of most popular girl in school or prom king. Others gravitate toward the top of small-group pecking orders—the chess club president, or the most popular kid among the computer nerds. All kids flow in and out of many pecking orders.

Brain-based research has shown us that girls who may be unpopular or not called on as much or not seen or not heard in the general melee of school life may also be less likely to fail in school than boys who are not seen or not socially aggressive. This research is nascent, and the next few years will flesh it out better, but again it throws recent gender theories into question.

These recent theories have argued that girls suffer because they are not seen and heard, while boys, who are constantly seeking attention in the classroom, flourish. Yet the girls who are lower in the pecking order are often getting better grades than boys who are low in their own pecking order. The girls, it appears, are not as dependent on pecking-order status for school performance.

Perhaps the fragile male "ego" is a very real phenomenon, though we can't "see" an "ego" with a microscope. But we can see the level of cortisol.

Brain researchers have suspected for a few years now that where a male is in the pecking order may have a great effect on how he learns because of the level of stress hormones (higher in males when they feel worthless). Biologically, males on the high end of a pecking order secrete less cortisol, the stress hormone. Males at the bottom end secrete more. Why is this significant? Because cortisol can invade the learning process; it forces the brain to attend to emotional and survival stress rather than intellectual learning. This is perhaps a "natural" reason for the male fragility so many of us have observed in boys who are humiliated or unliked, who appear weak, or who can't make any friends.

Use of Symbolism

Especially in upper grades, boys tend toward symbolic texts, diagrams, and graphs. They like the coded quality better than girls do, who tend to prefer written texts. Both girls and boys like pictures, but boys often rely on them in their learning—mainly because they stimulate the right hemisphere, which is where many boys are more developed. In literature classes, teachers often find boys inclined to make a great deal out of the author's symbolism and imagery patterns, while girls ponder the emotional workings of character.

Use of Learning Teams

Both girls and boys benefit from learning teams and group work, with boys tending to create structured teams and girls forming looser organizations. Boys spend less time than girls managing team process, picking leaders quickly, and focusing right away on goal orientation.

In Chapters Three through Six, we look at how teachers are applying these learning differences to their classrooms, and helping both male and female learning styles flourish. All of us, to some extent, adapt intuitively to the learning style differences we've experienced even if we didn't know we were experiencing them. With the new brain information available, we are now seeing the differences consciously, creating a plan of action to handle them, and of course never losing sight of the fact that these are only *trends*, not absolutes. Every child is an individual, and things like personality often are more powerful in creating a learning style than gender is.

This notwithstanding, the majority of boys and girls in the classroom or home fit many of these trends, just as they fit the various "intelligences" in gender-specific ways.

Learning Differences and the Intelligences

Perhaps you have gone to a training in Howard Gardner's seven intelligences (he has recently added an eighth one, which you can learn more about by logging onto pzweb.harvard.edu). Gardner has developed wonderful research into the kinds of intelligence with which children learn. Thomas Armstrong and many others have joined in this research.

Before discussing how boys and girls may differ in these intelligences, we want to identify five of them. They have been selected because in these five we believe you can best see male-female difference.

Time and Sequence

There are three forms of intelligence in Gardner's general category of time and sequence. Each requires the ability to rapidly process and communicate sequential information in a timely, orderly manner. These communicative forms of intelligence require an individual to remember the past, connect to the present, and anticipate what might be coming in the future.

LINGUISTIC INTELLIGENCE.   Linguistic ability lies in most people most demonstrably in the left hemisphere of the brain. For educators, of course, language is a critically important tool, both for the teacher and for the student. Language ability is not to be confused with talking competency; although the two are related, silent self-talk is every bit as important to the learning student as language used for communication with others.

MUSICAL INTELLIGENCE.   For the majority of people, music processing is located in the right hemisphere. Interestingly enough, rhythm is usually processed in the left hemisphere. Could this be why music can be such a powerful influence in so many aspects of classroom learning, from memorizing to expressing emotion, from concentrating to boosting self-esteem? It certainly is. Music is a whole brain activity, involving both hemispheres at once.

University of Oregon researcher Robert Sylwester analyzes this historically: "If music was a precursor of human language, it's possible that most of our brain's musical functions shifted over to the right hemisphere when the complexities of language began to dominate our left hemisphere functions. Trained musicians often activate left hemisphere mechanisms while listening to music, probably because they are also analyzing the music."

LOGICAL-MATHEMATICAL INTELLIGENCE. An enormous range of functions are involved in our brain (including both hemispheres and the frontal lobes) when we try to deal with mathematics and logic. It is certainly no accident that many students find math and, later, logic to be tremendously challenging, given the amount of brain energy required to do even relatively simple problems.

Space and Place

There are two forms of intelligence in the space-and-place category that help our brains focus on the nature of space and our place in it. Sylwester writes: "Intelligent action in this category allows us to *navigate* effectively throughout our environment." Although the term might be rather insulting in most usages, to describe one of our students as "spacey" might actually be a fair and accurate assessment of a certain kind of intelligence deficiency that can plague some students.

SPATIAL INTELLIGENCE. Spatial intelligence focuses on tactile and visual perceptual abilities to grasp a sense of objects, shapes, and forms in our environment. Engineers and architects are two examples of professionals who use their spatial intelligence to alter our environment. Normally, spatial intelligence is found in the right hemisphere.

BODILY-KINESTHETIC INTELLIGENCE. That wiggle-wart in the third chair from the back on the far left side of the classroom may actually, once put on a soccer field, have amazing control over the bodily-kinesthetic brain.

Tracking bodily-kinesthetic intelligence in a child's brain shows the interrelationality of brain functions. First, the basal ganglia are involved—at the base of each hemisphere of the brain, they coordinate the actions of the sensory and motor systems. Simultaneously, the amygdala, in the lower limbic system, produces emotional triggers for movements.

The motor cortex, connected above the inner ear in each hemisphere, helps coordinate the movements of each side of the body. The cerebellum, that bump at the lower back of our brain, coordinates and fine-tunes automatic movement that allows success occurrence of an entire action, such as all the steps up to and through a swan dive.

The wiggle-wart may not have good integration of these parts of the brain for sitting in a chair quietly, but he or she may well have the integration needed to perform a large motor task such as soccer.

Applying the Intelligences to Brain-Based Gender Difference

Differences between boys and girls show up as we observe intelligence styles. It is interesting to note that one gender's dominance in an intelligence style often grows in part from the other gender's brain hiding its ability to flourish in that style. The concealment is not conscious; it is simply that the brain puts forth into the world what it feels best at, leaving undeveloped (unless the brain is significantly aided) what it does not naturally feel as good at showing the world. A brain formed toward a certain kind of intelligence (for instance, bodily-kinesthetic) will probably never be as good at another as a brain already formed toward that other (say, linguistic), but both brains can get better at all intelligences with proper stimulation.

Although males and females show strong musical ability, both show increased development, especially at a young age, when they are musically stimulated. The "Mozart effect" controversially alleges that playing complex classical music to babies increases development of both hemispheres, which in turn helps girls and boys make up for any brain disadvantage they may have in either hemisphere. The ultimate effectiveness of playing Mozart to babies has perhaps been exaggerated by proponents and the media, but the theory is nonetheless accurate in terms of whole-brain development.

Boys are dominant in logical-mathematical intelligence, relying on it more heavily than girls do, but the last twenty years of effort to increase girls' brain development in this area is paying off as we see girls flourishing in math. The male-female brain difference still exists most clearly in physics, which is so highly abstract that males still dominate those classes; but most recent studies indicate females catching up (nearly) in almost every other category of mathematics class. Will males still tend to want logic, and females tend to accept emotive intuition as equally valid? Yes. There is less change there. Boys still tend to rely on deduction and girls on induction.

When it comes to intelligence based in space and place, boys tend to experience more processing, and thus both an advantage and a disadvantage. The advantage is that they are active in their learning, oriented to body movement, and thus further self-stimulate their spatial abilities, increasing right-hemisphere development. The disadvantage is that some boys are out there in everyone's space when they learn, as we said earlier—especially in the early grades, when they haven't learned to control impulses in the classroom. Thus they get in trouble for just being boys. Often we see teachers trying to calm down the spatial boys, and it may be essential to do so. But just as often, helping the girls toward physical movement in class along with the boys stimulates their cortical development in spatial intelligence, in the same way that calming boys down so everyone can read quietly stimulates their left-hemisphere and linguistic development.

The differences in male-female learning style and intelligence are, we hope, good aids in re-visioning school or home classrooms toward the reality of boys and girls being different learners. In Part Two of this book, we help by presenting innovations that have already addressed a number of these elements. Before moving fully to that material, let's take some time to explore how things are not going well for our "different learners." There's some bad news here. We hope it inspires you, rather than depresses you! Some of it, especially the material regarding problems girls face in school, may be familiar from years of media exposure. But some of it, especially regarding boys' problems, may not have gotten your attention as thoroughly until now.

The State of Boys and Girls in Our Schools

In the 1990s, we saws a wealth of statistics in the media about the state of gender bias in our schools. Until recently, most of these statistics (and their anecdotal support) have concerned gender bias against girls in educational culture. Since 1999, however, we've seen a surge of new statistics and studies that show, in fact, just the opposite: greater gender bias in our schools against *boys*. Perhaps the most powerful study is Christina Hoff Sommers's *The War Against Boys,* a comprehensive assessment of what is going on in our schools from a gender point of view.

To some extent, many parents and teachers already intuited that boys were in pretty bad shape, in many ways, in our schools. Now we have evidence for this intuition, evidence that in no way robs girls of attention but is also honest about what is really going on for the largest group of failed learners in our schools: boys.

We hope that the material here helps you filter through the available research as you wonder about gender bias in your school and community. Both boys and girls experience advantages and disadvantages in the educational community. Many of these outcomes, we believe, are due as much to our lack of understanding of brain difference as they are to inherent sexism. We have also come to understand, in our ten years of research in this field, that sexism against boys is as rampant as sexism against girls in our schools, if not more so.

Advantages for Boys, Disadvantages for Girls

Here are some of the advantages boys experience in general in our schools. These translate, of course, to potential disadvantages for girls.

- *Athletics.* The majority of sports funding and community support still goes to male athletics in most American schools. For instance, only 37 percent of high school athletes are girls, the rest boys.
- *Classroom behavior.* Boys tend to be louder, more physically aggressive, and more prone to attention-getting devices in class-

rooms than are girls, resulting in more teacher attention going to boys.

- *Specific academic areas.* Boys are approximately 2 to 4 points ahead of girls in math and science scores tracked by the U.S. Department of Education. This male advantage is mainly seen at the highest levels of calculus, chemistry, and physics.
- *Test scores.* Boys score slightly higher than girls on SAT and other college entrance exams.
- *Psychological disorders.* Boys are insulated from many girl-related disorders; for instance, most eating disorders in the teen years befall girls. Girls also suffer the majority of cases of overt depression. For every one boy who attempts suicide, four girls do.
- *Teen pregnancy.* When two teenagers have intercourse resulting in pregnancy and one of the mating couple drops out of school, it is generally the girl. Ninety percent of fathers of children born to teen girls abandon the girl and child. The immaturity gap between boys and girls affects girls in this and myriad other ways, including considerable harassment of pubescent girls by boys.
- *Sexual abuse.* Girls are the more common victim of sexual abuse suffered at the hands of teachers, parents, coaches, other students, or other school staff.
- *Culture gender bias.* In some school settings, good-old-boy networks still exist, teaching males that they are inherently privileged and bestowing advantage upon them, especially in access to employment networks by which they can get ahead.

This bias leaves females at a disadvantage in the workplace. In some classrooms, boys dominate discussions and girls' voices are lost. Furthermore, role modeling in literature is more often male than female, with male heroes dominating the cast of characters in a reading assignment.

Advantages for Girls, Disadvantages for Boys

Girls in general experience certain advantages (which translate to disadvantages for boys).

- *Extracurricular activities.* Girls make up the majority of student government officials, after-school club leaders, and school community liaisons.
- *Academic performance.* Girls choose to take the harder courses in middle school and high school at a higher rate than boys do; they also study harder on average for all courses than boys. Girls receive approximately 60 percent of the A's, and boys receive approximately 70 percent of the D's and F's. Among students performing in the top fifth of high school grade ranges, 63 percent are girls.
- *Specific academic performance.* Girls are approximately one and a half years ahead of boys in reading and writing competency, according to statistics tracked by the federal Department of Education. The girls' reading advantage exists at all levels, not just the highest. The department has been tracking the reading and writing advantage since 1981.
- *Educational aspirations.* Our colleges are now 60 percent female. Given that college graduation is the most consistent indicator of stable future income, this figure is particularly troubling for males. The federal Department of Education has found that eighth-grade and twelfth-grade girls have, on average, higher educational aspirations than boys. A nongovernmental study corroborated this finding: three-fourths of girls (compared to two-thirds of boys) "believe they will have many opportunities available to them after they graduate" from high school.
- *Learning and behavioral disorders.* Females are less likely to experience a learning, psychiatric, or behavioral disorder. For instance, boys make up two-thirds of the learning disabled and 90 percent of the behaviorally disabled. They number nearly 100 percent of the most seriously disabled. Girls constitute only 20 percent of ADHD (attention deficit and hyperactivity disorder) and ADD (attention deficit disorder) diagnoses and 30 percent of serious drug and alcohol problems, leaving 80 percent of brain disorders and 70 percent of these problems to boys. For every girl who actually commits suicide, four boys do.
- *Discipline problems.* Girls constitute fewer discipline problems and dropouts than boys. Boys are 90 percent of the discipline prob-

lems in school, as well as 80 percent of the dropouts, garnering the majority of school punishment for immature behavior and leaving school at a higher rate than girls.

• *Violence.* Girls are insulated from violence in the school in comparison to boys. Violence and harassment of children overall is higher than we would like, but when all the figures on violence are combined, boys are the more likely victims of violence on school property by about a three-to-one margin. The area of greater violence against females is sexual harassment.

• *Culture bias.* The educational system and the individual classroom are not as well designed for male brain development as for female. The system comprises mainly female teachers who have not received training in male brain development and performance; it relies on less kinesthetic, relatively unmentored, and less disciplined educational strategies than many boys need.

Applying Brain-Based Research to Gender Advantage

In our studies, you'll find that for the most part we avoid using the term *gender bias* in educational reform. We use, instead, *gender advantage* and *gender disadvantage.* We do this because we believe that most of what children suffer in schools such as ours—schools that are in fact very attentive to gender bias, especially against females—is not bias (which implies a directed favoring of one group)—but instead a basic lack of understanding of innate gender *differences.* In other words, our teachers are not biased per se, nor should they be attacked for being so; they simply do not have enough information to fully apply "ultimate" teaching to both girls and boys.

To understand this brain-based perspective deeply, let's explore each of the categories we have listed and discover not their bias-based, but rather their brain-based, element in causation. Given our understanding of the fact that both nature and nurture are together the cause of a gender bias, we do not offer brain-based causation as the only cause of a male advantage or disadvantage. The socializing culture plays its important, interactive part. But let's start with the brain.

ATHLETICS AND EXTRACURRICULAR ACTIVITIES.   Boys engage in more sports activities than girls and girls in more school clubs and government activities. This can be viewed as primarily a product of bias, or a product of nature. It is certainly a product of both, but our studies show us that this is mainly a product of the nature of the male and female brains.

Girls tend to choose interactive social activities that allow increased verbalization; boys tend to choose interactive social activities that decrease verbals and increase spatials, as well as physical aggression.

Whereas advocacy for girls in sports and boys in other social interactions is essential, the ultimate standard for a school ought not be 100 percent female participation in all athletics; that doesn't seem to us neurologically or hormonally realistic. Many girls don't like team sports and do not need to be pressured into them (of course, this holds true of many boys, too). By the same token, boys need a great deal of help directing themselves toward social interactions other than sports (the average American high school boy is more likely to be involved in *no* social interactive activity than is the average girl), but boys will probably never gravitate as fully as girls do to clubs that promote flourishing coeducational verbal interaction.

ACADEMIC PERFORMANCE.   Girls study harder, get better grades, and are quieter in class; boys goof off more, get worse grades, and are louder. Again, this fits the general nature of females and males: the latter tend toward impulsive behavior, the former toward the sedentary; males tend to be loud, females quiet; males tend to be less mature, females more considered; males tend to be aggressive and competitive in a classroom, females passive. Especially at puberty and in adolescence, females and males are even more different in their hormone-led strategies in classrooms, with many males seeking outward dominance and many females seeking inward excellence. Females also have longer attention spans than males and thus do not need, as often, to move interactive classroom activity from one subject or tangent to the next through verbal dominance and attention strategies.

Although the effort to calm boys down and give girls attention in the classroom is essential, the ultimate standard for a classroom ought not be parity in loudness, aggressive hands-up, or dominance. It is better to treat each student, female or male, with a clear sense of who she or he is, and help the student find a personal mode of expression that fits the particular brain system. This is certainly not what we are doing when we overdiagnose ADD and ADHD and drug young people (mainly males) with Ritalin—as early as the age of three.

SPECIFIC ACADEMIC AREAS. When we look neurologically at girls' dominance in certain aspects of reading and writing and boys' in certain aspects of math and science, we find that male and female brain structure is a direct causal factor. Even as we have removed gender bias against females in math and science (more girls than boys now take math and science classes), still females are outperformed by males at the highest levels of math and physics. This probably won't change (unless boys leave the educational system) because at the highest levels of math and science the male spatials and abstract cognitives will shine.

Furthermore, brain systems explain why girls on average don't like math as much as boys and boys generally don't like reading and writing as much. Even given all the exceptions—the girls who are math whizzes and the boys who write like Hemingway—brain systems always give a gender advantage in these categories. This said, because boys are so far behind in reading and writing right now, the most substantial pressure at all levels (local and federal) ought to expand from just advocacy of math and science for girls to improvement in boys' reading scores, and this shift to reading and writing priorities should be swift. We are damaging a generation as we neglect the tragic reading and writing gap.

TEST SCORES. SAT and other standardized test scores are nearly equal now, but there is still a slight gap in favor of males. It is very possible, given brain formatting, that this gap will always exist unless standardized tests move formidably toward an essay format (where females, of course, hold their advantage) and away from multiple choice (where the deductive male brain has the edge).

The male brain is better at storing single-sentence information (even trivia) than is the female. On game shows like "Who Wants To Be a Millionaire?" men outperform women in large part because of the brain advantage. The male brain holds a visual advantage in working with lists (as in multiple choice), and in making quick deductive decisions on lists. The female brain thinks more inductively (less like a deductive reasoner) and thus often needs substantial information to make a decision. This puts the female at a disadvantage in testing that requires very quick decision making in a short time.

Advocacy has helped girls improve scores in two ways, first by giving them confidence in themselves, and second by convincing testing services to create substantial essay formats that help the female brain compensate for its disadvantage in the standardized, multiple-choice format.

PSYCHOLOGICAL, LEARNING, AND BEHAVIORAL DISORDERS.   Males and females are quite distinct in the kinds of disorder they experience, mainly for hormonal and neurological reasons. New research into the brain, as we've noted earlier, shows the fragility of both male and female brains.

The etiology of eating disorders is related to hormonal and brain chemistry, though stimulation toward the disorder is often external, in cultural imagery and social pressure. Males do not experience a menstrual cycle, dominance by estrogen or progesterone, or so delicate a balance of serotonin cycles, and consequently they do not experience as many eating disorders.

The female brain, emphasizing left-hemisphere development, does not suffer as many attention problems. Females also secrete more serotonin than males and so are less inclined to a hyperactive disorder.

The male brain tends to lateralize its activity—compartmentalizing it in smaller areas of the brain—and therefore suffers more learning disorders. Thus, in some ways, the female brain is a better learning brain because it uses more cortical areas for more learning functions. If one area of the female brain experiences a slight defect, another makes up for it. Because the male brain lateralizes, a defect in one area of the brain may well affect the only area of the brain where a particular learning function is taking place. Special education, alternative education, and learning-different classrooms are dominated by boys for this reason.

Simultaneously, many boys are misdiagnosed with ADHD, ADD, and learning disorders because we have not understood their brains or created classrooms that help them deal well enough with natural impulsiveness, lateralization of brain activity, left hemisphere disadvantage, and learning styles. Chapters Three through Six attempt to right this cultural inadequacy.

Girls tend to suffer the majority of depression and boys the preponderance of alcohol and drug abuse. Again, in the brain and hormones lie the causation, from levels of serotonin and other brain chemicals to hormonal flow. But perhaps even more important is the idea growing out of brain research that our schools are creating overt depression in girls and drug and alcohol abuse (which is masked, covert depression) in boys because we are not creating bonding and attachment communities in our classrooms and schools to the extent growing children need.

MATURITY, DISCIPLINE, AND BEHAVIOR. The maturity gap between boys and girls, especially in the second decade of life, is one of the most pronounced brain-based gaps males and females ever experience. It is the root of many behaviors we have labeled as defective. Female hormones mature earlier and guide the girl toward long-term emotional attachments at the very time that male hormones may not yet be maturing or may guide the boy toward short-term experimental attachments. Teen fathers and those in their early twenties abandon pregnant females at high rates, and many teen females seek to birth and care for children as part of their unmentored biological imperative. Lacking enough guidance and familial attachment, they seek new attachments. Cultural and peer pressures to have sex too early affect both male and female biology, in very challenging ways.

More impulsive and thus less mature than the female brain, the male brain gets a boy into far more trouble in class and in school. The kind of classroom discipline that works for girls—often inconsistent, at times very friendly, and lacking profound authority—does not work so well for many boys in middle school and early high school. Male hormones are flooding, and many boys (especially at the high end of hormone composition) mature to a great extent through elder dominance systems—in which intense bonding and authority best manage them—until they learn to manage themselves.

Brain-based research holds many keys to maturity building and protection of both boys and girls; we apply a great deal of it in the next three chapters. The maturity gap may well be the most profoundly disabling feature of contemporary classroom life.

VIOLENCE. Violence statistics for girls and boys are very high, especially in comparison to the rest of the world. American culture is the most violent nation in the world not currently at war. Per capita, we incarcerate more young men than any other culture not at war. Our males perpetrate more violence on each other and on our females than all other cultures except those at war.

That we live in a culture of violence is by now accepted in all quarters. Schools may be among our safest environments, but they too are painfully aware of male violence. Female violence (and basic nastiness) is increasing, but males will always dominate violence statistics. Boys are testosterone-driven and brain-directed toward spatial expression of stress; they will tend to lash out physically (and with more sexual aggression and physical rage than school-age girls). This trend continues all through adulthood. Although statistically mothers are the primary physical abusers of their own children, they also spend the lion's share of time with their children, thus skewing the statistic. In every other area, males are more violent than females.

The hormonal and neurological factors in male violence, rape, and sexual abuse may never change, but our culture certainly must. In Chapters Three through Six we look at what schools and teachers are doing to curb male violence and better protect both girls and boys. It is important to note that although girls are the likely victims of *sexual* violence, boys are far more likely the victims of *physical* violence. It is essential to understand that males primarily victimize other males rather than females. Male hormones and the male brain cry out through their violence for a different classroom and school culture than many of us practice—one with closer bonding, smaller classes, more verbalization, less male isolation, better discipline systems, more authority, and more attention to male learning styles. The U.S. Department of Justice found that as early as first grade it can predict who the offender males will be. Most of these boys are doing poorly in school, which makes school performance a key factor in a male's self-conception of shame, inadequacy, and ultimately compensatory aggression against others.

My coauthor Patricia Henley directed the Missouri Center for Safe Schools and works with safe schools curricula around the world. She finds more and more schools interested in creating curricula based on brain-based research rather than the old "sensitivity training" models. Those older models have helped a great deal, but they do not help young people understand what is going on inside their own minds and hearts. Antibullying curricula, as we see in the next chapters, are gaining a great deal of effectiveness by enticing students to understand their own internal systems for expressing angry energy, sad energy, hurt energy. In other words, students are becoming self-neurologists, though they don't know it, and learning to manage their own hormones and biology.

In selecting these categories of male-female school activity, we have presented only a tiny portion of available research; but we feel we have left out no major category. Based on our analysis of available research on gender bias, it is difficult for us not to come to a conclusion: that *both* boys and girls are victims of gender disadvantage in our schools, with the harshest gender disadvantage falling against boys.

This conclusion differs, of course, from a great deal of national attention in the last decade to areas of gender bias against girls, especially in math and science performance, athletic participation, and drops in self-esteem. Why does our conclusion differ from those of Carol Gilligan, David and Myra Sadker, or the American Association of University Women, who have long argued that girls, not boys, are the primary targets of bias and privation in our schools?

There are two reasons we should mention. The first is how studies are carried out and reported, including underlying assumptions and lack of a biological foundation to the studies. The second is the desire on the part of women's advocates to deal with antifemale bias in the adult workplace by "proving" similar bias in the child-educational community.

Studies Based on Political Assumptions

For two decades, Gilligan (an early pioneer in gender differences), the Sadkers, and the AAUW studied American classrooms from a mainly sociological point of view, one that assumed gender bias against females throughout our patriarchal culture. When they began their research in the 1960s and 1970s, there was a great deal of bias against females in adult and child communities. They found bias because it was there, and then they continued to find bias even where it wasn't.

In terms of education, most of the "objective bias" they found was in SAT, math, and science scores. We are grateful for their findings, because in twenty years both SAT and math and science scores are now nearly equal between boys and girls. Unfortunately, most of their other findings were amorphous and dependent on interpretation. When they found that boys were called on more than girls in class, they assumed overall female victimization by patriarchal-institutional bias, without looking further into the fact that (1) much of the attention boys got in class was punitive, not rewarding; and (2) girls who were not called on often still outperformed the boys. "Being called on" was not necessarily an indicator of school success or failure, but these researchers decided to assume it was the prime indicator.

We all know that when a boy is called on but a girl is not, it affects the girl negatively. Because of the feminist research, we are all sensitive to managing gender energy in the classroom better. Simultaneously, the assumption that not being called on creates a crisis for girls and being called on ultimately rewards boys is an exaggeration. This hyperbole probably occurred because researchers were dealing with "self-esteem," an amorphous, undefined educational concept. When researchers don't include brain-based, or natural-science based, thinking in their research baselines, they often end up creating sociological conclusions that are, at best, incomplete.

Self-esteem research, done for instance by the American Association of University Women and provided to the public in their 1992 study *How Schools Shortchange Girls,* was burdened with this kind of incompleteness and inaccuracy. The AAUW study was based on a survey that asked boys and girls how they felt about their school experience. Girls were more likely to express negative feelings and detail negative experiences in the school environment. Interpreters at AAUW presented these findings as proof that schools were biased against girls, without informing the public that boys are, in general, more reticent to (1) share feelings about *any* experience and (2) share concrete details about an experience in which they have suffered pain or privation. Boys like to appear tough.

Girls have a verbal and cultural advantage in these areas. Although both girls and boys can experience repression, boys on average tend to repress more when asked direct questions of self-revelation and girls express more; this is true especially when suffering has taken place. Had the AAUW seen its own research through a brain-based lens, it would in fact have concluded that boys were worse off than girls, for in the study itself girls were only slightly more likely than boys to express feelings of privation and bias. This in itself should have been a clue, given how much more reticent boys are by nature. If boys even came close to girls in assessing their schools, then they were feeling a great deal of privation.

The Political Search for Workplace Privation

Perhaps an even more subtle reason for the disparity between actual statistics and the conclusions of certain girls' advocates has been the fact that women continue to suffer workplace privation in many areas of the job market. We spoke with a women's advocate who studied educational bias in schools in the 1980s and 1990s; she wishes not to be named. She told us: "Our thinking back then was that since the workplace is skewed against females, then the educational system, which feeds the workplace, must be skewed against females as well. We set out to find that girls were shortchanged in schools, and we thought we found it. Now, some of us are stepping back from that, especially women like me who have sons and are watching our sons struggle in school environments."

This advocate's early work paid off, as has the work of the Sadkers, Gilligan, and the AAUW: things are improving for girls in school as they have improved for women in the workplace. But once again, brain-based research would have helped our culture get to the truth of what is actually happening in schools much more quickly, had it been used. It would have shown us the real problems for girls *and boys*, problems the U.S. Department of Education has been tracking since 1981 when it first noticed how many more boys were failing in schools and classes than girls. "The Girls Report," published in late 1998 by the National Council for Research on Women, is important reading for anyone wanting to pursue this information, as is Judith Kleinfeld's study, *The Myth That Schools Shortchange Girls*.

It is important for us to realize that the school environment, unlike the work environment, is not generally a male-dominated one. In fact, just the opposite—it is female dominated. In kindergarten through sixth grade, for instance, almost 90 percent of our teachers are women. In the end, what often holds true for the workplace—that the male style dominates and many women are left out—does not apply in the same way in our schools. More accurately, the female brain's learning and teaching style dominates, and more boys are left out. A female-dominated educational environment does not need to let so many boys fail but will probably do so until the day when all teachers are trained in male biology and male culture.

Perhaps it's best now to develop a new assumption, supported by brain-based research: in a society that understands its children, we find that both boys and girls suffer privations and disadvantages owing, to a great extent, to their brain systems' disadvantages and advantages in learning. This assumption would have been hard to accept twenty or thirty years ago, because gender bias was so flagrant against girls in schools. But now, we must move on from old models and see what is really happening, not from political correctness but from the inside out—through the lens of the brain.

We have presented this material about the state of boys and girls in schools, and some of the brain-based reasons for their gender advantages and disadvantages, in order to set the stage for the innovations to follow in Chapters Three through Six. Let's move now to our plan for the best possible classroom for both boys and girls.

Creating the Ultimate Classroom

The next four chapters lay out components of what we call the ultimate classroom, one that works hard to best fit the very nature of each individual child. These chapters are divided chronologically into four stages: preschool and kindergarten, elementary school, middle school, and high school. The material comes from classrooms all over the world, among them a number that were part of a study we are carrying out in six school districts in the state of Missouri. We've included theoretical suggestions for ideal classes and schools along with actual examples of ultimate-classroom components at work.

The Michael Gurian Institute at the University of Missouri-Kansas City contracted with six Missouri school districts to train administrators, teachers, and staff in the kind of brain-based research you have read about in these first two chapters, and then train them in applying new models based on that research. You see the results of this training in the next chapters, in the form of anecdotes and stories from classroom teachers and people like yourself.

We are proud to say that after only six months of application, the brain-based research has already had a profound effect. For instance, in the Hickman Mills School District in Kansas City, Discipline Coordinator Michael Boothe wrote: "Hickman Mills has noted an appreciable drop in discipline referrals to the principal. In reviewing the middle school discipline statistics from first semester of the '98–'99 school year with first semester '99–'00 we can see significant drops. For example, we see 35 percent drops in fights, 25 percent drops in cafeteria misconduct. As we look at the variables, the only major addition to the mix this year was the district's participation in the Gurian Institute."

Dan Colgan, superintendent of the St. Joseph School District, noted: "In St. Joseph, an elementary school, Edison Elementary, was selected to pilot the Gurian Institute for the district. The institute has really changed the way we are doing business at Edison. Students are learning more with less disruptions."

From administrative agendas to classroom innovations, schools are systematically implementing positive, nurturing, and successful changes as they absorb brain-based research. The Gurian Institute brain-based training was part of many other wonderful things teachers and staff are doing and deserves only some credit. Simultaneously, it's great to know that sometimes theory actually does work!

As they read through the next section of this book, we hope that teachers find countless ways to create the ultimate classroom in their school. For most teachers, the students who are usually the most difficult to teach are the boys, so about 70 percent of the anecdotes and applications in the next chapters apply initially to helping boys. We found in our research that teachers are hungry for help for their boys not only because boys so often confuse them, fail in class, and fail in school but also because for about ten years research on girls has prevailed in our educational culture, so teachers have already received some training in it.

These circumstances notwithstanding, the ultimate classroom is a safe and generous learning environment for *both* girls and boys. It is one in which the teacher is challenged, by the innovations that fellow teachers are employing, to contemplate making changes to the classroom and the school: changes in school and classroom structure as well as function, in emotive opportunity for girls and boys, in how senses and physical activity are used in class, and even in how parents are advised to help their children learn.

As with most effective educational techniques, many innovations apply mainly, or only, to one gender. But it is wonderful that so many apply equally to both. It keeps us grounded, as educators (or as teachers in whatever way we work with children), in the fact that we are human beings who, though quite different, meet to learn on common ground, at this place we are calling the ultimate classroom.

Creating the
Ultimate Classroom
for Both Boys and Girls

A hundred years from now, it won't matter what my bank account was, the sort of house I lived in, the kind of car I drove. But the world may be different because I was important in the life of a child.

—KATHY DAVIS, TEACHER

Authors' Note

The next four chapters present action research that shows how to apply, in practical terms, basic principles of brain-based findings to a classroom or a school system. In many cases, teachers tell their own stories as they create the ultimate classroom in their environment. Many of these teachers are in Missouri, where the Michael Gurian Institute has provided training and support. Many testimonials in these chapters come from elsewhere in the country. Both public and private schools are represented.

When a teacher's name is used, a journal entry is sometimes quoted. Teachers in Missouri were asked to keep journals as they applied the brain-based theory to their classrooms. Their journals are often quoted verbatim, or with slight modification to fit paragraph structures.

In other cases, teachers asked not to be named, or they reported action research and practical strategies without including their names. A number of teachers appear many times in these pages, because their journals were specific, practical, and concrete, and because these selected teachers were asked to "upgrade" the specificity of their offerings as a favor to this project.

In the testimonials from around the country, names are sometimes used but just as often not; in some cases a teacher testimonial is a composite of a number of comments that say similar things.

These chapters are structured around specific sections that, quite often, repeat between the chapters. Thus if you are interested in a particular area, such as innovations for teaching math, you can move directly to that section.

For more than ten years, the three of us have explored techniques from many educational forms, traveling to school districts around the country, collecting action and practical material from the fifty United States, as well as personal experience abroad, searching through scholarly research from around the world, and personally applying techniques and strategies in schools and classrooms. The four chapters that follow are written in the hope of presenting the best of the best: the techniques and strategies that constitute the ultimate classroom teachers seek for the needs of boys and girls alike. In some chapters, you will find a section called Structural Innovations, which includes a number of recommendations for innovations that have not been widely tried out yet but hold great promise.

We know that we cannot cover everything here, and we know that many innovations have been missed. We can only report what we've had the good fortune of seeing and experiencing, and hope you will forgive our omissions. We have tried to avoid spending time on policies and programs that are already well known or commonplace; thus we hope to bring you many unique and wonderful ideas that will cause you to say, "Wow, I see how that can help!"

We have written these chapters with the idea in mind that many boys and girls can adapt to nearly any learning situation. We offer the ultimate classroom as a tool that adaptable children can certainly benefit from, but in the end we focus this ideal classroom on making sure to meet the needs of boys and girls for whom one must go the extra distance in adapting to their general and gender-specific needs. In selecting innovations to feature, we have not limited ourselves to those with a direct appeal to girls' or boys' brains; we have also selected major educational innovations that can have a particular effect on the lives of boys and girls. Although the title of this book is *Boys and Girls Learn Differently!* and though some of the best brain research available today is in this area of gender difference and the brain, we know that the ultimate classroom speaks not only to differences between boys' and girls' learning needs but also to similarities.

The particular service Patricia, Terry, and I hope to extend in books like this one is *constant practical application.* We hope that as you enjoy these chapters you will find so much practical help for your efforts to educate children that you will feel the educational lives of the children around you change to the high degree that they require, especially in today's world, where education of the child is increasingly complicated.

If you wish to share your own innovations with others, please contact us through the website: www.gurianinstitute.com. We hope you will send us your stories and your innovations so that we can include them in future editions of this work. All of us—teachers, administrators, parents, and others who care about schoolchildren—are in this effort together; we gain from constructive vigilance on the everyday and constantly changing teaching environment.

3

The Ultimate Preschool and Kindergarten Classroom

Early education of the child is as crucial as any other stage. In the early years, all future education is illuminated for the child.

—MARIA MONTESSORI

ONE MORNING, A PRESCHOOL TEACHER GREETED HER STUDENTS AT the door. She gave four-year-old Tessa a customary handshake and the girl said, "Mrs. Bingham, I got up on the right side of the bed this morning." Mrs. Bingham looked at Tessa's mother, who grinned, "Her father's been trying to get her to have a better attitude in the morning." Tessa gave her mother a last hug and went into the classroom, where she took off her "outdoor shoes," placed them in her cubby, put on her "indoor shoes," and then went to a small table where some other kids were coloring.

Mrs. Bingham now shook hands with Randy, watery-eyed from recent tears. At five, he was a year older than Tessa; he hugged his mother close. Randy's parents had just begun a legal separation and Randy had been showing, for a month now, both tension and grief in his everyday behavior, especially his separation time from Mom in the mornings. Mrs. Bingham worked with Randy's mother to reassure and engage him until he finally followed Tessa's routine.

On Randy's heels were the only twins in the class, Sarah and Anne, both four; they said goodbye to their father, who was dressed in camouflage pants and a shirt that read U.S. Air Force. While shaking Mrs. Bingham's hand, Anne said, "Daddy's going away, but we're going to do our lessons very well while he's gone." Mrs. Bingham responded, "I'll bet you'll miss your daddy." Sarah said, "Very much," and the children hugged their dad again. Finally, girls and father broke their embrace and good-byes were done; Mrs. Bingham shook both hands, and they too changed into their indoor shoes.

So went the first half-hour of preschool that morning. Teacher, parents, and children met at the door. The home world from whence each child came was an important part of the transition to the school world, not separate from it but overlapping. Hugs turned to handshakes, handshakes to the task of changing shoes. The children shook off hesitations and the preschool world awoke again with the sounds, tastes, smells, and commotion of young children learning lessons in that combination of work and play, order and disorder, freedom and responsibility that each early-education classroom tries to master.

Until recently, the general public has thought of a child's schooling as primarily a matter of elementary, middle, and high school. Over the last decade, brain-based and gender research is opening our eyes to a fourth essential era of child education: preschool and kindergarten. There is great debate in our culture about what is essential to the growing toddler and kindergartner, and what is pretty useful or just good if the child can get it. Because the goal of our research is to help teachers, parents, and communities create the ultimate classroom, we have gone through it all to cull the components, techniques, and ideas that we believe make a case, from the viewpoint of the brain, for innovations in preschool education.

The Foundation of Early Learning: Bonding and Attachment

The new brain research has resurfaced for us a remarkable notion, something that our ancestors seemed to know instinctively: young children learn best when they learn from someone with whom they are intimately attached. If a child, for instance, is securely attached to an important personal caregiver—his mother, father, grandparent, or teacher—he learns more, not only from that individual but in his total learning competency. Learning competence stays clear and unmistakable, from a research standpoint, long after the early years of attachment.

The brain needs bonding and attachment to fully grow and learn. We might think of the brain as a plant trying to grow toward the sun. It may grow in the shadows, but it does not grow as well as a plant that gets the necessary sunlight. The brain-plant makes itself crooked if it must to grow toward where it senses the sun is. It will put off, avoid, or be unable to achieve bloom fully until it finds the sun it seeks. It must bask in the sun before it can learn its full nature.

Does the sun grow the plant, or does the plant just wait to fully grow until the sun is present? This is the kind of spiritual question that neurology alone can perhaps never resolve. Neurology does teach us, however, that without the sun (attachment) the brain does not grow too well. Children from orphanages, for instance, have more behavioral and psychological problems and test out lower on intelligence tests than children not raised in orphanages. There can be a great deal of sun in the orphanage, but on average not as much as in a biological home.

In our ancestral human communities, children in infancy and the toddler years were raised in simpler nurturing groups than we have today. They generally had a "first mother" (the biological mother) and a second one as well (the grandmother, auntie, or other parenting female). They generally had a first father (the biological one) and a second father (a grandfather, uncle, or another male from the father or mother's kinship system). The first and second mothers were the main care providers for infancy and the toddler years, and further into growth. The fathers were present (usually at least one remaining with the family if the other had to travel far away to fight a war or to work) during the early years but became more actively involved when the child needed training in the works of the hand, or in adult male hierarchies. Fathers tended to be most active in protecting girls and in challenging boys. Mothers were less selective, we think, in what they taught children; we think they were more "generalists" among them than among fathers, but we don't know for sure. We do know that children were raised in these close, relatively closed communities.

Our present-day children, on the other hand, are likely to be attached to groups of strangers, in both physical reality and virtual reality. Instead of grandma, we have day care, preschool and kindergarten. Along with or instead of mom, we may have a nanny or other child care professional. In grandpa's place, we often have no second father. There may be no first father, either. The ramifications of these fractured intimate attachments for children are being felt in every part of child development. All preschool and kindergarten teachers know that their most problematic children generally come from homes or family situations where attachment is lax, dysfunctional, or dangerous. Some difficult young children have actual brain disorders, while most are under immense emotional stress—attachment stress—and are struggling to learn. To help the brain of the child become the best learning brain possible, we must first deal with these stresses.

Handling Children's Emotional Stress

Susan Colgan, family involvement coordinator in the St. Joseph, Missouri, school district, shared with us these experiences from preschool teachers and day care providers.

> Cleary was commenting that her "auntie" was keeping her and her siblings while her mom was in jail. She asked the teacher, "Who keeps your kids when you go to jail?"
>
> Destiny's daddy left the family and moved out of state. He returns for a few days to visit. The first three months, Destiny pooped her pants daily and talked continually about her daddy. After Dad leaves, Destiny is understandably very emotional and asks frequently, "How long until Mom picks me up?"
>
> Today, Andrew told the class that he didn't have a dad. Keilin found this hard to believe and asked, "You don't have a *dad*?" Andrew immediately shook two fists at Keilin and said in a threatening voice, "Don't *ever* talk about it!"

Case and Mary were in the house area. Case began to chase Mary with a plastic knife. She responded by grabbing a suitcase and stuffing clothes in it and yelling, "I'm leaving and I'm taking the babies with me!" With arms full, she marched out of the house area, leaving Case speechless. I'm sure she had recently seen this at home. Her parents just split up. The dad was physically violent.

Teachers like Susan are frequently faced with students like these, under immense emotional stress. The stress, in this age group, is generally founded in fear of attachment loss. The neurological path of this attachment loss might look a little like this: cortisol, the stress hormone, rises, flooding the brain and making some neural activity slower (for instance, in learning centers in the top of the brain) but other activity quicker (in the brain stem and lower limbic system, where anger and withdrawal responses of fight or flight increase). The stressed child learns less from the learning activities in the classroom than the well-attached child or the one under less emotional stress. The child under more stress is almost invariably the one whose brain is imprinting, or modeling, behavior such as Mary displayed (that of a mother trying to escape with her children from a violent father).

Imprinting of attachment loss affects memory, which affects learning quite comprehensively, inasmuch as memory is a foundation for learning. Areas in the hippocampus, for instance, where a great deal of memory happens, "fill up" with imprinted memory that is associated with emotional stress, signaling the limbic system to increase stress responses. Other lessons (say, about the alphabet or number chains) are not retained in the hippocampus, and the limbic system keeps the whole brain distracted from them as well.

Boys and girls overlap a great deal in how their brains and hormones handle attachment stress. Yet there are also differences, especially clear in these early years. Crying behavior is very common in this age group, but many boys have already begun to mask pain with "I'm fine." Many girls have already begun to mask pain by increasing responsibility behavior: becoming more responsible for younger children or as teacher's helper. Some teachers have noticed kindergarten girls in general, and overstressed females especially, already complaining that they are too fat and suffering body-image distortion. Teachers commonly report physical aggression from attachment-stressed boys as well as greater language delay. Teachers also note quick-to-anger and quick-to-withdraw responses from both boys and girls.

Teachers can't solve problems at home, but there is much that they and their communities can do. In California, through the auspices of the Palo Alto Medical Center, a community of philanthropic citizens developed and have sustained the Esther Brown Center in Palo Alto, an innovative school inspired by the idea that corporate health and community health are intertwined. As one donor told me, "Our corporations suffer the consequences of negative early-education experiences among the children of our community. The more of our new wealth we put into collaborating with educators, the better off we'll be in the long run. Many of us are especially interested in making sure every child has the bonds he or she needs, and we're ready to write checks in order to help." As this philanthropist was implying, it is easier, from a financial point of view, to implement the wisdom of creating bonding in schools and communities when the community is united around a research university (Stanford, in this case), a state-of-the-art medical center, and a booming dot-com economy. Yet it can be carried out anywhere at all, as so many schools and communities have discovered.

Bonding and Attachment Solutions

The first thing our research indicates as necessary is for our culture to reframe the early-education teacher's role. Day care providers and teachers of preschoolers and kindergartners are often a boy or girl's *second mother.* They are more than "just teachers." In the child's mind, the provider or teacher is often the woman who is second only to Mom.

Although this is an immense job, and teachers are not specifically trained for it in graduate school, it is nonetheless the reality we now live with. A nonblood mentor, not a blood-linked grandma or auntie, is the second mother to twenty-some children a day.

Our Western culture is now challenged to assist teachers and caregivers of young children in the same way our own, and other nations', ancestral cultures supported grandmothers, aunties, grandfathers, and other caregivers in their second-parent role. This kind of rethinking is foundational to all the innovations that follow in this chapter. Both boys and girls need their preschool teachers to become even more, not less, like second mothers.

CLASS SIZE AND TEACHER-STUDENT RATIO. Our brain-based research indicates that in preschool and kindergarten, not only is one second mother necessary but for learning purposes the presence of two teachers is optimal. If two teachers are present, classroom size can rise to fifteen or twenty students. If they are not, a ratio of one teacher to eight or ten students is suggested (infants are excluded from these suggestions). There are, in this scenario, enough teachers to go around, from an attachment standpoint. If there are any serious behavioral problems among the students, a second (or third) person—a "roaming" teacher—who is generally trained in the special education field can assist.

Ensuring this kind of student-teacher ratio has a positive effect on academic learning, psychosocial learning, discipline, and general growth; not surprisingly, it best attends to the gender-different learning needs of boys and girls. Kathi Winkler, an early learning specialist in the Hickman Mills School District, wrote in her journal:

> Our program has a maximum of twelve students in a classroom with a teacher and a paraprofessional. The advantage of this is that we are able to divide our time better to meet the unique needs of both boys and girls in the room. For example, I can be involved with monitoring elaborate block constructions and giving occasional suggestions for block stability or variations while my paraprofessional can be involved with children in a more sedentary writing or reading activity at the same time. Many activities that challenge young children take a hands-on, heads-up approach by an adult and these would have to be limited if I were in the room alone.

To give an example: At the same moment [that some boys were working on a big block model] my paraprofessional was involved with several children at the art area. Her constant attention was required there to help meet requests for assistance with materials and attempts at cutting, gluing, and writing. Having two teachers available allows for more activity, more choice, and less wait time for all the children. These elements make the program successful for all, but especially more successful for boys, who give us our greater difficulties.

Kathi's experience with boys is shared by most of the teachers in our research. Especially in early childhood, general difficulties haunt the young males, while specific area difficulties affect females—as in math learning, which we touch on later in this chapter. It's also important to note that in middle and high school, new difficulties emerge for girls. In preschool, however, the learning environment, when it errs, generally does so on the side of the female brain, giving girls learning advantages and boys disadvantages.

Furthermore, there is some evidence that the male brain does not return to stability and learning readiness as quickly as the female does after a traumatic experience or after a period of serious stress. Some research shows that the female brain adapts more quickly after emotional stress, for instance a problem at home in the morning. This may be especially true the younger the brain is, which would explain why more boys than girls have learning, emotional, and behavioral difficulties in preschool and kindergarten. Making a second teacher available is a matter of helping develop emotional learning skills as much as academic.

BONDING RITUALS. Because she understood the importance of attachment in learning (especially the fragility inherent in the male brain), Kathi devised a number of bonding rituals that she believes have increased learning in her preschool and kindergarten classroom. Although she initially devised them because she wanted to offset "the impact that lack of attachment is having on the boys in my class who have intellectual, language, and social delays," she quickly discovered that the rituals worked well for girls too. She writes:

Bonding with the boys in my classroom at times seems more difficult because they are in an almost exclusively female environment in terms of staff. Some of the activities such as wrestling and rough-housing are not comfortable for me. I have tried several other rituals with my boys and am pleased with my success.

Probably the most popular one, since it is now initiated regularly by the boys, is my "high five" game. Thrusting out my palm, I say "Gimme five." The child does so and then I put my palm up high and say "Up high." Again, the child high-fives me and I move my hand down low and say "Down low." As the child moves his hand to meet mine, I pull quickly back and say "Whoops, too slow!" and they miss my hand.

Kathi finds that two elements make this special, particularly to ensure bonding with harder-to-reach kids, most of whom, in her experience, are male.

First, the boys just seem to like the physical connection of a high five better than a hug and almost all will connect with me in this game. Secondly, the game has an element of competition attached to it that makes it a challenge for the boys. They will participate in it over and over in an attempt to not be too slow. The boys actually begin to have success and I cannot get my hand away quickly enough after a while so they are excited to beat my challenge. This game never seems to lose popularity and I can often use it to build a connection to a boy who is resisting me and resisting learning.

Last year, Carl was a little boy who usually responded to any request or redirection with the declaration "You aren't my friend," and with physical resistance. Yet I knew he wanted to meet my expectations.

Using the game in nonconfrontational moments allowed us to begin to establish a positive relationship that transferred over to more difficult moments. Now when I see Carl, he will both high-five me and then jump into my arms for a hug.

With this success in mind, I have added two other "I Love You Rituals" to help build attachment as I dismiss each child by name at the end of the day.

The first uses the song from the early '60s "The Name Game" (the children ask for the "banana" song):

> Toby, Toby bo boby.
> Fe fi mo moby—Toby.

The second choice is the little box.

> If I had a little red box,
> To put my Alan in,
> I'd take him out and [kiss, kiss, kiss]
> And put him back in again.

It seems amazing, but the children ask for this song daily. I usually let each child tell me if he or she wants the "banana" or "box" song. When they choose "box," I let them name the color of the box.

Like so many preschool teachers, Kathi finds a new smoothness in the school day and learning once it revolves around some rituals of love like these. She concludes that "little attachment games like this even make our transitions during the day more of a fun ritual than a struggle."

ROUTINES AND SCHEDULES. Bonding rituals work especially well when framed by other solid daily routines, like taking off outdoor shoes and putting on indoor shoes. All preschool and kindergarten classrooms benefit from ordered ritual and schedule. In young children, the brain needs freedom to discover varieties of information, but also an ordered environment in which to turn raw data and stimulation experience into learning, skill competence, and wisdom.

Classrooms that include one or more children with a learning or behavioral difficulty benefit especially from these essential components of early brain development. Actually, if a child has a particular problem, this idea, put to practical use, can be crucial.

Special education teacher Carrie Whalley wrote about

a particular kindergarten boy with pretty serious behavioral problems. We tried some interventions and they were successful for a while. But for the past few weeks he's been backsliding quite a bit.

He's back to hitting, kicking, name-calling, etc., when he doesn't get his way. For a while we couldn't figure out what was going on.

Then Mom explained to us that his home schedule has changed lately. Since his parents divorced, he would spend every other weekend with Dad. For the last few weeks, however, Dad has wanted to spend more time with him. His schedule is not consistent anymore and he has really seemed to have lost his sense of security.

Carrie and the other teachers worked on keeping this boy on a schedule during the day in order to offset his lack of stability at home. They have seen strong results.

BONDING TIPS. Principal Debbie Hughes and her staff at Edison Elementary School devised this list of simple tips after receiving training in application of brain-based, gender, and attachment research:

Be genuine with children.

Call each child by name.

Learn about the child's world, personal life, and personal interests.

Use "I noticed . . ." statements.

Smile, touch (when appropriate), and make eye contact.

Attend events in the child's life whenever possible.

Respect the child and the child's opinions.

Personally disclose your life as appropriate. Tell your own story.

Be nonjudgmental.

Listen, and then listen some more.

Give the child choices and options that compel healthy decision making.

Admit mistakes you have made.

These simple, commonsense tips can apply, of course, to children of all age groups. If we start focusing on these ideas in the early-childhood years, what a difference we make in the life of a growing brain!

Day Care, Preschool, and Kindergarten Community Building

There exist day care, play care, and preschool environments in which children are merely warehoused; television sets are on all day; parents do not return for children until ten hours after they've left them; near-strangers are taking care of children; child and sexual abuse occurs; and providers are paid so little they quit constantly, replaced by new care-givers who also soon quit, leaving the young children to form what con-sistency of community they can mainly among peers with whom they simply cannot learn the lessons of life as richly as they can with consis-tent, adult caregivers. The dangers of such a situation have been well documented and are obvious. We therefore move into specific areas that perhaps have not been as well defined, areas toward which brain-based research points us.

The Case for Preschool

There is some controversy today about the usefulness of preschool. "My child is better off at home," a parent might say, "at least till kinder-garten. The influences in preschools are terrible." "On the contrary," others say, "preschools help the child learn how to socialize, and the child develops a foundation for all later learning that the home can't as effectively create."

Our research indicates truth in the first assertion when the pre-school is run by professionals who are not well trained, but truth in the second when they are. The quality of the preschool defines its useful-ness. If the preschool is run by people of passion and wisdom, children are generally better off than when they spend the first five years of life in the presence mainly of one caregiver who is not trained in how the brain learns.

New studies indicate that good day care can increase brain devel-opment, and quality preschool increases it even further. An elemen-tary school teacher recently told us: "Especially these days, if a kid doesn't go to preschool, he's sunk. Expectations later in school and in life have changed so much that it's harder for the kid who gets no schooling until kindergarten." Social and academic expectations are indeed higher now than when we were growing up. Social technologies are vast and psychosocial demands more intense, both as the old extended-family systems break down and as children become entranced by global networks. If a child is not going to go to preschool, it is at least important that there be some "preschool time" worked into her day, in which she socializes with other children and accomplishes developmentally appropriate home-school lessons. At the same time, the ultimate classroom, the place of most stimulating development for the brain after the stage of potty training, is most probably a high-quality preschool program.

Parents as Teachers

It is immensely important that school and family life no longer be disconnected. It is especially important in the early years of a child's life to ensure that brain development at home is well accomplished and thus, when the child enters school, the brain is ready to learn. If it is true, as attachment research shows us, that teachers are in many ways like parents to children, then parents are very much like teachers. Thus the Parents as Teachers Program developed to help parents fulfill their crucial role. We highly recommend it for all school districts interested in expanding early-childhood learning. It is an immensely brain-friendly program. The state of Missouri uses it generously.

Parents as Teachers is a statewide program that focuses on helping parents understand the developmental needs of their infants and toddlers, and on providing advice and early help if a problem exists. It is a home visitation program where workers are trained and then visit the homes to support parents. Several other states have implemented Parents as Teachers programs, although Missouri was the first state to mandate and fund it. The Independence School District, in Independence, Missouri, has the longest operating Schools of the Twenty-First Century program. It began about eleven years ago and all the elementary schools in the district have all of the components except infant care.

The Parent Education Coordinator

Many busy (or harried) parents of young children are not trained in brain development and in gender-specific development, nor are they supported intergenerationally by elders, and they may be unable, during busy work schedules, to receive long-term, personal training in these essentials. To support them, we believe it is crucial that each school district assign a parent education coordinator, to disseminate educational materials, teach parents (by newsletter and workshops) how to provide good discipline to kids, answer any and all parent questions, offer books and other materials that chart normal child growth, and teach parents what boys' and girls' specific gender needs may be.

This position might cost a school district an additional teacher's salary, but it pays for itself by cutting down on parents' litigation alone. Many parents litigate because they feel disconnected with schools and pull back support—personal and financial—because of a communication breakdown or problem with their child, during whose schooling they feel disconnected and snubbed. By educating parents and being devoted to connection with them, the parent education coordinator becomes an invaluable link between parent and school. We hope this position becomes a part of every district's ultimate classroom, beginning with preschool, kindergarten, and early education.

Nutrition and Learning

Brain research has taught us that what children eat profoundly affects their ability to learn and behave. This is especially true of young children who have not yet developed the mature ability to control impulses when under stress. If a five-year-old is under emotional stress, she has great difficulty controlling herself or learning. If she is under nutritional stress, the same is true.

The ultimate classroom is a place where children eat the right foods at the right time; it is also a place where parents are educated about these same foods and appropriate nutrition. Parents want to know what their little ones should and should not be eating; they often need school professionals to help them filter through all the competing trends or coercive messages in the media. Nutrition is a fundamental element of parent education coordination and school-to-home liaison. Brain-based research compels us to set aside any illusions that food is not an essential part of the brain's ability to learn. It also shows us that girls and boys, though overlapping immensely in their reaction to stressful food or inadequate nutrition, also experience some neurological differences.

Carbohydrates, Proteins, and the School Day

Many children begin their day eating a piece of toast or a bowl of cereal, which is often high in carbohydrates. This actually dulls their ability to learn. If, first thing in the morning, the child is going to exercise, the high carbs are okay, as they generate quick energy for exercise (they bring blood sugar up from the overnight low that all of us experience when we sleep). However, since children mainly sit on a bus or in a car and then sit some more in a classroom, the high-carb loading in the morning is not advisable.

Carbohydrates with a high glycemic index (refined sugars, refined grains such as white bread) are fast-release carbohydrates that tell the brain to load the body up with glucose. In the short run, they build up serotonin quickly, which can give a temporary and pleasant feeling of calm, but this is accomplished by surges of blood sugar in the body that are often followed by either the jitters or feeling low. These come when the blood sugar crashes, which it must inevitably do.

The jitters tend to be a male way of experiencing the sugar crash; depression, or feeling low, tends to be the female way. Boys tend to become impulsive, and girls are temporarily withdrawn and distracted.

As boys get older, we may see them "carbo loading" more and more as they pursue high-endurance athletic activity (athletic girls often do this too, of course). A positive use for high glycemic carbohydrates that is uniquely female involves treatment of postmenstrual syndrome, and menstrual comfort in general. Sugary foods and drinks help the body navigate the stress of menstrual flow. Both these positive uses of sugary and starchy foods, however, come later in life. In early childhood, there is hardly a positive use for these foods if the goal of the day is for the child to settle into comfortable learning. *& play*

For both boys and girls, the first half of the day is not a time for bagels, pasta, rolls, donuts, and other sugary foods. Brain-based research leads us to recommend that preschools ban sugar snacks both in the preschool itself and in the lunchbox sent from home. Sugars and starches also ought to be deemphasized at lunch, as these carbs make the brain groggy, and the child neither learns nor tests as well after this kind of lunch. When, later in the day, the child is going to engage in athletics, there is some use for higher carbohydrates, but rarely until then.

High-fiber food, protein, yogurt, and milk (soy milk being just as good as cow's milk and in some ways better, because it distinctly and quickly builds alerting neurotransmission—what gets us up and thinking in the morning) are better breakfast and morning snack foods than carbs because they not only avoid inducing a minor serotonin crisis in the blood and brain, but they actually *build* learning ability by helping brain cell growth more than the offending carbohydrates do. They help the child stay more awake as well as actually challenge the brain to grow. A wonderful book for exploring the link between food and the brain is Robert Arnot's *The Biology of Success.*

Fatty Acids

Brain research has taught us an immense amount lately about fatty acids that help brains grow. It has also given us early warning about problems that our diet, both at home and in school, is creating for growing children. Unfortunately, in the United States we deemphasize omega-3 fatty acids (the kind found especially in fish and fish oils), and our brains are suffering as a result. We are setting our children up to fail as learners and as well-socialized human beings. Although the major problems for kids may not show up till later, it is in the early years that we need to grapple with this material.

The human brain is just over 60 percent fat and requires omega-3 acids to promote optimal brain performance. Psychiatric and neurological disorders such as depression (which hits girls in greater numbers) and ADHD (which favors boys), as well as learning and other behavioral disorders, are linked to lack of omega-3 acid. This link continues into adolescence, when bipolar personality disorders and schizophrenia emerge, again correlating to children with low omega-3s. According to Michael Schmidt, author of the very important book *Smart Fats,* "Preliminary studies indicate that an imbalance of essential fatty acid intake may well relate to such problems as social violence, aggressive behavior, and suicide."

The omega-3 fatty acid is not something the brain produces by itself. Instead, it relies on the environment—nutrition and eating habits. In our typical American (or Western) diet, we downplay fish, fish products, and fish oils, especially in children's diets. Disorders, depression, and violent behavior occur at a lower rate in cultures that emphasize intake of omega-3. Without intake of the omega 3s, the nerve endings of neurotransmitters can't function properly. Fatty acids are structural molecules of which nerve endings are made. Human synapses—brain connections—are membranes also composed of fatty acids, among them arachidonic acid, DHA (docosahexaenoic acid), and EPA (eicosapentaenoic acid). If the brain doesn't have enough fatty acids, both the nerve endings and the synaptic membranes are affected, and neurotransmission itself deteriorates. The very shape and constitution of receptors change. If the receptors are nuanced inappropriately for the normal brain process, neurotransmitters such as dopamine and serotonin are affected. Serotonin function affects violent, depressive, and impulsive behavior. Dopamine affects everything from mood to motor ticks.

For boys and girls, in brain and gender-specific ways, the lack of fatty acids in our diet can be devastating. In a sense, we are setting our children up to fail by keeping from their brains the "brain food" they need. We are setting our boys up to be impulsive and aggressive, to have problems with motor skills and motor ticks, and to suffer learning disorders. We are setting up our girls for overt depression, eating disorders, and emotional disturbance, and an increase in the rate of learning disorders.

During the preschool and kindergarten years, the brain is forming at a fast pace. Neurotransmission and synaptic processes are forming in patterns that will persist for life. It is important to protect a child's diet throughout life, but early childhood is especially the time to set the tone of life, and the rituals of eating that the child will follow. Some of what our culture is now (and will go on) handling through psychotropic medications such as Prozac and Ritalin can be handled more naturally for brain development by better diet. This should not astound us.

Dealing with Aggressive Behavior

One of the primary areas of difficulty in the preschool and kindergarten classroom is aggressive behavior, which has inspired a great deal of medication use. It has also generated debate among brain theorists and gender watchers. Boys are generally more physically aggressive than girls, and girls are generally more socially manipulative than boys. Let's look at the preschool and kindergarten classroom through the lens of brain and gender and then answer the question that educators continue asking after all the debate dust settles: "So where do we draw the line with our kids—how much aggression is OK, and how do we handle what isn't?"

First, let's hear some stories. A preschool teacher wrote this:

Jerrell always got in trouble. He was one of my favorites, if truth be told. He was with me from 2½ to 6, then went to first grade. I was like his auntie. But for maybe a year or more I just couldn't get him to stop pushing and shoving the girls. I had three brothers so I'm no dummy about boys. I've been in early education twenty years. I know how they like to push and shove and bump each other. I watch them growl in each other's faces and practice their karate kicks and Power Rangers. I like boys a lot and I'm good with them. But with Jerrell, I couldn't get anywhere.

Then one day, when he was about four, I heard him say to one of the girls, "You always do that. Stop it!" I went over to see what "it" was. The girl, Hannah, actually admitted her fault before Jerrell could figure out how to explain: "I called him an idiot because that's what he is," she said.

"Do you call him that a lot?" I asked.

She nodded. "Uh huh. Boys," she said, pushing her lip out. "I don't like them at all."

Later, when Jerrell and I were talking, he said that she and her friend Ruthie called him an idiot and stupid a lot and he admitted it hurt his feelings. I asked him if he pushed people right after that happened sometimes. He said, "Maybe."

From that day on I watched Jerrell and the girls more carefully. I also watched other boy-girl dynamics. I saw something that was really hard for me to admit was true, especially as a feminist. There were lots of times—I mean, *lots*—where the boys' aggressive behavior followed a verbally aggressive act by the girls (or even by another boy). All my life I'd known boys but this thing, right in front of me, had been blocked in my mind. I never wanted to admit that boys' [behavior] could be instigated by girls. I wanted to see girls as kind and boys as having aggression problems. I see things differently now.

Let's hear another story. A mother wrote us:

My son is five, in kindergarten, and goes to a preschool where the teacher does not allow karate kicks, even fake ones. The kids are not allowed to push and pull each other. She was an only child and I don't think she understands boys. My son can be very quiet and kind, but he also likes to be a "karate man." He and his father play it all the time at home and they wrestle. But when he goes to school, he has to be something so different. I'm thinking about taking him out of that school.

Another mother, experiencing the opposite, wrote: "I have a daughter and a son. She's four, in preschool, and he's five, in kindergarten. I find the kids there much rougher than my children are. There's a real 'Boys will be boys' attitude. The teachers let almost anything go. I don't like it. In some ways, I find my daughter better able to handle the roughness than my son. He's so sensitive. She's bossy enough to tell other kids what to do."

These are called the tender years in a child's life, and with good reason. The brain and body are growing rapidly, making them especially sensitive to aggression. Boys and girls often seem to follow gender lines, making teachers protective of girls and physically repressive of boys. Of course, there are exceptions to gender rules. Many boys are far more emotionally fragile than we have realized, their brains and psyches slower to develop than girls' or more aggressive boys'.

Almost none of the teachers who enter preschool classrooms have been trained in the differences between the male and female brain and thus have not studied possible behavioral effects of the brain on boys and girls. Nor have they had time, in their educational preparation, to develop strategies to handle the complexity of aggression that they encounter in the preschool classroom. Over time, all teachers bring their particular intuitive strengths to problems, but how wonderful it will be when teachers of young children are trained *before* entering the classroom, in this crucial part of human socialization. Here are some elements our trainings focus on.

Aggression Nurturance

Aggression nurturance is the term I use for nurturance that involves aggression activities, such as physical touch and talk of that sort, competitive games, and aggressive nonverbal gestures. Boys tend to practice more aggressive nurturance than girls, and girls more empathy nurturance than boys, but these general trends indicate no normality or "better" behavior; they simply indicate trends in gender difference. The male brain and chemistry impel males to practice less eye-to-eye contact and more shoulder-to-shoulder, less "Are you OK?" and more "You're OK, so get up," less "Let's talk about it" and more "Get out of my way." Clearly, also, social trends and pressure push males toward more of this behavior, and females toward greater use of behavior based in immediate empathic reaction.

It has been an assumption in our educational culture for the last three decades that some of the most important work we could do to aid both boys and girls is to help boys be more empathic and less aggressive. Some of this work is certainly worthwhile, but our research indicates that now another piece must be added to our vision of boy-girl differences in aggressive behavior, namely, to understand the value of aggression nurturance. This kind of nurturance is as valuable as empathy nurturance, but it differs distinctly from it.

When a teacher or parent laments that some of the children—generally boys—relate by bumping, prodding, and pushing each other, we might recast a lot of the behavior this way: "Wow, look at how those kids are nurturing each other by bumping, prodding, and pushing." If we look closely, we notice that a lot of what they are doing is indeed nurturing activity. They are building strength, focus, attentiveness, and hierarchy through these actions. Their use of this nurturance style increases into elementary school, and then when hormones hit—especially testosterone—it soars toward a high peak in the middle teens and into the twenties.

As the male becomes an adult, he learns many other ways to nurture, mixing aggression nurturance with everything else. Especially as he seeks romance, a male may modify his nurturance style to show greater knowledge of word-oriented empathy systems. Nonetheless, most males, even in middle age, rely greatly on the complexity of aggression nurturance. This gets them into relational trouble at times, especially with females and with less aggressive males, but it also pushes forward into greater hierarchical success, as in the workplace.

When they are very young, children experiment with all nurturing styles and can be taught—inasmuch as the brain is plastic and flexible—to increase how frequently one or other nurturance style is used. When we say to an aggressive child "Use your words," we are redirecting aggression nurturance toward empathy nurturance because we fear less the consequences of words to the human community than the consequence of aggressive action. It is crucial we do this, but it is also essential to take time to notice how much nurturance and learning takes place while it appears children are being tough on each other. Many boys are labeled defective in early childhood because they rely on aggressive nurturance more than a teacher is trained to mentor, teach, and understand.

Increasing Empathy Nurturance and Verbalization

Given what we've just said, let's recast what happens with Jerrell. In fact he was the benefactor—not the victim—of a girl's aggression nurturance. Her use of *stupid* and *idiot* was reprehensible—given the need for discipline and uniformly supportive language in a preschool environment—but her actions were meant aggressively, to aid Jerrell in reconceiving his behavior. He was doing things that bugged her, and she told him so. Neither she nor he acted as we wish—she too nasty and he too physical—but then again, unless they had acted this way they would not have learned the lessons they learned, nor would an astute teacher have intervened to take the lessons even further.

Jerrell was unable to see a connection between his aggressive behavior and the girl's verbal aggressions until he and his mentor "used their words." The teacher relied on empathy nurturance to continue, and perhaps complete, lesson learning that began in aggression nurturance between children.

Viewing Jerrell and the girl this way is different from what educators are used to. It runs somewhat counter to much of the training we've received over the last decades, which emphasizes the supposed wrongness of Jerrell's physical aggression and assigns the girl's verbal aggression to a less immoral status in children's dynamics. Even though she had brothers and was wise in the ways of boys, the teacher missed the fact that the boy was becoming aggressive because of verbally aggressive behavior by the girls; yet her intuition did guide her toward the ultimate solution: observation, then conversation, then one-on-one empathic assistance to both the boy and girl, in which she redirected both of their behaviors, especially teaching the boy to make a neural connection between his physical behavior and its external stimulant.

Even though it is certainly true that females tend toward complex verbal strategies, especially in preschool and kindergarten (when boys are up to a year behind in verbal skills), and boys tend toward complex physical strategies for nurturance, there are many girls who practice aggression nurturance better than boys, and boys who seek empathy nurturance more quickly than girls. This too is an area of difficulty for teachers and parents of young children, for the mass of boys seems to pull all of them into a certain kind of behavior, just as the mass of girls pulls girls in another direction. A distinct group of girls and boys don't fit the social interactive hierarchies and feel left out. For them, preschool and kindergarten are subtly frightening.

To take care of children who might suffer emotional harm in these gender-mass school dynamics, our research indicates teacher agreement that in the ultimate classroom *we must keep increasing children's use of words*. From a neurological point of view, we might add: "... especially use of *words that explain feelings*."

A typical situation is this one reported to us by a preschool teacher: "Our day care providers were teaching the children to use their words instead of actions. Tony, who is four, was upset because another child hit him. Tony told the other child, 'I don't like it when you hit me. Please stop.' Then Tony came to the teacher and told her what he had said and he was very proud of himself."

This "using your words" is valuable in increasing neural connections between the upper brain and middle brain and between the left hemisphere and the limbic system. Both boys and girls benefit from it, with male brains gaining neural connections they less naturally make than females do and females gaining a comfortable, less physically aggressive, and verbally safer school and playground that fits their natural brain development.

In the end, the brain-based gender research asks teachers to mentor *both* aggression and empathy. On the one hand, rules against cruelty must be a central component of all preschools. Children who are not directed to follow them are not well enough bonded with caregivers, nor experiencing appropriate discipline and mentoring. On the other hand, rules against *all* aggression show, generally, a teacher's lack of ability to fully bond, discipline, and mentor—especially her boys. In this case, rather than children learning life lessons through the aggression that is natural to them, they are learning that aggression is too difficult to manage in society and instead must simply be shut down. Because these same children will practice their aggression somewhere else, where adult supervision may not exist, they may come to learn that it is only adults who fear it.

It's better for aggression to be interwoven into the ultimate classroom, as Jerrell's teacher did. At a minimum, the playground can become an area for healthy aggression fantasy play, like shadow karate kicks. At a maximum, teachers can actually train students to understand what aggression is, where it comes from, and how to turn it into mission, service to others, and personal meaning—larger principles that we discuss in later chapters.

Discipline Techniques

Doing the right thing and training students in handling their own aggression is very much the goal of a classroom discipline system. Our knowledge of how the brain works directs us toward some common sense innovations in discipline. These work for both boys and girls, although there is generally more need to go beyond words toward other creative or innovative solutions in disciplining boys, since they constitute 80–90 percent of the discipline problems in a preschool or kindergarten classroom.

One key to improving discipline is the presence of older people. Our research indicates that discipline and behavior of children is heavily affected by the presence of elders in a classroom or other learning environment. Whether a grandparent visits or comes in for tutorials or is a teacher, the old teach the young. The Experience Corps is a very interesting organization that bases its work in this philosophy. It has placed eight hundred retirees in seventy schools across the country—and is now placing retirees in preschools. The presence of these elders inherently calms down a classroom, as does the healthy presence of parent volunteers, and even teens who come in to help out.

Here are specific, practical techniques teachers are using with success to manage their preschool classrooms. These techniques can work in nearly any similar environment.

- Show the child, in the immediate world, the effect of an inappropriate action. Direct his eyes to the bruise his hit causes.

- Redirect hitting and punching energy from animate to inanimate objects. A nerf bat and cushion in an "angry place" in a corner of the room can be a safe place for the child to hit and punch nonliving objects. Concomitantly, he is taught he should not hit a living thing in anger.
- When asking for an action to desist, the teacher says "please" once, maybe twice, but then becomes stern.
- Give the child a time-out as necessary, and encourage the teacher or other angry adult to take one as needed.
- Ignore a child's refusal; don't engage in a power struggle with it. Give sixty seconds to begin to do what you ask. If he or she is defiant after the sixty seconds, institute other techniques.
- Negotiate as much as is appropriate, and offer choices (usually just two: "You may put the block here or over there—which do you choose?").
- Whenever possible, rely on diverting or distracting rather than punishing.
- Take away privileges and toys as punishment.
- Present expectations in positive language: "Isn't it great how we expect you to carry those plants inside today? How important you get to be."
- Make things into games whenever possible: "Let's see how fast you can get your coat on. Look, I'm timing you!"
- Identify the *specific* challenge of a task or expectation. Don't be vague; point the child to it and help him focus on it, thus cutting down on failure and the need for punishment.
- Allow mistakes and failures, and use them as teaching tools.

Our discipline systems are often the result not of the need for discipline in the child but of our dislike of a behavior that, frankly, bugs us. A parent of an adopted child, Frankie, five years old, told me her son just couldn't sit still. Every day his teacher complained to Mom about it, and most days put her son in time-out for wiggling. As Mom tried to better understand her son's situation, she noted that he was impulsive at home but not problematic. Why the constant problem at school?

She discovered that her son's classroom did not stimulate him; he was bored. Bored kids wiggle. Frankie was being punished for a disliked behavior that grew, in large part, from his brain's very logical reaction to an environment that was inappropriate for his energy level and neural skills.

As we explore discipline from the point of view of the learning brain, all teachers are challenged to look at whether their classroom is creating a crisis of understimulation. If it is, they'll probably find girls more able to self-manage and boys likely (as with Frankie) to turn boredom to impulsivity and even acting out.

Frankie was also something of a bossy child, another characteristic that rubbed his teacher the wrong way. It's hard to blame the teacher too much—none of us like bossy people—but it is also important for us to know that brain-based research can now confirm a trend many of us may have intuitively suspected: bossy kids are often healthy kids. We must help kids control their bossiness, but we don't want to overreact to or shut down bossiness just because it bothers us.

Thomas Boyce, of the University of California, Berkeley, pediatrics, is one of the researchers who discovered the link between bossiness (something boys tend to do physically and girls verbally) and better health. Less-dominant preschoolers, he found, have high heart rates and significant secretion of stress hormones. More-dominant preschoolers experienced low heart rates and stress hormone secretion. In other words, their neural and central nervous system were under less stress.

For dominant and timid children alike, a better-ordered environment was most helpful, Boyce found. Punishing the dominating child, as we often do, may need to be rethought. We are, in fact, punishing him (or her) for being healthy.

The Outdoor Classroom

The Canejo Valley Adult School in Southern California is an excellent learning environment that has been concertedly set up in accordance with brain research. It offers day care and preschool for kids and trains parents in how to be co-teachers. A very fine trainer in brain-based gender research, Eilene Green, is on staff there. Eilene and her colleagues told us recently how they use the "outdoor classroom"—the grounds, garden, play area, and other nature areas—to help not only with stimulating the learning brain but also with handling young children's behavioral nuances. They found that many of the young males misbehave as a way of striving for the attention and power, albeit negative, that uncontrolled impulsive behavior can give.

One of the staff's solutions: behind the school are a set of stairs children can climb toward a meadow. They encourage the children to climb up there and be "above" the teachers and others below. "Look how high you are. You're a king up there," they say to the young person. The boy giggles and feels very important in that meadow above the others. "The more power the child feels, the less we find him misbehaving," said one Canejo teacher. What a wonderful innovation, using the geography of Canejo's outdoor classroom!

In the outdoor classroom we may find or use water. It is wonderful for the growing brain. Waterfalls, water falling on rocks, purling creeks soothe the working brain. Fountains inside classrooms can mimic this (if they are more than dribblers). This is another innovative use of the outdoor environment to guide young children's energy, calming them and thus opening their energy to greater learning.

The outdoor classroom is as important as the indoor, especially for younger children. It is their world of play, fantasy, and spiritual connection with the mysteries of nature and an essential component of the ultimate classroom. Even a school in the middle of a city is challenged to create an outdoor classroom, like one we heard about in South Dakota that built a playground on the roof. The snow melted fast up there; the roof was warm thanks to heat rising from the building. This school got the idea from a similar situation in Hong Kong, where space is limited but human ingenuity is not.

Young children are as much creatures of nature as culture, and nature is our great ally in teaching them. There is hardly a reading, writing, mathematical, scientific, or cosmological lesson that cannot benefit from being adduced and performed in the natural world. The classroom may be the laboratory for the young child, but the natural world is life itself.

The natural world is especially useful for boys (and some girls) who seem to need to move all the time. Millennia ago, young males had more space to move around in, and thus their impulsiveness was less an issue. Now, they don't hunt out in the world as much. Yet their brains still crave space to hunt in. The more time they can spend outdoors, the more space for them to discover and navigate comfortably. Especially in the preschool and kindergarten years, sitting down and learning during quietness, though useful, is also to a great deal about crowd control, not learning. Many children, especially many boys, need to move around in order to learn.

Directing Boys and Girls to Academic Excellence

The genders, of course, often show distinct psychosocial styles, gravitate toward their own gender groups, and often free play in their own natural sex and gender interests. Should we therefore teach them academic subjects differently? Before we answer this question, let's see if we recognize some of these gender differences in the preschool age group. These came to us from teacher observation in Missouri classrooms.

- Little girls stuff dolls in their T-shirts and deliver babies. Others carry on a pretend wedding. One teacher told us about a group of four-year-old boys who decided to stuff their shirts in pregnancy along with the girls and were told, quite logically, by the girls, "You're a boy, you can't have a baby." One boy was sad enough to cry, according to this teacher, which inspired a spontaneous lesson on how boys and girls are different.
- In this age group, when the class votes on an issue the children generally stand in different parts of the room. Almost always the boys stand in one area and the girls in another.
- Typically, the boys in a preschool class go to the block area to start their initial in-room play or learning activity.

- In the nursery, the girls wait more patiently than the boys.
- In one teacher's observation there is even a sex difference in sleep habits. She notices that the boys, upon eating, fall asleep immediately; the girls take longer.

There are many distinct gender differences in the preschool and kindergarten years in particular. Our research, and brain-based theory, indicates four general keys to ensuring academic excellence for *both* boys and girls during these years:

1. One-on-one lessons between teachers and students
2. Strong use of group work among students, especially the self-motivated
3. Use of manipulatives and interaction with the physical environment for nearly every lesson
4. A delicate balance between teacher interpretation of lessons for the student and student free play (uninterpreted)

Our research also shows that learning and teaching differences between genders at this age are as much a matter of when lessons are given as what they are. Because girls tend to mature many verbal skills earlier than boys, they can often be taught certain things earlier in their maturation, especially if the teacher likes to use lots of words and instruction. As the teacher deemphasizes verbal instruction and instead uses graphs, charts, and manipulatives, the boys stand a better chance of learning at the same time as the girls. As always, we are averaging male-female difference here.

In our brain-based teacher trainings, we asked preschool teachers which of their children have learning problems in preschool and kindergarten; not surprisingly, the response was, overwhelmingly, boys. So we asked teachers to deemphasize use of words, favor manipulatives, rethink the use of space and movement in the class, employ group work, and pursue a number of other strategies that would help *both* boys and girls.

One teacher, Kathi Winkler, volunteered to keep a very detailed journal of her process, teaching tools, and success. With thanks to her, let us share it in part with you now, and use her innovations as our template.

Teaching Math and Spatials

Kathi enhanced spatial learning in a number of ways.

USE OF CHARACTERS IN BLOCK ACTIVITIES. Kathi wanted to find an innovation that would help her get girls more interested in spatial-block activity, which was usually dominated by boys who liked to build high towers. She decided to give the girls "characters" or "people" to relate to.

"Including small toy people in the block area changed construction activities," she discovered, "from only the challenge of balancing blocks into the highest possible tower into an activity that facilitates cooperative building of settings for doctors, pilots, teachers, families, and police officers. In order to gain the interest of the girls, I directed the children to make sure the toy people were authentic in detail and sturdy enough to both handle and make stand up."

This addition of characters into block play linked the social element of play and language to the spatial learning that is inherent in block building. Kathi was creating an ultimate teaching moment for both male and female brains. "This past week," she continued, "I added some echo microphones into the block area to build a stage for a show and seats for the audience using large, classroom blocks. Often exclusively left to the boys, the blocks became an important extension of Jessica's and Tiffany's plans to sign over the microphones. With a vested interest in the use of the blocks, I heard Jessica take a more active voice in the construction." Adding "real characters" gave the female brain more investment in block play because it eased relationship with the activity; it also increased the girls' self-confidence to work in an area boys were dominating.

CONFLICTS THAT TEACH PROBLEM SOLVING, ESPECIALLY MATH. Kathi employed a similar basic strategy to get boys to solve problems, and again she wisely tied it to an innovation in teaching a math or spatial skill.

Developing problem-solving skills seems to occur most effectively when the problems are both genuine and interesting to them. In order to allow this to happen, I give choices during the day which can *easily create conflicts.* It seems to me that the boys in my class are more willing to work on negotiation skills as well as intellectual skills when *they are invested in the problem.* The following is an example of a problem created by a young boy's decision, the children's solution, and my assessment of the understanding gained during the process.

During snack time one morning, Tommy noticed that his "penguin" was on the helper chart next to the picture. That meant he could pass out the snacks today. Tommy looked forward to his role today, because part of the job of the snack passer is to decide how the snack should be distributed so that everyone gets a share. Tommy picked up the tray of cookies and we began a hidden math lesson.

I asked, "Tommy, how many cookies do you think each child can have today?" I have found that the answer to this question provides me with many insights to how a child is constructing the idea of numbers, quantities, and part-whole relationships. Some children always answer "two" because that seems to be a common number of cookies to get. Some children are really beginning to relate "big" numbers to understand oneness and so they answer "one." I accept whatever response unless another child objects, in which case discussion follows. I then get the chance to observe children counting out the number of the day, comparing amounts, and monitoring each other to see that they are "fair."

Tommy responded to my question with a wonderful idea of his own for deciding how the cookies should be distributed. As a very new four-year-old, age was an important issue on his mind these days. "Everyone can have as many cookies as they are years old," answered Tommy. He proceeded around the table and asked each child how old they were. "Are you three or four?" With each response, Tommy accurately gave each child three or four cookies.

I waited for a protest regarding who had more and who had less, but none came. The rights of age seemed easily accepted by all. Until . . . Tommy came to Mike.

"Are you three or four?"

Mike replied, "Four."

Tanner protested. "You aren't four because I'm bigger and I'm three. You are three."

"I'm four. I get four cookies."

Mike was indeed four. In fact, he was the oldest child in my class, having just missed the cutoff date for the older class by eight days. However, he was also the smallest and youngest-looking child in my class. And how the children saw Mike was the issue.

Cookie passing came to a halt and the discussions became lively. The children wanted to know if Mike was older than some of them [even though] they were bigger than him. I assured them that it was true that he was really four and had his birthday last summer. They became aware for the first time during this discussion that "old" is not directly related to size. They noticed that there were other children who were three years old that were bigger than some that were four years old. But, that didn't make them older. Finally, the excitement over this new and wonderful idea calmed down enough to allow Mike to get his four cookies and Tommy to finish his job.

Tommy's way of passing out cookies would probably never have been mine because I still tend to want things to work out fairly for everyone from my point of view. But, the children accepted it with no difficulty in terms of how many cookies anyone received. And from it, a whole new perspective of looking at age from a *quantity* of years instead of *perception* came into their thinking.

The combination of successful strategies in this incident is extensive. A child was given responsibility to complete a social task that involved developing personal responsibility and managing group interaction. Numbers, age, and social perception were all mixed into the task. The brain was already enlivened to the process, but then conflict kept the task interesting to the learning brain. The teacher was available to offer necessary information, and her presence kept the conflict from becoming one in which rancor outpaced learning.

Girls and boys both gain from this kind of learning situation: shy girls and boys find a great deal to understand through their observational learning style, dominant children practice learning in their way, and it is difficult for any student to remain disengaged. Kathi's intuition about boys liking conflict and excitement in order to learn led her to an innovation that is good for both boys and girls, just as her knowledge that girls can better do spatials if attached to a kind of living character led her to create an innovation that all the children can enjoy.

SELF-DIRECTED ACTIVITIES. In many classrooms, self-directed activities make up a quarter to half of the child's day. Brain research asks that at least a third of the day be reserved for self-direction. A successful teacher in these early years often finds that some students can support more than half a day of self-direction. For the developing brain, self-direction has many advantages, especially that in a supportive, well-led environment the mind gravitates toward learning what it needs to learn in order to grow. The brain has, to a great extent, its own blueprint of how to grow itself, and if a classroom is set up to let the brain explore, it moves in the neural motions required.

Kathi reported her success with this process. "At least one-third of my daily schedule is devoted to allowing the children to self-direct their activities. This is particularly important in early childhood because the social interactions that occur between peers and between the children and adults during this time impact development tremendously. Language, intellectual challenge, and social/moral development of all children in early childhood flourish in an environment of choice, movement, and activity." In this she observes a gender difference: "Girls, I notice, can still maximize their potential in a more sedentary, language-oriented environment. My boys seem to grow best when they are active and setting up their own challenges." Self-directed activity works for both genders, but teachers may find it a kind of panacea for those boys (and some girls too) who are not learning as successfully in other ways.

INTEGRATED USE OF THE PHYSICAL ENVIRONMENT. The brain at this age is not capable of much in the way of a leap of abstraction or of verbal ideation; it learns in the concrete world. All early-education teachers know this, yet we often do not use as well as we can the concrete environment around us. Since young children learn by working to make sense of the physical environment, and since the brain grows when it has to work in the concrete world to decode what it does not understand and manipulate objects into patterns it can understand, the physical environment is for the brain a garden of Eden.

Kathi wrote: "Recently, Kailin and Shawn worked together in the block area to build a precarious structure that was approximately four feet tall and encompassed a floor area of about 50 square feet. During that time, they constantly were confronted with challenges of balance, decisions of purpose of the structure, and use of the blocks. My constant attention was needed to keep them safe and help them negotiate with one another using words and not violence. The result was a complex building that incorporated over a hundred blocks, cars, and play figures."

Group or paired activity brought success here, as well as teacher involvement; perhaps best of all, the children had to work in physical space in order to learn. Also, the more the various parts of the brain made neural connections, the more learning was likely to become sacrosanct. This is the kind of spatial activity from which girls often get excluded, both because they may not feel as naturally comfortable in it and because a boy may seek to dominate the space. This is an opportunity for teacher vigilance about including girls, while not damaging the spontaneous and gender-defined play of the male group.

USING GAMES FOR MATH. Kathi wrote:

Mathematical thinking is primarily stimulated by using games in my classroom. All of the children are more interested in learning to use numbers in meaningful ways when context is challenging and interesting. Since we can work in groups of no more than six, I can use lots of manipulatives and small game pieces to make it interesting.

Our current theme is transportation. Counting, sorting, and playing games with cars and trucks as the tokens especially capture the boys in my room into working to use numbers effectively. Last week little Sandy worked hard with several other boys to sort out transportation counters of planes, trains, cars, trucks, and buses into categories. He then counted objects in each group and compared the quantities of each group. These types of activities take time and are best done in small groups, so wait time is short and hands on time is increased.

This again is an opportunity to use male-brain learning, which tends to gravitate to a spatial task, as the challenge base of the learning experience. It is also important to make sure females participate, as they naturally favor it less yet need it just as much (or more).

SARAH, CHLOE, AND TERRY. Kathi told us a wonderful story of a "treasure game" and its effects on the learning process of two girls in particular. As she realized ever more that "one strategy for encouraging children to explore logical-mathematical thinking is through the use of games," and that games are "successful with girls because they meet their need for social connectedness while challenging them to become 'players' in problem-solving activities rather than just passive learners," Kathi decided to open some school days with a brief, introductory period and then set out games for a choice of activity during the children's self-directed work period.

Sarah and Chloe, both five-year-old girls, recently chose to play the "Treasure Game" together. Terry, a four-year-old boy, was invited to join them. The Treasure Game is teacher-designed material and has several elements essential to encouraging mathematical exploration.

For the young child, interesting manipulatives invite extended play. I have noticed that the girls in our class choose games that contain pieces that are attractive to look at and handle. Games with realistic animal or people tokens or treasurelike qualities seem to have a particular appeal. This game consists of individual game boards

picturing ocean scenes and treasures with a path to follow. The tokens are small plastic sailboats just large enough to collect small,
brightly colored gems along the way. Each time a player lands on the
treasure spot, she collects a gem and continues her move to deposit it
into her cache.

A successful game allows for some open-ended choices and more
than one strategy to be employed. I keep games in my classroom that
allow for children of varying developmental levels to play together.
Sarah, Chloe, and Terry each chose a game board and their favorite
color of boat as their token. They chose to use a large die as a move
indicator, although they also could use a spinner or cards if preferred.
During my observation of their play, I saw that all three of the children were fully engaged in the game.

The first problem-solving activity was determining who would go
first. My children are not taught the traditional "girls first" but rather
are shown ways to negotiate this decision. Sarah suggested that the
three of them draw straws and got the basket containing straws of
varying lengths. I find that as girls learn to use a variety of strategies
such as drawing straws, paper-scissors-rock, or flipping coins, it
moves them past the passive realm of gaining or being denied privileges based on their gender.

The children drew straws and Sarah got to go. As the children
commenced play, I observed that each used their own developmental
level of counting. Sarah's skills included a good understanding of
one-to-one correspondence and an emerging understanding that a
whole number could be the sum of two smaller numbers. Each time
she rounded the board, she was able to split her roll in order to collect a treasure and then continue her move. At one point, she was
three spots away from the treasure mark. She rolled a six. Counting
out "One, two, three—treasure!" Sarah loaded a gem into her boat,
and then continued along the path, counting "Four, five, six."

This move was confusing to Terry, who had always stopped his
move when he reached the treasure mark regardless of the quantity he
had rolled. After Sarah used her counting strategy for the second time
during the game, Terry challenged her thinking. He insisted that

Sarah must stop at the spot, as he did, and that she was cheating. Rather than giving in to Terry's strong insistence that the game be played according to his understanding, Sarah attempted to explain her reasoning. She argued that she should get to move a full six jumps since she had rolled a six on the die. She took a boat and physically modeled for Terry and Chloe how loading a boat should only be a pause during the count instead of an ending point to the turn.

At this point, the game almost ended in contention, but Sarah persuaded the other two to keep playing. During the course of their play, both Chloe and Terry attempted to imitate Sarah's strategy.

This move to higher-level thinking allowed all three to play more quickly and to collect more treasures. Play continued until Chloe suggested that the first one to get five treasures would be the winner. The children agreed and Chloe collected her fifth treasure on her next move.

This type of game playing provides girls with an opportunity to not only think mathematically but to defend their understanding of number concepts. It gives girls the opportunity to operate both in the forum of social language to communicate mathematical understanding [and] engage in play designed to encourage their understanding. Without challenges to their thinking, girls often get caught in the mode of looking for the right answer instead of multiple solutions that can be examined and defended.

USE OF PHYSICAL OBJECTS.   Kathi reported:

Three-year-old Charlie in my classroom is an example of a young boy who needs constant involvement in a sensory-motor activity to learn effectively. Last week, Charlie spent most of his time at the water table exploring pumps and boats, experimenting with things that sink and float. During this time, I was able to notice his learning in several areas. Charlie made comparisons of the boats in the water table, noting that some were big, some little, and some were the same size. He learned that a boat remains buoyant when empty but will sink when pumped full of water. He began to coordinate his point of view with another child as they took turns with the pump and sorted out the boats.

His language skills were practiced as he talked with me and the other child about his explorations. He worked on learning colors and counting as he noticed the attributes of the boats in the table. These are skills that could be taught in a teacher-directed group activity. However, I believe Charlie's involvement with learning would have been less enthusiastic and intense if all his senses were not a part of the activity.

In many of the strategies we've been discussing, there is a kind of pattern. When, by intuition and by training, teachers create innovations to keep the harder-to-handle and easily distracted boys involved in the learning process, the innovations mainly excite their brains toward gender-specific learning comfort. By making these difficult students comfortable, the teachers also reveal strategies and innovations that ultimately help girls expand their learning strengths beyond their dominance in verbal skills and into spatial competency.

By the same token, teachers find that fully discovering how to use the female strengths helps create the best classroom for males in verbals and language. Again, teachers find that using the concrete world is the most fail-safe strategy for language development.

Language Development

Self-directed activities and many other strategies useful for spatial development enhance language development as well. Kathi shared with us some of her innovations.

USING MANIPULATIVES, PROPS, AND MOVEMENT FOR LANGUAGE DEVELOPMENT.   Kathi writes:

Research shows us that boys' brains are "wired" in such a way that language is a more difficult skill for them to acquire and use effectively in learning than it is for girls. Thus in our early-childhood classes, most of my language activities are paired with movement and/or the use of manipulatives. This strategy seems to work especially well with young boys.

For instance, I use songs and finger plays together on a daily basis to encourage language development. I have noticed that the boys participate most readily and request most often songs where their whole bodies are involved. Joshua, who is a twin and has significant language delay, frequently asks for a song called "Late Last Night." In it, someone puts different shoes on your feet while you sleep. The music then encourages things like riding a motorcycle with boots on or running around the room to score a touchdown when you have cleats on your feet. The anticipation of running, galloping, or jumping around the room has encouraged Joshua's attempt to sing the song and is one of the techniques I use to help increase his vocabulary.

Our speech and language therapist, Laurie, tells stories to the children that involve them each holding a prop central to the telling. Taylor is a four-year-old with many articulation errors that make him difficult to be understood and, thus, at times reluctant to answer. However, I have noticed that with a prop in his hand, he is more attentive to the story and his spontaneous language increases.

ABDUL'S STORY.   Kathi recalls Abdul, who had language learning problems.

Abdul, age five, started preschool at three years of age. His mom is a bright, outgoing single mom raising her only child without any help from Dad. Her biggest concern when Abdul began school last year centered around his moderate language delay and the fact that he did not want to spend time being read to and learning to write his name. Mom loved to read and had beautiful writing and was frustrated that Abdul would not sit still for long periods of time and pursue these activities with her.

My first goal with Mom was to help her understand what skills were really developmentally appropriate for a three-year-old and then to help her appreciate the intellectual and language gains Abdul would make in an atmosphere where he could build with blocks, experiment with sensory materials, and be allowed to make choices.

In December I spent some time observing Abdul's development after twelve months of preschool as he played with two other four-year-old boys in the block area. Abdul had set several ramps up on the top of the shelves containing blocks and was rolling cars down them. He quickly obtained the interest of the other two boys as they noticed that cars released down this elevated ramp took flight, landing several feet away from the shelf. As Abdul worked to keep control of this activity, *I heard him speaking in clear, complete sentences of five to eight words.* Right on target for his age. He employed language effectively to describe how he wanted the ramps set up and to assign roles to the other boys. He also used it to persuade them to do things his way.

Abdul's brain development was, in many ways, on target for a young male. There was, for Abdul, some difficulty in these early years with straight language use, but once language was attached to a spatial task, his brain developed good patterning and language came out articulate. Attachment to a concrete and spatial task was the key.

Kathi continues:

As the cars flew through the air off the ramps, they often were lost for several minutes under shelves and our coat racks. This result became a problem for the boys, and I watched them work together to come up with a solution. Bryan, age four, got a plastic mixing bowl from our dramatic play area and put it on the floor below the ramps in an attempt to catch the cars as they fell and before they were lost. Three boys worked together, with lots of verbal argument, to come up with a satisfactory adjustment to the ramp and the bowl which would work. When they realized that different cars sometimes went different distances, they added two more bowls and a basket to their target area. This verbal exploration of physical knowledge in the area of ramps, inclines, and trajectory went on for forty-five intense minutes.

The role of leader for the activity was vied for, and at times the discussion became pretty loud. As the boys worked and struggled, I observed some real verbal negotiation skills being tried out successfully. I intervened at one point to say that in order for the activity to continue, the boys had to figure out how to give and take in terms of the use of the materials, turn taking, and setup. This did get resolved verbally.

A little later, my role as an observer crossed over for a few minutes to facilitator as I attempted to insert some emerging writing (and math) skills into the activity. Since the boys tend to be pretty competitive during activities such as this, I suggested that they try keeping score of how many times their cars hit the targets. We brought out paper and pencil, the boys made their own effort at writing their names, and I showed them how to keep a tally score.

This single activity seemed to encapsulate the rich opportunity boys have to grow in an environment where they are allowed to be mentally, physically, and socially active. Abdul's developmental level in the area of language and emerging writing skills came to normal levels at this time and were used to solve problems, record results, and work with other children.

Kathi has wisely illustrated how a child's right and left hemispheres can help one another develop. The right-brain spatial work and the left-brain verbal and language work came together through an activity of such whole-brain quality (requiring spatials, verbal language, social courage and interaction, and emotional self-management) that the child with a learning difficulty became a child without one. In the area of verbal difficulty, we generally find more males than females, but when the child with the language difficulty is a girl, a similar whole-brain, body-movement strategy works. The challenge is to create one that the girl likes. It may not involve trucks and ramps; it may involve a verbally interactive game, like Hospital, in which the girl is asked to take out pen and paper and record how many patients come in and what their symptoms are.

Special Education

In later chapters, we spend more time on special education and learning disorders, most of which appear after age six. At this early-education stage, we have found that many or most learning disorders can be "cured" by rethinking expectations of a child's learning. For example, our educational culture is relatively obsessed with learning through early reading and labels nonreaders as disordered or "behind." How much of this is cultural expectation? In Hungary, reading is not generally taught until the child is seven years old. Hungary consistently tests out at the high end of European countries in its children's reading skills by third, fifth, seventh, and later grades. Sweden's culture of literacy is similar. Obviously, then, learning-disorder diagnoses in the first six years of life can depend on the culture's expectations. Since males have a disadvantage in learning to read early, it is no wonder that so many in the United States are diagnosed with a learning disorder in the area of reading and writing. Rethinking expectations can rethink diagnosis.

The same holds true for behavioral disorders (BD). The United States is far ahead of Europe in BD diagnoses per capita. We medicate earlier than in Europe and use more of it; 85 percent of the world's Ritalin is consumed here (more on this later in this chapter). Rethinking our cultural expectations of children is an issue that educational culture must face in the years to come, as it further embraces brain-based, brain-gender, and multicultural research, discovering that the culture's definition of normal brain development may not, for many children, be accurate. Thus the child thought to need special education may simply need different expectations, in and out of the classroom.

On the other hand, many preschoolers and kindergartners do need special help. They can benefit from our knowledge of how bonding affects their brain development.

Creating a Tribe: Bonding and School-Home Alliances

Carrie Whalley, a special education teacher, worked with a BD kindergarten student who has problems with kicking and biting. She decided to try dealing with his problems not head on but by bonding with his family. She met with the student and his extended family, including parents, stepparents, grandparents—the "tribe." Since these sessions occurred, she reports, she is having much more success with teaching this student.

Carrie told us another story:

In my special education caseload, I have a kindergarten boy with a behavioral disorder. For the first seven days of school, he would have multiple incidents throughout the day of hitting and kicking other children. When teachers intervened, he would hit, kick, and bite them also.

We are a basic school and believe that teaching character is one of our highest priorities. But how could we teach him character when he could not remain in the classroom for more than thirty minutes without an outburst?

We also believe that developing a positive relationship with families of students is vital. We have met with Mom four times in two and a half weeks and now we realize why this boy is the way he is. He doesn't have and never has had a "*tribe.*" Mom and Dad [have been separated] for a long time, so he splits his life in two houses with two different expectations, rules, and discipline patterns. In trying to create a sense of a tribe at school, everyone who deals with this boy met with Mom and came up with a behavioral management plan. This plan gives him a goal to work towards and rewards for doing the right thing (instead of acting out to gain attention). Now everyone praises him and he earns celebrations for positive behavior.

Since we've done this, he has turned himself around—Mom does this plan at home, too, so he knows everyone is on the same page. It's amazing the changes you see when adults really take the time to help a struggling child.

As with so many aspects of early child education, if we increase the bonds, attachment, and supervision and learning that occur through these interventions we give the growing brain the sense of safety and stability it needs to move from being a disordered brain to a learning one. Our culture has, of course, been going in a different direction for many of its special ed children. Let's look at that problem now.

Use of Psychotropic Medications

The use of such drugs as Ritalin and Prozac is increasing among toddlers and children under seven. Statistics for exact use are hard to come by, but it looks as though somewhere between one-half million and one million children under seven are prescribed psychotropic medication. The situation, which has alarmed early-education theorists for some time, has now caught the attention of politicians. The Clinton administration convened a task force to better understand why such use has increased so steadily, and especially in the United States; the task force will also plot a future course for parents, teachers, and other child care professionals.

At this point, Prozac tends to be prescribed to girls and Ritalin to boys. Given inherent brain differences, this makes biological sense. Because of naturally low serotonin levels, boys tend toward impulse problems—hyperactivity—and, because of brain layout and functioning (less left-hemisphere activity), issues with attention span. Girls, on the other hand, tend toward overt signs of depression but fewer impulse and attention issues.

Nevertheless, our research indicates that prescribing psychotropic medications for children of this age is potentially dangerous not simply to the child but to human society as well. They have essentially no place in the ultimate preschool and kindergarten classroom. We estimate that more than 90 percent of the medication taken by children younger than seven should not be prescribed. (Exceptions include highly violent children and those whose lives seem to be at stake.)

It is true that the rate of depression among this age group is increasing, as well as presentation of disorders such as ADD and ADHD, but using psychotropics betrays our reliance on medication to solve what are mainly attachment, bonding, and gender-brain-based learning issues.

This fact is masked by the incredible power of the medication. "My son is getting better!" we cry in relief after he has been on Ritalin for a month. "My daughter seems happier," we point out to the teacher, thus reinforcing the power of medication. Teachers themselves are often relieved to have the problem child calmed down or pepped up.

On the other hand, the medication has interrupted the natural flow of child brain development within human society. It allows parents to continue whatever disengaged parenting style they have practiced, and it permits the school and classroom to continue the trend of warehousing the child, rather than one-on-one bonding through (1) funding more teachers and care providers to stay longer at day care and preschools, (2) better classrooms, (3) engaging lesson plans, (4) teacher training in brain differences, and (5) clear discipline systems and character education.

Furthermore, it is important to remember that the medications are gateway drugs. Children who take psychotropic medications are more likely to become drug and alcohol addicted in later life. These young children can develop internal coping mechanisms that mimic the chemical effects of the medication. This can be healthy, but the success rate is unclear, and children are just as likely to become medication-dependent and not develop internal psychological coping mechanisms at all, instead finding themselves adrift once off the medication in early adolescence.

What is most frightening about the rapid increase in drug use among young children is the fact that so many presumed presenting behaviors of disorder are actually not indications of real disorder but rather indications of (1) caregivers' and parents' lack of training in normal child development and (2) cultural pressure to create a kind of uniformity in children that is, ultimately, unnatural.

Ken Jacobson, of the University of Massachusetts, conducted a cross-cultural study of children using and not using drugs. In England, for instance, he observed one group of schoolchildren diagnosed with ADHD and another not, using a grid of thirty-five behaviors that include giggling, blurting out answers, squirming, and tapping fingers. He found no significant difference in the presence of the thirty-five behaviors in the diagnosed and undiagnosed groups.

Untrained in normal development—and overwhelmed by our own and others' children—teachers, parents, and the human community in general are often tempted to diagnose a child with a spirited or shy temperament—one that steps out of an amorphous uniformity that we believe makes the classroom and the home "easier." Once diagnosed, the child gets medication.

Paul R. McHugh, professor of psychiatry at Johns Hopkins, calls this use of medication "mental cosmetics." It should be, he argues, "offensive to anyone who values the richness of human psychological diversity." McHugh's objection is that, from a neurological point of view, it is not through overly forced uniformity but through well balanced diversity that the human species ultimately flourishes. We have not, from an evolutionary standpoint, thrived by shutting down diverse temperaments, ideas, and ways of succeeding. Nor do we enjoy success, in the end, by labeling impulsive boys as naturally defective, or shy girls as natural victims. Yet in our very young, we often shut down diversity of temperament with drugs that increase a child's chance of addiction later and demean humanity's love of children.

One-on-one attention is generally the best antidote for what ails the toddler or kindergarten child who appears to need medication. A minister and father of a four-year-old boy wrote us of his experience with this truth: "My four-year-old son's preschool teacher recommended Ritalin this year and we even considered it, but then we decided to try a smaller, more structured class with a different teacher. Our son is thriving and one of the top kids in the class!" The child's story is a common one. A new structure, a small class, well-connected parents or grandparents, or a connected teacher can change the life of the child. Because it is generally too early in brain development to say with certainty that a child of three, four, five, or six needs a brain-altering medication, we must instead increase parental, extended-family, and teacher bonding whenever presented with a difficult child.

Recent studies show success with these nonmedical options:

- A parent moves from full-time to part-time employment so as to mentor a difficult or spirited child for an additional two or three hours each day.
- The spirited child is moved from the present preschool to a smaller, more intimate one where there are consistently present at least *two* caregivers or teachers.

- The child is led through the day with set routines and discipline systems in place.
- The child is shown a "stress" area where he can hit a small punching bag or otherwise release energy.
- Alternative medicines are used.
- Grandparents and other concerned caregivers provide new (and nearly daily) support, especially in single-parent homes.
- Talk therapy and counseling augment structural changes in the family and classroom; several promising new therapeutic programs are showing good results.
- Teachers and parents offer as much art therapy as possible, allowing the child who is in psychological pain to paint or draw when experiencing stress.
- The natural and outdoor world is used more than previously.

The highest increase in use of medication in the preschool and kindergarten age group is among boys; of medication used, nearly 70 percent is given to boys. This creates a specific male-brain issue. We cannot stress enough that, to a great extent, using medication in this age group is a cultural resignation to the perceived defectiveness of the male brain system, and it hits parents and teachers of boys especially hard. Boys who are medicated at four, five, or six learn very early that they are "sick" or "defective." The label sticks in the soul of the child in ways we have not fully understood yet.

In the end, our research shows that in this age group, for perhaps 90 percent of medicated kids, the presence of medication in a child's life is proof that the child is less loved by humans than he or she needs to be and that his or her brain, therefore, is not developing as gracefully as human culture wants it to. This situation is frightening in the human community in general, but especially in America, where we use more psychotropics on young children than any other country—while perceiving ourselves as the wealthiest, most luxurious, and most advanced country on earth.

The Ultimate Preschool and Kindergarten Classroom for Both Boys and Girls

Let us conclude this chapter with a bulleted list of simple things preschool and kindergarten teachers have reported doing to facilitate learning in both boys and girls. In some way, each suggestion is good for both genders, though each has grown out of, or been noticed, because of inherent strengths or weaknesses in either gender. We've assembled this list from answers given to us by teachers when we asked, "What 'little things' do you and your classroom do to help boys and girls?"

For the Boys

- Teach sewing and beadwork to help boys learn fine motor skills, an area in which they are weaker than girls.
- Have books on shelves and elsewhere around the classroom, so that boys who don't feel comfortable with reading can get used to the omnipresent book.
- Make everything experiential, and have lots of blocks and other manipulatives for play and lesson learning.
- Keep verbal instructions to less than a minute before going to the activity.
- Have a permanent "feeling corkboard" on which balloons are taped above the words "angry", "sad," "happy," and "mad"; let the kids throw safe, plastic darts at the feelings they are having, which gives them an action for accessing and then talking about the feeling.
- Personalize the child's desk, coat rack, cubby, and other storage area to increase the sense of attachment and identity with the environment.
- Bring in male mentors and other men from the community, or boys from upper grades to promote male presence; this is done especially to make male role models available to fatherless boys.

- Teach the child to use concrete, emotion-laden words such as "I don't like it when you hit me."
- Enjoy the boys' high energy and put it to work in cleaning the classroom, helping you move things around, and helping other children in their learning and work.

For the Girls

- Play kickball and other ball or movement-related games to help girls learn gross motor skills, which is an area where they are comparatively weak.
- Have portable and digital (immediate-result) cameras around, and take pictures of the children being successful at a task; they can admire the pictures later, which seems to really help young girls feel good about what they're doing.
- Use a water table and sand table to make scientific things experiential.
- Help facilitate working groups and working teams in which girls learn to take a leadership role; this also obliges them to work out their in-crowd, out-crowd arguments with each other.
- Use lots of puzzles to help perceptual learning.
- Build lofts in the classroom with safe steps, and encourage kids to climb up to the top and otherwise experience three-dimensional space.
- Use manipulatives, such as number rolls, to teach mathematics, a process that compels the brain to make math concrete and particularly aids girls (or boys) who are not inherently talented in math calculation or design.
- Praise more than you think you need to, especially for activities well accomplished.
- Make sure not to miss the hidden high energy of girls, who may pull back because a few loud boys dominate; help these girls become leaders.

The preschool and kindergarten classroom is our first professional look into the boy's and girl's minds. In the end, how wonderful it is when we see our classroom and the home as part of the same family, both concerned with creating environments of attachment and stimulation that grow the child's brain. Parents as well as teachers can employ many of these girl-friendly and boy-friendly techniques. In many communities, such as those using Parents as Teachers programs, this is already happening.

And now at the end of this chapter, as with the next three, we present specific tips for parents.

Tips for Parents

- Become an advocate for gender-specific educational tools and forms in the preschool or kindergarten classroom.
- Be especially cognizant of your son or daughter's learning strengths and weaknesses, and how the preschool or kindergarten is compensating for them.
- Hold yourself to the highest bonding standards, whether as mother, father, or other caregiver, because in these years of life if you even suspect your child needs more love, attention, and direction from you, he or she most probably does.
- Be especially vigilant about the class size and teacher-student ratio in which you place your child; select only a preschool or kindergarten that carries the highest standards in these criteria.
- Ask your child's teachers how you can support both his or her general education and education as a boy or girl; institute any changes at home that are necessary.
- Insist on good discipline at home, as well as daily rituals and routines.
- Whenever your child needs help with homework, give it.

- Create daily reading rituals, reading to younger children and then (once they begin to read) letting them read to you for a brief portion of the reading time.
- Create math games of your own at home to augment math and spatial learning.

Our culture is moving more and more in the direction of community collaboration with schools, after a number of years of keeping the family and school units separated. Brain research shows us, moreover, that instilling a sense of collaboration between home and school is the best approach to educating both boys and girls. From this approach comes something that no book can quantify: the human intuition and intelligence that emerges when parents trust teachers and teachers trust parents as an integral part of an extended family. In this system, issues of maleness or femaleness in the child are so fully discussed and observed among these members of the extended family that human ingenuity does what it has always done best: raise the next generation well, laying a foundation for all later learning in the so-called tender years.

4

The Ultimate Elementary
School Classroom

When I was in elementary school, I really liked school. When I taught elementary school, I taught young minds eager to learn. Now I work to help construct a school where no elementary student doesn't absolutely love coming. Elementary school should be a place a kid can't wait to get to.

—TERRY TRUEMAN

AT A ROUNDTABLE DISCUSSION OF ELEMENTARY SCHOOL TEACHERS, we asked, "What are three areas of your classroom life you wish you could improve?" Many of the thirty teachers in the room had taught a number of grades, most at least two, and all now taught between first and sixth grade. We ended up getting a longer list than three areas, of course. Some highlights:

- "Wish I could spend less time on discipline," said some of the teachers of higher grades.
- "Getting some kids motivated, especially the bright ones who just won't perform."
- "Having enough time for all the different contacts and bonds I'd like to make, not only with each student but with parents," said a group of lower-grade teachers.

- "Wish I could be more innovative more of the time—there just isn't time."
- "Need smaller class size."
- "Want more training, but not training that's boring or treats me like an idiot."

"OK," we said, "now let's bring it right to boy-girl issues. List three areas where you are having specific trouble teaching boys, and three areas where you are having trouble teaching your girls." Here were some of the responses.

- "Girls are definitely getting nastier these days. It's sad."
- "Higher levels of math are harder for the girls. I have to be pretty innovative and really encouraging when I teach some girls."
- "Getting some of the shyer girls to hold forth. They'd rather just watch everyone else shine."

For the boys:

- "Impulsive, undisciplined boys . . . there are more and more each year. Sometimes we just have to stop all learning to deal with them." ·
- "Reading is hard for a lot of boys, and getting some of them to focus on writing is even worse."
- "It's sad how many underachieving boys there are, and so many with learning disorders and unable to focus. I almost worry more about those problems than the hyperactivity."

Teachers listed many more issues in teaching boys than girls, and many more serious issues—failures, low academic achievement, and mental and emotional problems.

Elementary school (generally, first to fifth or sixth grade) is a time when boys and girls have gradually become fixed in their gender identities. Girls are very much girls, and boys very much boys, especially by about fourth grade. Male and female cultures often afford enjoyment of each other, but just as often they pull back. "Oh, those boys!" girls murmur sardonically, disgusted by "boy behavior" (even if a little enamored as well); "Who needs girls?" some boys murmur, with an equal show of sarcastic bravado.

Over the elementary years, girls appear to develop learning abilities with more flexibility, on average; even if brain research didn't show this, school and grade results would. Girls generally have less trouble than boys in elementary learning environments. Ninety percent of teachers at these grade levels are female, and 99 percent of those teachers have not been trained in how boys and girls learn differently. It would stand to reason, then, that if structural mistakes in classrooms are being made, girls—learning in a female-oriented environment—can make natural adaptations more so than boys can. Given that so many of the learning and classroom problems involve males in our elementary schools, you see more innovations in this chapter regarding boys than girls. For teachers, there is more of a sense of emergency regarding boys. Nonetheless, we offer some wonderful innovations for teaching girls as well.

At the same time, many of the innovations that make an elementary classroom ultimate—that is, so many of the innovations that help boys—also help girls (and vice versa).

Structural Innovations

One of the joys of being a teacher or administrator in a school system is the possibility of enacting not just small innovations but very large ones as well. In our present educational culture, though, especially as it faces myriad pressures from parents, communities, and legislators, being an innovator is often so difficult that school districts give up their freedom to try new things. We hope that the school districts in your area consider trying at least one of these innovations that have been successful in school districts around the country.

We have chosen for this section those innovations that have direct application to the brain-based learning needs of boys and girls. Some of them are being used in Missouri districts, as a result of training received there, and others are found outside Missouri, indeed around the world. Some are major structural changes—notably year-round schooling—that apply universally to all children, not specifically to either boys or girls.

We include these changes toward the beginning of this and the next chapters because they enable (and set a background for) gender-specific innovations we discuss later. Teachers, administrators, and legislators often try to solve such problems as girls' math-science performance or boys' behavioral problems with specific, functional solutions, neglecting major structural solutions. The latter, though, are entirely possible, and not as hard to accomplish as we think—and they can solve classroom-function problems at higher structural levels.

Use of School Time

We need to rethink the time that our students spend in school (daily and annually) as we pursue what is an ultimate classroom from the point of view of the brain. The human brain, whether male or female, seeks a certain kind of learning schedule. The schedules themselves are much debated, but we've combed the research and discovered that specific areas are of great importance in improving our children's elementary learning.

YEAR-ROUND SCHOOLING. Presently, there is great pressure from legislators to improve students' academic performance. Many states have third- and fourth-grade testing (and beyond) that legislators have decided ensures better student performance. Teachers almost universally denounce the efficacy of this testing, criticizing it as an invasion of normal curricula and added academic pressure on students and classrooms.

There is another way to raise academic performance: year-round schooling. In many countries—Japan and France, for example—schools are taught year-round, with breaks of three to four weeks occurring three times a year. Interestingly, when politicians suggest that America's schools are failing, the comparison is often made to high scores in Japan and France, but without noting the year-round school regimen those countries follow.

The United States has a long tradition of summers off. Young people were needed at home to help the family with summer farming and ranching duties. Things have changed today, of course, and young people are not needed for such duties; actually, their enforced free time creates great concern for many working parents, especially in the elementary school age group, where kids are not old enough to be home alone.

There is an assumption in our culture that teachers would dislike year-round schooling—that they would rebel against it because they would lose their own summers off, an important time for personal renewal and curriculum planning. Teaching is one of the most difficult jobs in our civilization and one of the least rewarded with monetary compensation, so this protest must be taken seriously.

However, teachers are not universally opposed to year-round schooling. Far from it. In our decade of research, we have interviewed countless teachers who support it. Veteran teacher Greg Capanelli's comments are representative: "Year-round school, even maybe eight weeks on and then ten-day breaks, with holidays at Thanksgiving, Christmas, and so on, and maybe four weeks in the summer . . . this would actually be better for teachers, and when teachers understood it, they'd support it. We could avoid the month we waste in September reteaching fractions and everything else the students have forgotten. We could avoid the big hype in June that 'school's out.' Our students would generally learn and retain more. And teachers would have a smaller block of vacation but more blocks of available vacation time."

If we add brain-based research to this dialogue, we find good reasons for year-round schooling for students of all ages, but particularly in the years between fourth and sixth grade. This is a crucial pruning, or "use it or lose it," time when the brain retains what is used and loses what is not repeatedly used. Summer vacations cut down on retention and thus, ultimately, on one measure of intelligence. Furthermore, no proof exists that there is any reason to keep summer vacations as they are now set up. Brain-based research supports year-round schooling; there is no logical reason not to have it. Only an old tradition keeps us locked in an inferior mode of learning and teaching.

CHANGING THE SCHOOL DAY. Because to an ever greater extent parents are both working away from home, and because schools are required year by year to teach more material, the school day running from 9:00 A.M. to 2:30 P.M. is becoming less effective, especially for students in the higher grades.

One of the most serious pressures parents feel is worry about children in the latchkey hours, after school is out and before parents return from work. The hours of 3:00 P.M. to 6:00 P.M. are the time of most juvenile crime, delinquent behavior, and sexual activity. Parents are often desperate to make sure their children are engaged in learning and useful activity during all or part of these hours. Athletics and clubs can help, but so can an extended school day.

Furthermore, as our culture relies increasingly on schools to add character education, success theory, coaching in group dynamics, homework achievement in school hours, study halls, computer training, and more art and music curricula, an extended day is needed. Schools don't want to rob existing basic curricula in order to add what are clearly also important components of a young person's training in social and other technologies. The solution?

A school day is from 8:30 to 3:30. This kind of school day would not impede athletics, except during the winter, and adjustments can be made in gyms and other school buildings. It would add additional time to a teacher's workday, but once the logic is understood by legislators, pay increases for teachers would hopefully follow, commensurate with worktime increases.

Both these time changes in how we now do education depend first on experimentation in schools (some experiments have already begun and data are forthcoming) and then on pay increases. Few structural changes will occur soon unless education becomes a financial priority for our culture; thankfully, the trend is already under way in many states, and at the federal level. In the states with which we the authors are most familiar because of our residence—Washington and Missouri—governors Gary Locke and the late George Carnahan have made education a high priority. Throughout the recent presidential and congressional elections, most major candidates declared education a top funding priority.

A number of the innovations featured in this book have been possible because funding, from the top level of government, supports the search for the ultimate classroom.

Class Size, Number of Teachers, and Teacher-to-Student Ratio

The ratio of teachers to students varies greatly among elementary schools by virtue of year-by-year developmental needs. A learning brain that, in second grade, experiences the presence of more than one teacher in a classroom for at least part of the day enjoys more neurological variety in learning culture and experience. This is optimal for that age brain. By the time the brain finds itself in a sixth-grader's body, variety is less essential for learning a specific intellectual subject. However, depending on class size, a second adult presence (a volunteer) for part of the day might be equally valuable in helping manage psychosocial energy so that bonding, order, and discipline are improved.

In the ultimate classroom, a second teacher, intern, or volunteer is a daily presence in first through third grade, perhaps not for the whole day but for part at least. One teacher for every fifteen students is at the high end of the optimal ratio. A ratio higher than 15:1 is more difficult for both teacher and students unless a second teacher (even in the form of a parent volunteer) becomes an important presence. Vertical mentoring is useful in helping keep teacher-student ratios healthy—when, say, a sixth-grader comes in to tutor a first-grader, and when this happens many times over. In this case, a "second" or "third" teacher is helping out, and more students can be served in the classroom.

With only one teacher, no more than fifteen students ought to be present in a classroom that is not self-directing. Those fifteen brains do not get enough one-on-one attention in an instruction-oriented classroom. This is especially difficult for boys' brains during the early elementary years because of their great need for environmental stimulation to grow cortical areas that girls grow more quickly and completely by nature. If the classroom is one in which self-directed lessons are the norm (for instance, a Montessori-type classroom), the teacher-student ratio can increase; but volunteers are still necessary for part of the day.

Furthermore, we recommend that for the sake of bonding and attachment (on which so much learning depends) students keep the same teacher all day. By fifth grade this might change, with teachers rotated every hour or two. However, it is important for a school district to notice that a well-respected teacher who keeps the same class all day, even in fifth or sixth grade, has fewer discipline problems than are found in a classroom and school in which students move between classrooms every hour.

An experiment worth trying is this: have all fifth- or sixth-grade students stay in one classroom all day (thus remaining in a known environment with which they are bonded) and have specialty-subject teachers (calculus, physics) come into that classroom for an hour or two during the day. The students are thus bonded with one teacher and one set of classmates, forming a yearlong community into which specialty teachers commute from elsewhere in the building, just as many special education teachers now commute into classrooms. (Lab work would, of course, have to occur outside this classroom.)

The advantages of keeping students in a daylong bonding community are as much neurological as social; in particular, the students who have great difficulty learning do not have the constant distraction of new communities and new environments. The students who do not have difficulty learning enjoy a socially ordered community in which they can flourish. Problems that may emerge for any and all students in the learning community have to be worked out, by means of which maturity increases. There is no escaping healthy conflict, which must emerge when students are, as it were, constantly wedded to each other under the guidance of one or more respected mentors.

SMALLER SCHOOLS ARE OFTEN BETTER. Deborah Meier, formerly the principal of Central Park East schools in East Harlem and now head of the Mission Hill School in Boston, recently wrote of her experience in New York City: "Where I taught for thirty years . . . we organized hundreds of small, unique schools. Parents, students and teachers created communities where they could get to know each other well and work closely toward shared goals. Folks around the country who have tried similar reforms have found the same thing: it works. The hard data prove the case: they are not only good for achievement, they're cost-effective. At our school in East Harlem, more than 90 percent of our graduates go on to college."

This is a very high figure, and Meier credits the long-term learning environment of that school, based on small class size beginning in lower grades, as one key reason for this success.

Trying to educate students in huge schools with one teacher for twenty students can work; it works every day. It is also a fragile way to educate the growing brain. More students are lost in the long run than in smaller schools with more teachers and better ratios.

Using Group Dynamics and Group Work as a Basis of Pedagogy

Education is a group process much more than an individual one. This is truer of elementary school than high school. Brain development and social development during the elementary years are extremely intertwined. The brain learns because it is part of group learning. Human psychology in the first few grades puts individuation lower on its list of priorities, especially where learning and achievement are concerned, because in many cases the brain is not yet able to act alone. It depends on the group for help in its processing, as well as for reflection on what it is accomplishing.

For this reason, brain-based research cries out for teachers to make group process a basic component of learning. The more projects that groups of two, three, or four students can accomplish together, the more varied the human learning experience. This is crucial for both boys and girls.

REVISITING MULTIGENERATIONAL CLASSROOMS. Only a few decades ago, multigenerational classrooms were the norm. Older students sat in the same rural classroom with younger students. Older students learned by teaching younger students. Young students grew up in the embrace of mentors. The mentors themselves grew up because they took responsibility for their actions—responsibility forced on them by the elder role they played. Everyone learned together. Sometimes this led to boredom for the high achievers, who lacked challenge; but the benefits were also immense.

Educational and economic trends in the early and middle parts of the twentieth century began to cut out multigenerationality in learning groups. First-graders went to school with first-graders, second-graders with second-graders, and so on. Yet as we look toward an ultimate classroom, it is essential to revisit multigenerationality in classrooms. The human brain loves the stimulation not only of a teacher (who is of a different generation) but also of multigenerational peers who can help provide order, challenge, wisdom, direction, and intellectual focus.

Montessori classrooms are well known for their multigenerational component. First grade through third grade learn together, as do fourth through sixth. For those districts curious about the logistics of this kind of classroom, it is worthwhile to visit a Montessori elementary school. Throughout our chapters on the ultimate classroom, we present various ways to use multigenerationality in classrooms.

TEACHING TEAMS AND TEACHER-TO-TEACHER SUPPORT. Many of the schools in the Kansas City area use teaching teams with great success. The teachers meet in the morning to plan the day. These teams are becoming a greater part of school districts nationwide, and we hope they will become universally acceptable. They meet with nearly unanimous praise from participants.

For instance, Anthony Alvarado, chancellor for instruction in the San Diego city schools and former superintendent in New York City's District 2, has seen great success with teacher-to-teacher team contact. He openly encourages teachers to visit one another's classes. Alvarado expressed himself this way: "We all know that our classrooms are generally separate units and teachers are essentially isolated from one another. [But] in a school where classrooms are open, teachers talk to one another, and are in each other's classrooms, frequently and with purpose. This isn't social visitation. Rather, I am going into the second-grade classroom because I'm looking at 'writer's workshops' and I want to find out how this master teacher uses them to link reading with writing in this grade."

Parents parent in teams, workplaces are team efforts, and the ultimate school is a team community in which teachers and students work well as they work together.

Use of Computers and Other Media in Elementary School

Elementary teacher Denise Young told us: "I have started having the children use the computers in our room more often. Several of the children, especially a couple of our boys, had been having trouble with fractions. After using a computer fraction game they seemed to really catch on. The fast action and excitement of the game seemed to make the difference."

There are many essential uses for the computer, with advantages to boys who often learn better with games than "boring lessons" and girls who do not as naturally gravitate toward spatial stimulants and can increase spatial connections (and later-life business and workplace competency) through early computer use.

Computers are an important element in the ultimate classroom, yet it is essential to be cautious about computer use for children under nine. Recent brain research shows us that, as with everything else we put into a child's brain, computer and media stimulants are potentially harmful.

Jane Healy's *Failure to Connect* is a crucial reference for this kind of research, as is Gloria De Gaetano and Kathleen Bander's *Screen Smarts*. Brain-based research guides us to make sure all teachers and parents familiarize themselves with the wisdom of these researchers before turning a young child on to a computer. Here are some of the things we are discovering about young students' use of computers:

- Our plethora of attention-span problems in the present generation may be due to early brain attachment to mechanical stimulation that does the brain's work for it and thus does not compel areas of the brain (such as the temporal lobe and left hemisphere) to grow normally. This is a special problem for boys because the young male brain does not naturally grow as quickly in these areas anyway; it is also the young male brain that tends to be attracted to spatial stimulants like moving objects on computer screens. In a very real sense, the boy's right hemisphere is attracted to stimulants that, somewhat tragically, ensure his left hemisphere grows less well.

• Imagination functions of the brain, especially in the right hemisphere, do not grow as richly when young brains are attached to mechanical stimulants.

• Reading and writing functions—verbal skills—develop more slowly if young brains are mechanized too early. Reading and writing are whole-brain activities that require use of many brain functions at once; spatial stimulants, especially when images move fast on a TV, movie, or computer screen, reduce the time the young brain spends on whole-brain activity, increasing its time on partial-brain activity. Thus the whole brain does not develop as well, and given the fact that most screen stimulants are less verbal than spatial, it is again left-hemisphere development that is generally lost.

It is crucial that school and home collaborate to discover how long a young child is using a computer, watching TV, or playing video games in a day. Often, a second- or third-grader's brain is getting more than enough screen time at home and does not need more than a few hours of "computer research time" per week at school. By about fourth grade, the brain's imaginative, verbal, and attention functions are better developed by natural design, and computer time can certainly increase.

Computer and technology programming is becoming a structural component of many elementary schools, and we support their value—but not for younger children in the massive engagement with computers that some schools, and even politicians, are recommending. As districts and communities debate computer use, it is very important to remember this fact: a child who learns to use a computer at six and a child who learns at sixteen show little or no difference in proficiency after a few months of use. Quite simply, to learn computer or other screen proficiencies is not complicated—it is not like learning a foreign language—and they can be learned later in life, thus with no risk to natural brain development.

All districts discover structural compromises for computer use in their own way. In the ultimate classroom, the computer is a tool to be used in moderation, not a machine that should be permitted to invade group dynamics, development of fine and gross motor skills, verbal and social development, or natural learning curves.

The Outdoor Classroom

A developing structural trend in some schools is the decline or elimination of recess. Nearly 40 percent of our public schools are (or have recently considered) eliminating recess.

Eliminating recess is a profound mistake, though our culture has come to it with the best of intentions. We strive to increase academic excellence, but we are untrained in brain development, and we assume that play and outdoor life do not markedly enhance academic skills; the result is that we diminish recess and play in schoolchildren's lives. In our effort to assert discipline, we've deleted "cutting-loose time" from a child's daily regimen and used the threat of staying indoors during recess as a discipline tool. Many schools are also diminishing (some nearly obliterating) the physical education component in child education.

In considering whether this trend is useful to the child, we might stop to think that 25 percent of American schoolchildren are overweight, and a quarter of American schoolchildren do not regularly participate, according to the surgeon general, in the vigorous activity that is necessary for full child development.

It is useful, also, to consult the brain itself and watch how it grows in relation to the connection with physical activity and natural environments. What we said about preschoolers still applies to elementary students. To grow, the brain needs the body to move about, in fine motor tasks such as bead work and gross motor tasks such as running and playing. If the brain doesn't get physical movement, especially in early and middle childhood, it is more likely to impel that movement inappropriately. The mind wants movement and will wreak some havoc if it doesn't get it.

Given high male metabolism and energy level, on average boys need physical release in order to self-manage behavior more than girls do. In some neurological ways, then, boys can become almost desperate for recess. Nonetheless, recess is just as important a physical and socializing time for girls, who need nonstructured time to develop friendships and challenge relationship systems. Furthermore, in regard to body-image issues for girls (notably their fear of being overweight), which begin for them at around third grade, it is essential that they get exercise. All of our children, eating nonessential fats and carbohydrates in junk-food nutrition and spending less time in physical labor than previous generations, need planned physical exercise even more than their grandparents did. Spending more time inside closed rooms than our ancestors used to, our children also need more time outside.

Joe Frost, a playground expert at the University of Texas, recently told Principal Abigail Wieberson of Washington, D.C.'s Lowell School, "The best classroom is both outside and inside." Few teachers and parents have not intuited the same in their dealings with children. Brain-based research gives us wonderful clues about why. As the brain develops, especially until just before puberty, it develops sensory functions constantly. For instance, a seven-year-old might be observed smelling a rose in a way that an adolescent or adult might not; the seven-year-old is building the cell patterns, tissue, and neurotransmission throughout the brain that the adolescent and adult will rely on throughout life for patterning smells. The garden is very much the brain's classroom.

Play that goes on outside and in nature usually involves a complex near-chaos of social relations. That each child must manage the constant possibility of random experience is also good for the developing brain; it further involves neural challenges regarding how hierarchies work, and how the limbic system should accept or reject certain emotional impulses, from anger to joy. It provides all this in a few minutes of concentrated experience. Because the outdoor natural environment is open (not boxed in like a classroom), it also affords more space for physical movement, which in turn develops the brain. Again, for boys this becomes especially important because of their emphasis on the right hemisphere, and thus their natural need for space area in work and play.

Eliminating recess (and physical education) in search of academic excellence is another example of educational and political culture making a decision to enhance academic excellence in a way that actually runs counter to complete brain development. A brain that has fine and gross motor skills is a smart brain; likewise for a brain that can manage social hierarchy well, move the body without awkwardness, and relate to others freely.

The theoretical learning advantage to cutting out recess lies in the idea that the best brain is one that is mechanized to learn certain intellectual lessons, such as computers or mathematical calculation. Cut out everything else but these, the theory goes, and the brain learns undistracted. This theory is the logic behind cutting our recess and phys ed in order to raise test scores in math and verbals. But (especially in our culture) the logic is flawed.

Early tracking and mechanical learning work better from a behavioral point of view in cultures where emotional repression in young children, especially high-energy boys, is commonplace. If we compel children throughout our culture to sit down and shut up or speak only when spoken to, then we create a kind of child who does somewhat well without phys ed and recess. But since our culture values freedom in a child's emotional expression, and given that we want the brain to actually be better at *varied* learning, academic, and social skills, our elementary classroom must include an outdoor component where the body can breathe so the mind can grow.

Bonding and Attachment in Elementary Learning

As we have shown earlier, the brain requires profound one-on-one attachments in order to work fully. To some extent, the ultimate classroom cannot exist unless teachers and other mentors have formed these profound bonds with students. Teachers most often find that students who aren't learning are also students the teacher just isn't able to reach. "I can't get him to open up," one teacher said of a fourth-grade boy who is underachieving. "She is like a brick wall," another teacher said of a fifth-grade girl; "I try to get her to trust me, but she won't."

As American elementary school classrooms grow larger and larger, we are decreasing opportunities for bonding and full teacher-student attachment. The results are seen around us constantly, but the source is little understood and poorly tracked. The problem lies fundamentally in the fact that a brain that tries to learn its lessons when it doesn't feel the stability and comfort of secure attachment cannot fully learn or grow.

In the earlier section on structural innovations, we started looking at innovations to handle our problems in this area. Let's go deeper into it now. In our research with school districts and teachers, we found almost universal acknowledgment from teachers of the need for greater attachment. Some teachers who have taught overseas argued that we have a particularly American problem with lack of attachment and bonds in our schools. This is an interesting matter for debate.

Bonding issues in the schools were brought home to me a number of years ago in Ankara, Turkey. In the late 1980s, my wife and I lived in Ankara, where I taught literature and language and my wife worked as a therapist. There we met a teacher, Selay Hanim, who had received her M.S. at Tulane, taught in the United States for three years, and now taught back in her home city of Ankara. She loved teaching in America, she told us, and especially enjoyed the richness of technology and wealth of information available to students here.

"But you know," she said frankly, "sometimes it seemed like your school systems forgot to protect the love teachers and students need from each other. There's no country on earth right now with discipline problems in schools as severe as you have in America. I think your learning process is being interrupted by discipline problems much worse than we have in Turkey. I think a lot of what you're facing is a lack of bonding. I think many of your kids have trouble learning because they don't feel cared about. I think your schools will not be as safe as you need them to be."

In the context of school shootings, her comments in 1988 were prophetic. As the new millennium begins, we are confronted with safety concerns in our schools as never before. I have confirmed her generalization about the severity of American discipline problems compared to other cultures in my research of thirty cultures to support *The Good Son: Shaping the Moral Development of Our Boys and Young Men.* We do have the least disciplined school environments I can find anywhere in the industrial world. Of course, what Selay wanted to point me to was not just the symptom, but the source. In her opinion, *too many of our students don't fully trust teachers as elders, leaders, mentors, and role models.* Too many of our students do not feel they can fully bond with us as teachers.

Recent gender research—especially by the AAUW, David and Myra Sadker, and Carol Gilligan—has explored bonding issues from a feminist point of view, showing that girls' self-esteem is lowered by lack of trust in the teacher's call-on performance. Girls are called on less than boys by teachers who favor bonds with boys, according to this research. Because of the bonds favoring boys, girls' self-esteem drops. Girls feel outside the loop and less connected to the teacher, classroom, and learning process.

Who gets called on in class can be one indicator of how in-class bonds work. And it crosses genders. Carrie Whalley, an elementary special education teacher who has taught both mainstream and special ed for grades between first and eighth, told us that in her experience boys' bonds with teachers appear stronger based on who gets called on (boys are likely to receive attention from the teacher and thus appear bonded) "but it's more negative attention they get," she says, "which leaves most of the positive attention to girls."

Our research supports her statement. Boys do get more attention, on the whole, in a daily classroom environment, and so in some ways they appear to have clearer bonds with the teacher. However, the bond is often a *negative* one. Girls often get less moment-by-moment classroom attention and appearance of bonding, but when they do it is generally not as negative. Carrie noted, "I have had many girls [so quiet that] you wouldn't even know they were there in class—I'm not sure I could say that about one boy." The double-edged sword here is painfully clear: boys force us to bond with them in negative ways during class more than girls do, while many girls hang back during class, often ending up with bonds that are less dramatic and forced but also positive.

Call-on experience in class is, of course, only one indicator of bonding experience among teachers and students, though a much discussed one of late. In our ultimate classroom teacher training, we look at bonding from a brain-based point of view, presenting research on how much better the brain develops in circumstances of secure attachment. Teachers have found this material helpful, they say, not simply because it helps them create innovations for reducing discipline problems and increasing educational success but also because it speaks, at some deep and inchoate level, to the instinct we all have: to constantly challenge ourselves to increase our ability to love the growing child.

Let me share with you now some innovations teachers are using to increase bonds and brain-based learning for elementary age boys and girls.

Carol Myers, a fourth-grade teacher at Edison Elementary, told us:

Each morning at the top of the stairs I give my students some directions or a problem to think about. While they are thinking I invite each student in one at a time in order to greet them personally. I am able to make eye and physical contact (handshake or a hug) with each child every school day, thus building relationships.

At the beginning of the year we talk about how to work as a successful family. Respecting others is talked about at length. For the next couple of weeks (and the rest of the year periodically) the students and I write down "good things" they see people doing or saying to each other, on an easel with chart paper at the front of the room. This way, students get to see their name in print in a positive way; students love to write on the chart paper, and they are also practicing written language.

Every day we have "yays and yuks." Each student is given an opportunity to tell his or her yays and yuks that may have happened the day before or will happen in the future. If students begin to become long winded, a time limit can be put on each student. Of course, students may choose to pass. This is wonderful way to build a family relationship within the classroom; it also provides the teacher with much insight into the goings on of each student's home life.

Sometime within the beginning of the school year I participate in some type of physical activity with my class (mile run, climbing the rope, kickball). I make sure it is something I can do well and beat or at least compete with all the boys! By participating in this physical activity, I earn a new and different kind of respect with the students, particularly the boys.

Carol's innovations are universally usable. Like Carol, teachers who use some or all will generally find improvements in both classroom discipline and learning.

Jenny Peterson, also a fourth-grade teacher, talked in inspiring terms about her results from increased bonding:

RELATIONSHIPS, RELATIONSHIPS, RELATIONSHIPS! Now that we're in the second quarter, some of my relationships with students are finally coming together.

Jamal [with whom Jenny had had some of the worst discipline and learning problems] is a new person. I really can't believe the change that has taken place. I think that through all of our trouble together, Jamal has finally realized that I care about and believe in him. I think part of that has come through his realization that I really care about his mom and that she and I are working together.

Tyrell and I are finally coming together as well. This is just so hard to believe. For the last couple of months, I didn't think I was ever going to meet his needs. When I sat down to work with him one day in math, he realized that I wanted to help him, and he basically told me what he needed from me. It's still difficult, but we have connected!

After months, Joseph and I are finally connecting. Some days are better than others, but we're having more good ones than bad ones. I realized that our whole problem was that he thought I didn't like him. I couldn't believe it. Now he knows that I do, and most days he's really trying. He had C's, D's, and F's in the first quarter. When I figured grades for mid-second, he had A's, B's, and C's. All because we have connected—it's the only thing that's changed!

The influence I seem to have is overwhelming to me. It's almost too much to ask of a human being. But it's also encouraging to know that if I stick with these guys I can get them! In the beginning, I didn't think we'd get here. I didn't understand when people told me that the students still didn't trust me. Some of them, like Joseph, have probably been in situations where they've lost trust and it takes a while to build that—especially with a white female teacher.

It seems almost a truism that the finest insights and innovations in education come from the hard work of the teacher. With all three of these students, Jenny followed her instincts to bond even more closely with difficult students; she was supported by brain-based training, colleagues, and home environments to form the all-important bonds. The jump in Joseph's grades are not a fluke, but a reality for so many students who fully bond with teachers.

Susan Colgan, a family involvement coordinator in St. Joseph, Missouri, told us about a program for girls that increases bonding and has shown growing success. "We have an after-school program for girls and their moms called Monarchs. The program is for fourth-grade students. Moms and daughters participate in craft classes, cooking classes, field trips, and various other classes that they are interested in. The final program is a dinner at a restaurant. The two teachers serve as role models to the moms and daughters. This has been a very successful program, and we hope to continue it."

Oftentimes, there is teacher and institutional resistance to increasing bonding and attachment activities in elementary classrooms and schools, especially in relation to later elementary school (fourth grade and above) because actual hands-on instruction time is so valued and might be reduced. The prevailing idea seems to be that the more time taken away from instruction, the less well students perform on year-end testing and later, in middle school and beyond.

Bonding activities must be balanced with instruction and academics; still, cases like those we've shared here show us that quite often the track to better academic performance is not rote academic instruction but love and attention. It is common sense, in a way—but a piece of common sense that instructional pressures have made many educational communities forget.

Elementary teacher Lois Hedge and a coworker went out of their way to bond and help difficult students, choosing after-school time. She wrote:

> A co-worker and I conduct a tutoring/homework help club once a week after school. Our students are fifth- and sixth-graders. Most of them are boys who are easily distracted, have some behavioral problems, or both. These students have been signed into the class by their parents. They are not completing their work during the class time. With about eight students in the class each week, we find ourselves giving lots of positive feedback. The boys especially seem to like the small group. They open up more to the teachers and each other. Their attitudes toward getting their work done are better.

A number of teachers place bonding activities not only at the beginning or end of their class time but also right in the middle. Julie Ogilvie, a third-and-fourth-grade teacher, uses journal writing. She told us about one particular day: "We did a journal writing activity that was based on a song 'Life Together.' One of the lines of the song says, 'Friends forever, till the end / On this my friend, you can depend / When you are weak, I'll be strong / When I fall back won't you pull me along.' The students were to tell what they thought the song meant. It was awesome to hear them talk about the friendships that they had made and the looks on faces as they were talking."

It just so happened that soon after this day, Julie's class, which was very large, was to be permanently divided, half the students moved into a new classroom with a new teacher. Especially in a classroom like hers, where bonding and attachment were emphasized, this structural change was heart-wrenching. She would not see many of the students again in class, nor they her; and they would be separated from their peer support in learning. Julie told us:

> Just before noon, the principal came in and told the students about the change. Many started to cry as soon as they realized how this change was going to affect their world. I cried along with them. We spent the afternoon celebrating the time that we had shared together. Tears had

passed and we ended the day with laughter. As we were dismissing, the tears began to flow again. Many children cried again. Some of the boys cried for the first time. A few of the boys whom I thought I had not made a connection with were crying. Jimmy, my student who didn't like to be touched, was crying terribly and clinging to my side—this broke my heart. I had to send my students home in tears. I called home to talk to [the parents of all of the students] who were leaving my class.

The pain experienced by teacher and students alike shows the immense success of the bonding systems in the class. Despite the grief that accompanied the division of the class, true to her style of teaching Julie worked on building bonds as the foundation of her new class, to which some new students were now added: "I began the school year all over for the new class. We all did team building activities. We began to build trust among the class. As a class, we talked about expectations in our classroom community. The students talked about what they expected out of their classmates and me as their teacher. I asked them to think about what I expected out of them."

After a rocky transition, filled with emotion, Julie's bonds with her new class flourished, and she found herself in the midst of another class in which love between teacher and students sat at the center of the learning experience.

Bonding is, in some ways, the most hidden, least measurable way to ensure good learning. It is, for some, difficult. It takes more work and time than we may think we have. Thus it needs the support of the whole educational and institutional system. Legislators rarely, if ever, propose that our educational policies should include funds for training in bonding and attachment. Legislators assume bonding probably has low-level effects on learning, in the same way it is assumed that a doctor's relationship with a patient doesn't really matter; what matters is the medical model and pharmacology he provides.

The ultimate classroom is a place where common sense and brain research prevail over these assumptions. Joseph, Tyrell, and Susan Colgan's girls learn because they are loved. In the years to come, as more research emerges in the field of emotional literacy, and as more children suffer from lack of adequate bonding in their nuclear and extended families, schools will be forced to create bonding opportunities. Using bonding activities at the beginning, in the middle, and at the end of a classroom hour or day is each teacher's practical and personal step toward bypassing decades of argument and simply doing what is most humane, *now*— loving students, one by one.

Handling Students' Emotional Stress

The decrease in home-family bonding that nearly every teacher is noticing today has a profound impact on the level of emotional stress among students. Even if only one or two students are feeling the stress, all the students soon discover it, for the stressed student often acts out—causing disturbance—or "acts in"—withdraws from achievement— in an unconscious effort to make sure the other students and the teacher experience their stress with him.

Girls and boys often differ in how they "announce" their stress, girls tending toward increased passivity (acting in) and boys toward increased aggressiveness (acting out). There are, of course, many exceptions to this, many boys who passively watch their grades decline, their friendships wither, and their level of depression increase; girls who curse, hit, and rebel against authority. Yet teachers have themselves confirmed biological differences in how girls and boys express stress.

Sarah, an elementary teacher, wondered over this difference and so used the technique of asking students to draw what they thought about when under stress. "Most of the boys," she reported, "drew about war, space ships, or violent things. The girls had a tendency to draw food or their play area." Another teacher noticed gender difference in this way: she heard girls say they are fat, even in first grade. She heard no boys express this stressor. "I have first-grade girls drinking Diet Coke with their lunches," elementary teacher Kimberly Walter reported to us. This too is a rarer occurrence among boys. Teachers have noticed clear differences in how the child handles emotional stressors, and in how the teacher instinctively aids the child.

Third-grade teacher Maxine Meyer, for instance, told us: "Anger in girls often masks a severe rejection of the self, and an enormous sense of loss." Maxine uses a lot of open-ended questions, and she listens to the answers, without guiding discussion too heavily, in order to encourage girls to find out what's behind their anger. Girls generally talk enough, she finds, to lead themselves to answers.

On the other hand, with boys teachers often find it fruitful to ask questions in which the teacher guides the emotional mind toward an answer. "Has someone hurt you today? Were you just in a fight with so-and-so?" These questions are directed and concrete, and discussion is often led by the teacher, not the child. With boys this often works as a mitigator to the inherent slowness in the male brain's processing of emotive information. The teacher helps by trying to point the child in a specific direction in order to find the emotional material hidden there.

DEALING WITH PROJECTION STRESS. One key area of student stress that heavily affects the learning curves of both girls and boys is student-teacher stress, resulting from transference onto the teacher of child-parent or other environmental stressors, such as absent father or mother, poverty, or lack of extended family support.

Elementary teacher Jenny Peterson captures some of this complexity in these free-flowing thoughts she presented in her own journal:

> There are some boys in my class about whom I am really worried. They seem to be angry at me, themselves, and the whole world. I know that part of it must be the world in which they're living, but anger is hard for me to understand. I particularly worry about Larry, who really can't read. Cleery runs around the room all day, and I'm wondering how I'm ever going to help him.
>
> It's funny, but the girls are such a stark contrast! For the most part, they come in, sit down, and get to work. They aim to please. For example, I don't really feel like Brittany and I have a relationship, but she still works hard and gets her work done.

The boys, on the other hand, aim to get attention. I'm wondering if I'll ever get a word in edgewise. Sometimes I think we're from two different planets.

Jenny has been especially troubled by one student, Darryl, whose home situation is perhaps the most important piece of the puzzle:

I really struggle with helping Darryl. It is hard because he thinks that he should be in charge, but I think that I should be in charge. He really tries to engage me in power struggles. I know, though, that he has lost his father and that makes things difficult (his father committed suicide the year before). I really think defiance is his way of being in control—by making decisions in the classroom about what he will and will not do no matter what I say. Because now he is the man of the house, he's trying to be the man of my classroom and that's why we're having trouble. It must be awful to feel as if you must be in control of your feelings and be able to handle everything when that's really not possible. I know that I have to be the bigger person because I'm the adult, but it is hard. I know that I am at least partly responsible if he fails, and I need to help him.

Jenny's commitment to this student appears almost saintlike; yet most teachers, if they can figure out why the child is acting as he or she is, feel called to the maturity Jenny shows. In the ultimate classroom, teachers need help identifying the family stresses that affect the child—help from parents, the child, and counseling professionals. Darryl is projecting his home situation onto his classroom, something many troubled children do. So many of the stressors that students bring to the teacher are ghosts from home, ghosts the school environment cannot be blamed for.

To go even more deeply into this material, in supporting the ultimate classroom our general culture must educate parents and teachers on how differently boys and girls often carry the ghosts and shadows of major stress. Many teachers have Jenny's experience, one in which the boys act out the stress through power struggling and the girls act in the stress by pleasing. Similarly, many teachers find that girls talk out stresses among their friends or with the person who is the source of the stress, perhaps a parent; by contrast, boys often bring the stress to school and seek attention for it there—usually negative attention.

Teachers cannot solve or heal all student stresses. The teacher can be vigilant in trying to guide the child (and, often, the child's family) toward solutions; but the teacher's job in relation to this stress is ultimately to help the child learn to manage his or her own stress wisely. In accomplishing this, the teacher mentors higher character in the child (self-esteem), removes blockage to academic learning by removing distracting stress, and teaches valuable life-survival skills.

How does the teacher do this? Here are some innovations teachers are using.

Elementary teacher Denise Young has her class make "stress balls": "To make them, we use round (fairly large) balloons and fill them with a variety of soft items—one with flour, another rice, beans, etc. We keep them in a basket by my desk. When a child is stressed or nervous, he or she can ask to get a stress ball."

Denise also revealed another wonderful method for stress release:

A team of us teachers use another technique. When a student is ready to "blow," I ask him to run to another room (way across the building) to get a book I have loaned out. The teacher there knows to tell him that she loaned it to someone else. She sends the child there, and so on. We usually send them four or five places, and, of course, the book is never found. All this running around seems to get rid of the aggression the child is feeling. The child is usually calmed down and has forgotten all about being angry.

Jenny Peterson now allows more physical movement in her classroom, both to help with stress and to increase good thinking and academic performance. Part of her inspiration to use physical movement came from the reality that her boys just move around a lot anyway. It was also partly from learning that movement can actually stimulate imagination and learning because of increased blood-flow activity in the neocortex of the brain. In her words:

I found that boys definitely need to move more than girls. As a girl, I don't ever recall needing to get out of my seat or to run around the room. Brandon, however, is moving all of the time. Today, he had his assignment notebook in the air and he was looking through the little holographic window of it. The other day, he was walking around the table while thinking of an idea for a story. I've finally gotten to the point where I can tell this "thinking" movement from "trouble," or "I'm under stress" movement. Paul has the same thing going on. He and Brandon and some of the others just frequently stand up.

In my class we have a deal now that some of these kids can stand at their tables when they're working, but not when I'm teaching.

I think I'm finally getting used to the movements going on around me. I'm beginning to see that they're even productive. Kids are learning better, getting more done.

Adding a recess in the afternoon has really helped break it up, too. This has even helped me!

Physical or body movement in class—especially when rules are promulgated as to what movement is and is not acceptable—is a powerful asset in managing stress, and it leads to learning advantages in all areas. Blood flow to the top of the brain does indeed increase when the body moves in space. Movement of blood—or, more accurately, glucose—increases in limbic areas of the brain, where emotional processing occurs. Teachers often find it helpful to let a child move around the room while he or she is trying to talk about a painful, humiliating, or otherwise emotional incident.

Brain-based gender research has taught us something fascinating about the need for movement in the male brain. It appears that the male brain does not as quickly move neurotransmission in the upper limbic areas; nor does it as naturally direct emotional material between the right and left hemispheres for analysis and verbalization. But engaging the whole body in the task of emotional processing seems to enhance neurotransmission to limbic (emotive) and left-brain (verbal) areas. When we think of boys punching a bag or doing karate or riding their bikes fast through the bike trails when they are angry, sad, or frustrated, we are seeing this theory in practice. The boy is naturally moving energy through his own brain by making his arms, legs, and whole body move.

Though we see this starkly in boys, use of movement with girls is also important, especially when a girl is blocked in her emotional processing or cannot release her stress through traditional sitting-and-talking strategies.

As always, in our ultimate classroom what works for one sex can potentially work for the other. The experience of one gender focuses our attention on a solution from which both genders can benefit. This has certainly been the case in teachers' increased attention (over the last two decades of the twentieth century) to engaging all kids in talking about feelings. This is a strategy that we've seen work well with girls; since the late 1960s, it has been increasingly applied to boys as well. Many teachers notice, as one recently put it, "When boys cry and talk about their feelings, they do it just as well as girls. We shouldn't think anymore that boys can't do these things just because more girls do them more easily."

Some teachers have instituted a talk-based check-in time at the beginning of their classes, for about five minutes, in which all the students have to say something about how they are feeling. This can proactively reduce emotional stress and open the rest of the hour or two hours of class time to real learning. A student may even say, "I'm all right, I guess," but the teacher can tell otherwise, and after lesson activities have begun, the teacher takes that student aside for another five minutes or so of talk and check-in.

As brain-based research is showing us (popularized in Daniel Goleman's *Emotional Intelligence*), a great deal of intellectual intelligence depends on emotional intelligence. Teachers find they must deal with the emotional stress ghosts in the child's life before the mind can be educated on a given day. One teacher, of the fifth grade, has applied this concept and reported:

At least two or three times a week, I see stress in a student I wouldn't have seen, and we get at it right away. The rest of the day goes better for that one kid, and so it goes better for all of us. I can't even say how many kids just feel better and less stressed because they've been able to "check in" with everyone else and hear how everyone else might be having some trouble too. I think lots feel connected and so they learn better. I certainly know things are going smoother in class since we started this.

The Role of the Mentor

When we think of improvement in bonding, attachment, and trust in the classroom, we often think only of what the teacher can do. Yet as we've seen earlier, other allies are available to an ultimate classroom, from the student body and from the family systems of the students.

In the last ten years, I have found some of the finest innovations in classroom life among schools that support three mentoring options:

1. A second teacher in the classroom
2. Intergenerational (or vertical) mentoring, between grade levels
3. Adult mentor volunteers from the community

Inserting a second teacher in classrooms is generally agreed to be useful, but it is not usually found after kindergarten. The primary reason for the dearth is funding. Student teachers or interns are relied on, and when there are none the single teacher continues her hard work on her own. Until more funding exists, this first option of the three will not become commonplace. There is no reason, however, that the other two cannot become an integral part of classroom life. In many schools they are already, as these testimonials affirm.

Kimberly Walter, an elementary teacher in Kansas City, Missouri, uses a "study buddy" program in which each first grader has a fifth-grade study buddy. The two children even eat together many days of the week during lunch. The fifth-graders are trained by the teachers to be responsible for such things as instructing the first-graders on proper etiquette. Kimberly reports that though the fifth-graders sometimes feel frustrated by having the responsibility, they are more than thrilled to live up to, in her words, "the role model expectation."

Carrie Whalley, her colleague, has found "that even the fifth- and sixth-grade students from bad environments are positively influenced by the opportunity to work with and help primary grade students." The older child's natural propensity for compassion and service shines when challenged by the reality of a younger student—who becomes like a younger sibling or cousin—in the school. Even the hardened older elementary student comes to enjoy responsibility, just as a first-born child can be both frustrated by his or her responsibility for younger children but also thrilled to be looked up to.

For Carrie, comparing the school environment to a family is very important, especially for children who do not get enough attention at home and thus may act up at school, or who see themselves as failures and need to reframe themselves as young people who belong in the world and who can be successes.

Concerning the bulk of her problem students (boys), Carrie writes, "The elementary years are a critical age when a boy first discovers his 'clan' or 'crew.' A boy will choose a clan to grow up in, and hopefully it will be a positive clan. Teachers can be part of a boy's clan, steering him in the right direction. Teachers who are female can help link up boys to positive male role models in the school and in the community."

Carrie goes on:

In our school, we have a team of teachers who meet once a month to assist teachers who need strategies for dealing with certain students. During this time, we come up with many ways different teachers and students can form relationships with the child. For example, we have a fifth-grade boy who is having a lot of behavioral difficulties in his classroom, many of which stem from lack of academic success. One of the strategies we came up with is to let this boy go into a kindergarten classroom, during reading instruction, and help out. This way, he gets key reading skills by helping out younger students. Working with younger students seems to make the older students feel really good about themselves.

A sixth-grade teacher corroborates this experience. She discovered that even the boys in her class who have discipline problems "turn

themselves around when working with their kindergarten buddies."
Part of the success of her young people comes from her emphasis (as
with Kimberly Walter) on the importance of the student being a good
role model not just when visiting the kindergarten classroom but also
in the hallways, so the kindergartners observe proper hallway behavior.
She finds that her students really want to be good role models to their
buddies.

In many private schools, vertical mentoring is mandatory. In the St.
Mark's School of Texas, a very successful private school in Dallas, older
elementary students mentor younger ones, and the mentoring is an
honored, long-standing tradition. The headmaster of the lower school,
Barbara York, believes that much of the school's success actually rests
on the results of mentoring. Among public schools, vertical mentoring
has been considered a logistical difficulty. But it is not so, as the public
schools in Kansas City can attest. It is wonderfully workable and already a success.

Community Collaboration: Mentors from Outside the School

As with in-school mentoring, using outside mentors is often considered "invasive" or logistically problematic. But many schools find that
it is not at all hard, especially if the community is trained to realize the
importance of parent, grandparent, and other volunteers. The ultimate
classroom comes to depend ever more on mentors and falls short, we
believe, if mentoring bonds and the instructional advantages integral
to them are not fostered by the school district and the teachers. Beyond
the help of any one teacher, the learning brain needs the variety of elders available to it in the human community.

The most common and simplest use of adult mentors and volunteers is in the reading tutorial. Parents, grandparents, and others come
into class for an hour or two a week to read to and with younger elementary students. Some school systems actually require adult volunteer time from participating families. These obligatory hours can be
fulfilled by a reading tutorial (or by a parent helping teachers with cleri-
cal work, such as photocopying). The Apple program, which is attached

to many public schools around the country, requires ninety hours a year from its families. The bonds that parents in the Apple program establish with the school and the teacher, as well as with the students, more than compensate for the extra time they give.

Fathers and grandfathers are especially in short supply. Their presence is extremely worthwhile in classrooms, for both boys and girls, and especially for boys brought up without fathers. Tracy Sharp, who teaches remedial reading at all elementary grade levels, told us this story:

> I started in the field of education twenty-five years ago. As a classroom teacher I never thought about doing anything to address male issues. At the time I started teaching, the majority of young men had positive male role models in the home. Families were more stable in the seventies.
>
> It didn't occur to me until I started teaching remedial reading (classes boys mainly have to take) that it was imperative to connect males with books that had male characters, and with men themselves. As a classroom teacher one year I used a father to portray the lion from the *Wizard of Oz*. I was teaching a lesson on the difference between a question and a statement, so it was presented in an interview format. The students had to interview the lion. Another year I had a father come in and share his experience of staying and living with an African tribe.

Our children are hungry for the presence of role-model males. They bring that hunger to classrooms. Elementary teacher Jenny Peterson writes about her students:

> Many of them do not have male role models, and it shows in their discipline issues. Two who lack discipline especially also have no father, and one has a stepfather who seems dangerous. Four male students all have male role models, and they seem to be good ones. These are all boys who get into trouble here and there, but their acts are never malicious—they seem like regular boy/kid stuff. It's obvious that they have a certain level of security that the students without fathers don't

have. They have an understanding of a certain code of behavior—one I'm guessing that is modeled by their dads. The boys who lack this seem to possess a certain amount of insecurity that, I think, shows up in their aggressive behavior. It seems like they need to be in charge and put others down so that they can feel powerful. There's no one at home showing them what it means to be a man or what having power means. It is obvious that they're out there trying it on their own— trying to figure it out.

Though perhaps most obvious in boys, father hunger is also a distinct problem for girls, especially in the broad area of character development. Quite often girls who are raised without fathers, or who hunger for a father's love and discipline, can overwhelm teachers with what elementary teacher Jan Miller has seen in some of her female students: "a lack of a moral compass."

In the ultimate classroom, our children's father hunger is fed by fathers and grandfathers who come into school. Supporting this innovation requires the men to reach into the school; but first, the teachers must reach out to the men. In making father presence a large part of every elementary school, we have to buy fully into the idea that school and family are not separate but intertwined, as we discussed in Chapter Three. Children do better at school if they are fathered, and if this means that schools must increase the fathering or male-mentoring opportunities within educational culture, then they must do so, reaping rewards in fewer discipline problems, better academic excellence, and more humaneness.

How to Provide Discipline in the Elementary Classroom

When we think of the school as a second family system, we think of teachers not merely as instructors but as family members, as mentors and role models whose instructional capacities are either enhanced or diminished by the extent of their bond with their students. By the same token, we notice that a teacher's ability to create a well-disciplined classroom, and her capacity to handle discipline issues as they arise, also depends on how well bonded she is to students.

To some extent, this was not the case a hundred, or even fifty, years ago. Discipline could be a matter of fear—fear of God, fear of the rod, fear of parents. The teacher might not utterly bond with a student yet nonetheless instill fear because the child feared other forces—perhaps family and God—that supported the teacher. Furthermore, the child was taught from infancy to respect elders, including teachers, as inherently right.

Both innate respect for the teacher and fear of punishment by supportive religious and family forces have diminished. Teachers are now required to adjust to methods of discipline that are relatively new to the profession. It is no wonder, then, that discipline issues are among the most discussed in our classrooms and schools.

Learning from Past Mistakes

Recently we held a group discussion with elementary teachers of all grade levels. We asked them what did not work well to ensure discipline. Their comments are enlightening, especially because many confessed to certain realizations about previously used discipline techniques, in the wake of training in the brain-based and gender-based material. Because most of the discipline problems the teachers faced involved boys, the discussion in this group largely related to the male population. Here are disciplinary measures teachers took in the past that they realize now to be ultimately counterproductive:

- Time out exacted at recess. Exacting time-out during recess ended up quite often creating problems later in the day as the child was unable to engage physical energy and movement.
- Overreliance on trying to force a confession, or immediate self-assessment, from an offending student. Boys could not talk about what had happened as quickly and accurately as the teachers wanted them to. Learning that the male brain is often slower at

processing important emotive material helped the teachers change their expectations.

- Embarrassing the offender in front of classmates. Teachers agreed it could be effective, at times, to confront an offending student in front of classmates; yet there was consensus that this should not be overdone. If the boy's (or girl's) pride was hurt too much, the rest of the child's learning experience for that day, and sometimes longer, was ill affected. Confronting the momentary offense by "getting in the child's face" in front of others was usually counterproductive.

Many teachers in this and other focus groups confessed happily to how they had cut down on discipline issues by realizing that many normal boy behaviors did not require discipline. Boys are normal Huck Finns and Tom Sawyers. The teachers, nearly all of whom were female, confessed to needing to "stretch their minds" to accommodate the normality of some boyish behavior. Teachers who had been raised with brothers found this stretching less difficult than those who had not spent a lot of time as children with groups of males.

Claire, an elementary school phys ed teacher, recognized boyishness in an experience she had with a second-grader earlier on the same day. The second-grader shaped his hand into a gun and replicated shooting her. She privately told him how disappointed she was in his behavior and decided to leave it at that, recognizing that the boy had not crossed over the line between aggression and violence. Claire confessed that prior to receiving training in the male brain, hormones, and culture, she used to be very hard on boys who made gestures like this, or did fake karate kicks at friends. She saw these acts as violent behavior and wrote the boys up. Now she understood that in some cases, like the present one, this was just aggression play and aggression expression (expressing self through physically aggressive activities and gestures), not violence (attempting to destroy another person, place, or thing).

As the group discussion continued, many of the teachers agreed that it is important not to overreact to situations like this, nor to let them interfere with the bonding relationship with the student. On the other hand, certain standards emerged from this discussion for when to do more than just express alarm or disappointment about the aggressive gesture:

- If the student is, by use of the gesture, dissing the teacher in a way that inappropriately challenges teacher authority
- If the student has a history of violent or overly aggressive behavior
- If the aggressive gestures disrupt the class (that is, are done to get attention at a time when that is inappropriate)

All the teachers agreed that showing one's disappointment at a student's gestures is always the teacher's right, yet if the child was expressing his nature rather than offending on purpose, expression of disappointment is enough and no other discipline is required.

In our research into discipline at all grade levels, we have found that the ultimate classroom is one all these teachers want, wherein teacher authority is sacrosanct yet each student feels free to express the growing self. Walking the line between allowing strong student expression and retaining strong authority is the core challenge of all discipline systems, especially in the present day and age.

Discipline Techniques After an Offending Act

No single discipline system or act is best. A combination of efforts generally helps return the child to self-discipline, the classroom to stability, and the educational community to a sense of justice. Here are some techniques any teacher or school can use.

THE FIVE-STEP SYSTEM. At Balboa Elementary School five steps are followed once an offending act has been committed. Depending on the severity of the act, the teacher may never need to go beyond step one.

1. *Teacher-student contact.* The teacher talks to the student or otherwise works with the offender, without outside help.

2. *Teacher-parent contact.* The teacher makes two attempts to contact parents. If she can't reach parents, the head office keeps trying.

3. *Notifying principal.* The child sees the principal, or the principal otherwise gets involved.

4. *Teacher–support personnel contact.* This usually calls for a counselor or school psychologist, but it may be another teacher or coach with whom the child is bonded.

5. *Excluding student.* If necessary, the child is excluded from the class. All previous steps are documented before resorting to this one.

QUESTIONS AND ANSWERS. When offending children are sent to Jan Miller, an acting principal in a Kansas City school district, she presents them with paper and pencil. They are to write responses to questions that help them work their way through their problem. The first question is usually "Why are you here?"

Jan reports, "This technique seems to give boys more time to think about their responses and, because they do not want to write any more than they have to, they carefully select and limit their words." The technique works well for girls also, since they ordinarily write more words and have less difficulty than some boys in writing.

The experience of special ed teacher Carrie Whalley with some of her boys indicates a difference many teachers have found regarding how questions are asked. When Carrie has to confront a boy who needs discipline, she has noticed, in her words, that

> boys find it difficult when we corner them. It's hard for boys to open up when you say "Look at me—I'm talking to you—what is wrong?" I find myself and other professionals doing this all of the time. I want a boy to look at me when I am talking to him, but I am finding that's not how we go about getting boys to open up. Lately, I am trying to be very conscious of what I ask a boy to do when I am trying to get information. I try to get something in his hands (crayons, blocks, cards) while I'm talking. I find this tends to relax the boy and also prevents a lot of frustration on my part.

Quite often, discipline of an offending child becomes exacerbated by the child's reluctance to talk and explain. By allowing the boy or girl to lower the head, play with a crayon, and move slowly in response if needed, the teacher gets to the heart of the matter with less need for angry second-stage discipline.

THE TIMER. Carrie has found a timer works well in a situation where the child (likely a boy) is angry. She wrote, "Today one of my fifth-graders was very upset with me and I set the timer for five minutes. I told him I'd talk to him when the timer went off. By the end of five minutes we were both calm and could talk."

This technique allows cooldown and lets the brain prepare for processing of emotion surrounding an action or an offense. It is generally helpful to let time pass before expecting clarity from a child who requires discipline, especially boys, who generally need time to collect themselves enough to talk.

BUDDY ROOMS. Students who do not respond well to their teacher's discipline are sent, in Denise Young's school, to a buddy room. This becomes a safe place to work out their problems. The buddy room can be the room of another teacher. For instance, new sixth-grade teachers often send their problem students to Denise because she is an experienced teacher and has excellent rapport with the students. The students normally respond respectfully to her.

Denise told us about one sixth-grader who refused to go to her room when sent there by his classroom teacher, so the teacher sent for Denise and asked that she help get the student to move to the buddy room. Denise went to the other classroom and directed him to come with her. He did without argument. When they were in private, Denise notified him, "If you ever fail to respond to your teacher like that again, I will come get you and take you home." She foresees no further problem with him.

When buddy rooms are used, it is important to use a teacher who has clear authority and is respected. Using a buddy room can backfire if the teacher is not bonded with the student she mentors; the offender can end up causing trouble in two classrooms rather than one.

RUN-AN-ERRAND METHOD. Elementary teacher Jan Miller wrote generously in her journal about the errand method, which we mentioned briefly earlier. Here is more detail:

> Our staff developed a code to use on kids that need some time away after creating a disturbance, time to get it together.
>
> We have a card that states, "I need the Love and Logic book." There is no Love and Logic book. But you can send a child on an errand to anyone to get it and they pass them on to someone else and then back to you and by that time the child has cooled down and is ready to settle into class.
>
> Recently, this worked extremely well with a BD boy that I have in my class. When coming in from recess, the basketball was thrown and accidentally hit him and he was immediately mad and went off. I saw how he was treating the people around him and knew I had to help him regain his self-discipline.
>
> On the way in, I asked him to do an errand for me, gave him the card, and he went to three different teachers, returned and said no one had the book. I said, "OK, we are on page 32" and he sat down and began working. The whole process only took minutes and was a great cool down for him.

ONE-ON-ONE MENTORING. Alison Jabosky, a parent liaison at an elementary school, told us that her best discipline method is one-on-one mentoring. She reported particular success with a second-grade student who was creating major disruptions in the classroom. People nearly gave up on him, but she mentored him for three weeks. This mentoring proved to be quite successful; he has transitioned back into the regular classroom with ongoing mentoring from her. "He needed structure, attention, and positive reinforcement," she says, "which I was able to provide in a one-on-one mentoring situation."

Both boys and girls need this kind of mentoring, but teachers find that, once again, undisciplined boys seem in the most need of ongoing mentoring. Given the structure and functioning of the developing male brain, this makes biological sense. Males often take longer to process all of the emotional and social material that goes into restabilizing themselves. This notwithstanding, when girls are being disruptive, one-on-one mentoring can be the best method for reaching them as well. A teacher in a large school in Maine told us about a third-grade girl who was especially disruptive. The student intern made this girl her focus for a week and finally, after that time, discovered the girl's parents had just divorced. The girl returned to stability after that revelation. Sometimes, nothing but one-on-one mentoring can solve a discipline problem because no other method builds enough trust for a breakthrough revelation to occur.

THE BIST MODEL. BIST stands for Behavior Instruction Support Team; it was developed by the staff of the Ozanam School in the Kansas City area. They now market this model to other school districts. The primary support for school personnel is a consultant who helps them when they have issues they can't seem to successfully resolve with offending students.

BIST uses a "recovery room" for major offenses (throwing a chair, screaming and cursing at a teacher, hitting another student in class). In some cases, the BIST system can result in substantial time out of class. However, it also results in fewer suspensions and expulsions as the students get older. How much better it would be to teach students responsibility and self-control at the elementary level!

Kimberly Walter has noted how helpful BIST is in handling student anger. As Kimberly has employed it, the disruptive student remains in the safe spot, or recovery room, until he or she owns up to responsibility for the problem. This means the student may be there for more than one school day. Once the student believes he is ready to accept responsibility, he "checks out" with the teacher at the teacher's convenience. The offense is processed, and a commitment is made to improve behavior.

If the student does not comply with the direction to report to a specific safe spot following an offense, the teacher notifies the Crisis Response Team (or CRT, a group of trained teachers) over the intercom. For example, if the teacher in room 101 wants the CRT, she announces over the intercom "CRT to room 101." Kimberly reported that kids in her school have heard the message enough to determine that CRT stands for "come rescue the teacher."

Once the CRT arrives, all the other students are taken out of the room. The CRT then works with the disobedient student, physically removing the student if necessary. Students typically become obedient as soon as the CRT is involved because it is embarrassing to them to be carried down the hallway. Use of the CRT is rarer than an offending student simply removing himself from the room and to a safe spot.

The BIST model is obviously not needed in the case of a small disciplinary action; but for those times when a larger action is required, it comes highly recommended by the teachers in our study.

Discipline Techniques to *Prevent* Undisciplined Behavior

Kimberly Walter has found that her first-graders transition better from task to task, and thus require less punishment or reprimand, if she gives them forewarning. About three minutes prior to the transition, she announces to the class that they have a few minutes to finish up or get to a stopping point, as well as what they will be doing next. Without this preparation time, her boys especially are not ready to move on, and she wastes time getting into discipline situations with them.

This is a wonderful example of a small thing teachers can do to manage the classroom effectively. Males do tend to have difficulty in multitasking and switching from one task to another quickly. Brain-based research posits that this comes from the fact that in the female brain there is less lateralization to do activities—in other words, the female brain is doing a given activity in more parts of the brain than the male and thus overlaps between activities more easily. Even given this brain difference, Kimberly's practice of giving lead time is certainly good for the girls in the class too.

BUDDY ROOMS. Kimberly uses the buddy room not only in the context of the BIST model but also as a preventive technique. If she is going to be out one day and a substitute must take her class, to prevent a problem with a particularly difficult child she arranges for him to spend that day in Mrs. O'Dell's class. He works well for Mrs. O'Dell but always has difficulty with substitutes.

This is entirely humane. When a teacher knows a student's weaknesses and insecurities, nothing is gained by watching him dissemble in a difficult situation—not by the student, the teacher, or the class group that will be disrupted by his attacks on the substitute teacher.

FEWER SECOND CHANCES. Quite often, when I consult in classrooms I notice teachers diminishing their authority in favor of a second chance. Haven't we all, sometime in our career, heard ourselves say:

"Jimmy, if you do that again. . . ."

"Jimmy, I told you, if you do that again I'll. . . ."

"Jimmy, I've told you already how disruptive that is."

"Jimmy. . . ."

The teacher (like the overwhelmed parent) does not realize that one of the best ways to preempt discipline problems from escalating, and one of the keys to managing classroom discipline in general, is to use the child's sense that the teacher is an alpha—a powerful leader. This sense is thwarted if the child gets a number of second chances, especially in the late elementary and middle school years. Although a zero-tolerance policy generally erases good bonding and often does more harm than intended, a "ten-tolerance" policy (allowing a thing to repeat ten times) does great harm as well to the whole learning environment. It is better to say, "Jimmy, if you do that again, you will lose your _____ privilege." Then, if he does it again, he suffers the consequence.

PULL CARDS. One elementary teacher has had great success with making her students responsible for their actions by keeping a tally of offenses on "pull cards," which are analogous to punch cards at a workplace:

Lately, my students have had a problem throwing little things at each other. Everyone is sick of it. I wish I was able to trust the people who report the violation, but I can't. It seems as though those who are the most vocal are also the guiltiest. Yesterday, I actually watched a student throw a crayon at himself then yell out during class blaming another student.

We had a class meeting today to work out solutions. The class suggested we use pull cards to help manage the classroom. The students are very visual—they need to physically see that they have a certain number of violations and what their limits are.

Her class now tallies violations, and once a child is over the set limit, he or she goes to the principal. The method is working very well, her class is restabilizing, and, most important, new discipline problems such as throwing objects at each other are preempted.

PUNISH THEM ALL! Carol Meyers, an Edison Elementary fourth-grade teacher, has had success with a kind of peer pressure to behave. She writes:

Towards the end of the year students sometimes begin bickering on the playground (usually the girls). When it first occurs I bring all the students involved together and place their names in a container. I tell them that it is just too difficult to decide who is really having the problem with whom. Girls tend to change best friends frequently, so new problems can develop daily. So the next time a problem occurs between any of them I will just pull three names out of the container and they will be the three people to receive the consequence whether they were involved or not.

This may seem draconian to some, but Carol responds that "it has taken care of the petty bickering every time I have used this method so far; it also keeps me from being the bad guy because the names in the container are predetermined; and I let a student pick out the names to see who received the consequence."

Many of the best discipline techniques have developed, whether consciously or unconsciously, to fit male-brain and male-behavior needs specifically because 90 percent of the discipline problems in schools are associated with boys. This does not mean they don't work with girls; they do. At the same time, some teachers have definitely found less need for a long cooldown time with girls. Girls also tend to be quick at clearly verbalizing problems and not so reliant on imposed authority. Perhaps most of all, teachers in our study noticed a great need to encourage a girl's ability to give voice to her own hidden agendas and feelings.

Motivation Techniques

Another area where teacher intuition has favored boys' learning difficulties is in motivation development. Between 70 and 80 percent of the students with motivation problems are boys. Therefore, as with discipline, many teachers have had to seek male-brain solutions to motivational problems. Our research indicates that many techniques used to inspire motivation, though perhaps linked to male-brain issues, can work for both boys and girls.

Carrie Whalley has found success with seriously unmotivated students by using time limits. "I challenge them," she writes, "to do something in a certain amount of time: 'Let's see if you can do these three math problems in two minutes.' This can work wonders."

Elementary teacher Rita Oglesby says that pride and embarrassment play a role in the measures taken at her school to motivate students, particularly boys, to take responsibility for their behavior. This school has identified those primary-grade teachers who have been there for a number of years and who have good rapport because of their consistent discipline. Undisciplined and unmotivated boys are directed to these mentors, many of whom are teachers in younger grades. Rita has seen success, she says, "in part because these are the teachers who the unmotivated boys respect the most, so the boys are embarrassed to be sent to them for messing up. They are also embarrassed to be in a primary grade classroom."

Character Education

Such classroom issues as discipline and motivation can be aided and normally resolved by practical, moment-by-moment strategies, but schools
have even more success if character education is in the foreground of activity in the ultimate classroom. For a generation or two our schools have
emphasized "soft" values, such as self-esteem. It is important to nurture
self-esteem, but unless it is grounded in "hard" values such as respect,
honesty, and integrity, it can easily become a path of self-indulgence for a
child. A school system or classroom that does not emphasize character
development is not fully serving the growing moral needs of the child.

There are many wonderful character-education programs around
the country. Twenty-eight states either require or encourage character
education. We feature in this book a program called CHARACTER*plus*,
developed and applied initially in Missouri and now used nationally.
We choose this program not only for its integrity and success but also
because we know its compatibility with the brain-based research at the
Gurian Institute and in the Missouri school districts.

CHARACTER*plus*

The program came about through the encouragement and support of a
St. Louis businessman, Sanford McDonnell of McDonnell-Douglass.
He noted that many of his new employees did not have a positive char-
acter base. He approached the Ferguson-Florissant School District in
St. Louis County with a partnership offer, which has since evolved into
the CHARACTER*plus* Center. Through the work that the center in St.
Louis has done, dozens of school districts and communities now work
together to build the character base of their young people.

According to Linda McKay, the director of CHARACTER*plus*,
"Character education creates the climate our schools need for learning
to begin—it is the internal engine and the heart of student learning."
Here's how CHARACTER*plus* works.

The process starts with community members, including educators,
working in a series of meetings to identify and define the character

traits they want their community's young people to demonstrate. Once the traits are agreed on (in a moment, we present a list of possible traits), teachers are taught to integrate them into their existing curricula, and community members make a commitment to support, model, and teach them as well.

Having facilitated these community processes, Patricia Henley has seen community members move from actual distrust of one another and of the possible outcomes of designing a "value system" for children, to relationships of mutual respect and commitment. An example is the Hickman Mills School District, where community members were still grappling with the fact that the community makeup and dynamics had changed in recent years with the influx of many families from the inner city. In writing a working definition of the value of diversity in a school district community, participants came to a much better understanding of the position, hopes, and fears that each of them held.

This large community committee also came to consensus as to which character traits would be taught and reinforced within the school district. After selecting the traits, they also defined and adopted the traits and their definitions:

- Respect: showing positive regard for self, others, and property
- Accountability: willingness to be responsible for our actions and to accept the consequences of those actions
- Empathy: ability to relate to and understand the feelings of others
- Responsibility: being accountable for one's actions
- Recognition of diversity: acknowledging differences and appreciating individuals as equal members of society
- Honesty: willingness to be truthful in both words and actions
- Compassion: carrying out action sympathetic to others in an effort to assist
- Cooperation: the action of working together for mutual benefit to accomplish a task
- Self-confidence: positive belief in oneself and in one's ability
- Resourcefulness: creating ways to achieve positive solutions or outcomes

Although the character traits and their definitions can vary from community to community, similarities outnumber differences even though the communities vary in terms of location, size, and cultural makeup. For example, practically all communities agree on the character traits of honesty, respect, and responsibility.

Integrating Character Education into the Whole School

Character education works best when it is integrated into all the departments of a school. For instance, a science teacher might ask the class to analyze the ethics of a given science project. The teacher might, on another occasion, assign a meta-analysis (a character analysis) of certain scientists themselves. In an overarching way, superintendents and principals trickle down their interest in character education, extending to teachers training opportunities in how to teach character education and supporting arts and history teaching, which inherently touch on character-related themes. Even education about the historical development of religions can generally work in a history class, especially if the religious history is taught as a way of tracing how our civilization has or has not acted with "character plus."

Dealing with Cruelty, Hazing, and Violence

At Lowell School, a private school in the Washington, D.C., area, the staff made a conscious decision in 1996 to focus on teasing. As at most schools, private and public, they had seen an increase in teasing behavior over the previous few years. Because they trained staff in the problem, the Lowell community was able to hold students accountable for teasing behavior; those who were teased became articulate about when it was happening, and the teasers or bullies took responsibility for their actions, including understanding what actually constitutes normal teasing and what is hurtful. Lowell made a special point to ban most cross-gender teasing and completely banned any racial teasing.

Recently the courts have gotten involved in the matter of teasing and humiliation behavior in the schools. Though the obvious reason appears to be school shootings—such as the Columbine murders at Littleton, Colorado—the increase in inappropriate humiliation behavior throughout our nation's schools has been noticed by educators and parents. This behavior, we now realize, can be a character issue.

When does teasing become humiliation, and when does humiliation become illegal harassment? At what point do all of these behaviors become violence? These questions are decided over and over again by the courts, but the ultimate classroom must exist in safety and enjoy standards of behavior that are both realistic and enforceable.

Definition of Terms

Our study of schools, as well as our research into brain-based reasons for cruel behavior, have led us to some information we believe is helpful for schools deciding on their policies.

TEASING. Teasing is a normal activity among peers, in which children focus on a real or perceived weakness in another or others. Especially in elementary school, friendships are just as frequently cemented by teasing as they are destroyed. Teasing is a way of one-upping, but just as often flirtatious. It exists in human relations as a means of building strength in a peer community. Most children adapt to it and grow stronger from the process. Some, especially those who are less confident, are harmed by it.

HUMILIATION. Humiliation is also a normal activity among peers, but it is generally practiced by children who are perceived (or who perceive themselves) to be at the upper end of a hierarchy. These children generally pick a variety of targets.

HARASSMENT. Harassment is repeated targeting of one or more individuals, over a prolonged period, which generally uses one or more psychosocial traits (physical feature, race, sexual identity, gender, social class, intellectual disability, emotional vulnerability) as the seat of the harassment.

Teasing and humiliation are generally normal—though painful—forms of human aggression, practiced by both boys and girls in gender-specific ways. But harassment is generally a form of violence and can escalate into physical assault.

AGGRESSION AND VIOLENCE. By *aggression* we mean an individual's attempt to control or manipulate another individual or system. This is normal in all humans. By *violence* we mean an individual's attempt to destroy the core self or very existence of another individual or system. This destruction can be accomplished on a behavioral spectrum that runs from incessant shaming to physical attack and, in the extreme, systematic annihilation.

Zero-Tolerance Policies

Our school culture is crueler than we'd like. Simultaneously, many teachers and parents are not trained in basic brain and human development, to say nothing of knowing how boys and girls experience aggression differently. In lieu of deep understanding, many policy makers are opting for a stark solution.

Zero-tolerance policies are presently in vogue. They are useful, but just as often too rigid and inhumane. Though zero tolerance for carrying a weapon in school seems essential, even this can be overdone. For instance, we were recently informed of a fifth grader who was expelled from school for carrying a pocket knife he had been given by his father over the weekend and put in his backpack. He had forgotten it was there. He committed no offense except forgetfulness.

From the point of view of brain-based and gender-based research, zero-tolerance policies are easier to support in small private schools than in large public schools. These private (as well as small public) schools are structured as comparatively intimate communities on account of their generally small classroom size, increased mentoring, and increased one-on-one attention to students. The behavioral range of students in these schools is generally not as wide as in a large public school.

When, therefore, the argument is made—as it recently was on a radio forum on school discipline—that "private schools have successful zero-tolerance polices, so shouldn't public schools?" we must look closely at the configuration of mentoring and bonding systems in the school structures. If a school is set up to prevent student unruliness by providing constant supervision, then zero tolerance is compatible with the school structure (as the students experience the structure). If two thousand students go to a school and many do not get the mentoring and bonding they need from elders, then zero-tolerance policies are—like Ritalin and other medication policies—often a show of how overwhelmed the school is, not how humane.

Zero tolerance of actual violence and of gang attire or activity is generally essential, an exception to our warning about unfair zero-tolerance policies. San Diego–based gang expert Jesus Villahermosa offers this profile of a gang member:

- Poor achiever in school
- Frequently truant
- Dresses in gang attire (including bandanas worn on the head or back pocket, sagging pants, and baseball caps with monikers or graffiti written inside the brim)
- Uses intimidating body language
- Uses street names as gang alias
- Draws gang symbols (in block-style lettering) or flashes gang hand signs

Gang involvement is frightening to a school, a kind of antithetical example of students seeking bonding opportunities in isolationist, violence-based gang systems rather than in school systems.

VIOLENCE PREVENTION TRAINING.   In tandem with character education, violence prevention training is essential not only for teachers and staff but for students as well. Many of the school shootings of the late 1990s were preventable—not necessarily by teachers, who have far too many students to fully read the violent intention of any one, but by students, some number of whom are intimate with potential offenders. As these students are trained in their community responsibility, and as they learn options open to them, they are forthcoming, motivated by empathy for a depressed classmate and a sense of responsibility for the whole school.

HARASSMENT RULES. Now that the U.S. Supreme Court has come down on the side of harassed students, it is essential that each school promulgate and post its harassment rules. We suggest a posting in this vein:

- A student or group of students may not repeatedly taunt another student.
- A student or group of students may not hit another student.
- Students witnessing harassment or violence must report the act.

After posting a list of rules of this kind, enforcement policies, appropriate to the given school and its legislative mandates, should also be declared.

Posting without student training is less successful than promulgation of rules in conjunction with student training in such terms as "aggression," "teasing," and "harassment."

HONOR TRAINING. Honor training and honor codes should be considered by all schools. St. Mark's School of Texas has a model for honor codes and training. If possible, the school should make sure all students are involved in designing and then signing the honor code. At present some parents (and children) resist honor codes as too restrictive, but so too did they resist character-education training a few years ago. Once we begin the effort to make honor codes a part of every school, we will see success in making them universal within just a few years.

NONBULLYING CURRICULA. There are many wonderful training programs available to aid educators and communities in stopping violent behavior. One we find especially helpful is On Target to Stop Bullying, which began with research by the Missouri Safe Schools Coalition and is now marketed by the Stop Violence Coalition in Kansas City. It uses principles consistent with brain and biological information in violence prevention.

Whatever program a school uses, it is essential that all teachers be trained in a stop-bullying curriculum that is rooted in understanding how boys and girls actually think and feel. Programs of this kind feel very supportive to teachers and staff; they teach skills for handling misbehavior and they edify teachers in the mysteries of their students' very confusing behavior.

THE ROLE OF MEDIA.   The effect of media influence, especially on male violence, must be courageously dealt with by every school district. According to media literacy expert John Caputo, "By age 16, the average child has seen 16,000 murders on TV alone. Acts of violence exceed 11 per hour on evening TV. By the end of high school, the average student has spent 11,000 hours in the classroom, watched 15,000 hours of television, listened to 10,500 hours of popular music, seen 350,000 commercials, and witnessed 18,000 media deaths."

Years ago, there were arguments as to whether media images affected growing children. These arguments existed because brain-based research was not commonly understood. Now we know that the human brain is affected by these images in problematic ways. *What Stories Does My Son Need?* by Michael Gurian and Terry Trueman analyzes this research and then lists one hundred books and one hundred movies that build character in boys (and in all children). It is one attempt to link media literacy to character development. All schools will benefit from building media literacy programs into their curricula.

In many ways, the media itself can help. Pokemon, for instance, the Japan-based card and movie craze, is a highly values-based game. Japanese elementary schools use the game to instill empathy, responsibility, and cooperation in students. We can use it similarly, by asking for reports from students on what the characters mean and how they help each other succeed.

Community collaboration in this area is crucial: teachers and parents alike need and want training in media literacy. This is because the media—especially its violence and amoral content—are ghosts from the home that visit many schools by way of schoolchildren who are allowed at home to surf the net inappropriately, watch whatever television they want, and see developmentally inappropriate movies. In the near future, through using parent-education coordinators, schools can take the lead in training parents on good standards for media use and thus make schools themselves safer.

Innovations for Academic Excellence

Teasing, bullying, and other psychosocial issues tend to be featured in most discussion of elementary discipline issues, but the two areas of most pronounced difficulty—and the most copious brain and social research—in the academic realm are reading and writing, and math and science. We asked the teachers in Missouri to pay special attention to these areas.

Innovations for Teaching Language Arts, Especially Reading and Writing

Reading and writing are rudimentary to academic and social excellence. If a student performs well at them, the teacher feels as if she can teach anything. If a student doesn't, the road to excellence seems very long indeed. Similarly, it is immensely gratifying to see a child enjoy critical thinking in social studies, or historical analysis in history class, and demoralizing when the child just seems bored.

In general, boys are further behind in these skills, for neurological reasons we've already noted. But many girls show reading and writing difficulties as well, becoming bored by subject matter in social studies or history that does not speak to them. In our research, we have grouped all subjects not in the math and science area as "language arts." Here are some innovations that have worked for teachers of these classes who focus on the learning-brain and gender issues.

READ AND DRAW. An interesting experiment was shared with us by a second-grade teacher. She wrote that her students, despite gripes (mainly from some boys) about reading, love to be read to. After learning about how the brain processes, she decided to allow her students to draw as she read. Many of them were especially attentive and creative in this modality.

She reported: "It is really neat to see what students choose to draw. This is insightful to their lives. I have noticed that the boys tend to draw military, violent scenes, robots, or sports themes. The girls on the other hand tend to draw flowers, natural scenes, or realistic situations."

This is an experiment any early elementary teacher can try. Reading time, which is already an important part of many classrooms, becomes a time for spatial and art functions, expanding its use. Drawing is not a substitute for reading, but can take the pressure off those children who read poorly but use aural and verbal stimulation to better code and decode words.

USING MANIPULATIVES FOR READING. Elementary teacher Jan Miller told us that following new insight into how the brain learns language, she increased her use of manipulatives in literacy education: "I tried the magnetic letters on the overhead today for a spelling lesson. Students loved it." She also created letter packets for each child in reading: "We used these to create new vocabulary words for reading a story. Kids became more involved and seemed excited about finding the words in the new story." By essentially making a game out of letter learning, she had great success. "Each child," she said, "was given a bright index card to follow along with the reading of a story. This seemed to keep students on track with the story." Jan allows students to handle a stress ball while she is reading a story aloud or while they are reading a story. She has found that many of the boys perform better if they have something to do with their hands.

Along the lines of the "yay and yuk" approach used by Carol Myers that we described earlier, Jan has each student journal each day on a "yum" or a "yuck," something in their day they did or did not like. The students with poor writing skills find it difficult, of course, but the action of journal writing gives them a good ritual, and good practice.

Jan also uses macaroni in several shapes as a manipulative to represent apostrophes, quotation marks, and commas. She reported: "This hands-on activity made writing fun and the boys related to it better since they had concrete objects to work with as they developed writing skills."

WAITING FOR AN ANSWER. Denise Young told us she has noticed that some students, especially boys with less-developed verbal literacy, need extra time to formulate thoughts. "I have begun to try the sixty-second wait time with boys when asking a question," she says; "I have noticed it often does help, and I am getting better responses from them." This technique is also very useful with girls who are not quick to answer when asked a question about a story or other process.

MULTISENSORY READING AND WRITING STIMULATION. Denise employs a multisensory approach worthy of universal application in our classrooms. In her journal, she reported: "I asked my students to write a Halloween story and decided to play scary music and light candles for a more realistic effect. They all enjoyed it, but I really got great stories from the boys. They used a lot more describing words after listening to the tape." Stimulating the mind via more than one sense led to greater literacy.

One of the finest resources we have found for improving a teacher's ability to teach reading and writing is *Teaching Children to Be Literate,* by Manzo and Manzo.

PROVIDING VARIOUS LEARNING MODALITIES. Our research has found that although both girls and boys can enjoy a variety of learning modes, girls usually shine through when provided with numerous ways of learning. Angie Hathaway, at Spring Branch Elementary School in Missouri, told us, "My girl students enjoy tutoring other students, male or female, same age or younger. They like writing their thoughts down in a journal. Every day, I put a journal question on the blackboard that may be academically related or something the kids do outside of class. They like debates. I teach social studies, so we very often hold discussions or debate issues that are controversial to their needs or interests. (Example:

Would you rather have recess or PE?) We also do a lot of cooperative groups which seem to help the girls be more creative and confident."

Angie's intuition about girls is shared by many teachers, who use varying learning modes. This helps boys, but teachers often find that many boys find one mode they like and stick with it, whereas girls generally like moving from one mode to another. Given our knowledge of the multitasking female brain, it is quite possible this male-female trend is directly related to the brain itself.

SEPARATE-SEX LEARNING. For over a decade, powerful research has filtered through school systems on the benefits of separate-sex learning for girls. In our next chapter, on middle school, we focus on its benefits for both boys and girls. Many elementary teachers trained in brain differences find great benefit in this experience in their classrooms. Ruth Whertvine puts it high on her list of strategies for teaching girls: "This year our school separated the girls into classes by themselves away from the boys. It has helped the girls to concentrate. They are more focused, and I have noticed things about girls' behavior that I never really noticed before."

EXTRA ENCOURAGEMENT FOR GIRLS. Ruth goes further to "make sure I call on every girl every day." Teachers like Ruth notice that girls often need more verbal feedback than we give. Perhaps all of us have seen the girl in the class who just did not believe in herself until we kept encouraging and encouraging her. It is crucial for teachers to realize how personally girls can take perceived failure—whether in a relationship or in academic performance.

Patricia Henley shared this wisdom from her own teaching experience:

Everyone can win at something—it really just takes a teacher helping the girl find that ability or perseverance to get to be a winner. If I hadn't been pushed to achieve beyond what I thought I could accomplish I wouldn't have believed I could ever have done it. I remember a student of mine at the elementary level who thought she couldn't speak publicly. I continually gave her opportunities to speak to me, to groups of students or teachers. Finally, she was selected to be a peer mediator. She was really good, but she couldn't have done it without being encouraged and praised each step of the way. In my experience, girls especially will stand back if they don't think they can do it, rather than risk failure.

PROVIDE FEMALE ROLE MODELS AND NONBIASED MATERIALS. Lois J. Hedge, of Edison Elementary, has been vigilant about what reading materials that girls learn from in the classroom. She wrote in her journal:

> Since I am female, I hope that I am a role model for all students, but especially for girls. Making sure the playing field is even is a good way to get girls to participate. I use literature and materials that are not gender-biased. Allowing girls to see females in many positive roles is another way to instill a sense of worth. Girls like to work together and help each other or other students. I look for their strengths and help to steer them to that interest. Any little thing that might empower them can be a big thing.

Jennifer Hull, an elementary teacher in Hickman Mills, echoes Lois: "I teach English, which is often easier for girls. In my situation, I role model behavior, dress, and courage. I attempt to show girls how to be strong, intelligent, and feminine. In teaching English, I make smaller groups and speak to girls in a manner they are comfortable with. The girls enjoy grouping around my desk and talking about how literature relates and affects them. They enjoy telling their story, and I listen to their stories."

The importance to girls of paired conversation, one-on-one encouragement, and role modeling simply cannot be overstated.

Innovations for Teaching Math and Science

Math and science classes are, along with language arts, a common area of discomfort for many students. Armed with gender-based and brain-based training, teachers have developed innovations that can be readily used. Some are already familiar to teachers, but many are quite new and creative.

EXTERNALIZING THOUGHT PROCESSES ABOUT MATH. Jill Lamming, of Spring Branch Elementary School, makes sure to help a student understand the thought process of doing math by seeing math work outside the student's head:

> To help teach math and science (especially to girls) I include in lessons the strategies of outlining thought processes and self-questioning techniques. An example of this might be how to figure out the value of numbers with decimals. The first thing the student needs to ask herself is, "Is this a whole number?" The next step would be to locate where the decimal falls in the number. She does this outside her own head by asking the question, writing the answer, or "seeing" it on a graph. I have found that talking through strategies and outlining processes on a chart or overhead as we go helps girls to better visualize and work through what might seem second nature to boys. Diagramming information has also proven to be a useful visual tool for girls.

MIXING VARIOUS MODALITIES AND STRATEGIES. In teaching language arts we noticed how many girls enjoy variety in teaching mode. Teachers have found this quite true of math and science teaching as well. Generally, when a student is having a problem with a subject such as math, science, social studies, or writing, he or she becomes bored or feigns boredom. This is one way the learning brain defends against the subject in which it feels it is inadequate. Boredom is, in this case, a mask. Variety in learning modality stimulates the brain past the mask so that real learning can take place. We asked some teachers what varieties of focus they used to teach girls.

One elementary teacher in the St. Joseph School District told us: "I try to implement a variety of strategies. Many of my girls are communication oriented, so I try to incorporate writing and role play into all subjects. Also, many of my students benefit from peer tutoring and teaching other students. I also try to include many concrete tactile experiences for those who lack abstract or spatial perception. I try to make sure all students have an equal opportunity to participate in class so that all recognize their value."

Denise Young, in the same district, told us:

> I make sure to give girls activities where they can act out or role play. They seem to enjoy being "on stage" during the reading of a play, poem, or story. They often want to make props, etc., to use with it.
>
> I like to mix things up, too. I find this works with girls. When I see girls doing group work in an area they don't feel as comfortable in, I add a boy or two to their group. For example, in science, we had a unit on simple machines; the girls really got into the activities when the boys encouraged them.
>
> I always try to add role models to the mix of learning experiences. To be a role model for girls is so essential. I take a Tae-Bo kickboxing class, and I often talk about it with my children. I pick girls often for activities or jobs that boys usually do, such as carrying boxes.

As we regularly hear from teachers who are focusing on the brain, gender, and girls' learning needs, issues revolving around role modeling and encouragement often outweigh other specific academic issues in a teacher's mind. One teacher told me recently, "With girls, I feel like most of the time her brain can do just about anything we ask, if we just encourage her will and her spirit." Many teachers echo this sentiment: they have confidence in a girl's mind but need to constantly encourage her heart.

I've thought a great deal about this teacher's statement. None of us wants to pretend girls don't have inherent and neurological learning issues. Nor do we want to pretend boys don't need equal encouragement. But it is important to look honestly at gender strengths and weaknesses in the classroom, from a neurological point of view. It should not surprise us that when teachers sit silently over coffee at the end of the day, contemplating their students, they see fewer inherent weaknesses in the girls' learning brains. Statistics bear this out, as we know: most learning disabilities are in fact suffered by boys. At the same time, it should also not surprise us that girls may well appear to have a weakness in the area of risk taking. This fits their general, inherent, natural difference from boys. Every opportunity we take to encourage a girl toward risk taking in academic learning enriches the individual girl and the classroom too.

USING MANIPULATIVES WHENEVER POSSIBLE. Perhaps the most important conclusion that recent brain research has come to, regarding teaching of math and science to kids—quite often girls, who do not so naturally learn it—involves using real objects and manipulatives.

Jan Miller has had great success using a unique manipulative. She writes: "We used hula hoops to create a Venn diagram in a fourth-grade class. The hoops were placed in the chalk tray and sticky notes given to students to place in the correct part of the hoops to create a Venn diagram. Then students wrote in journals what the Venn diagram told them. This got everyone involved and was a hands-on writing and problem-solving experience that the students enjoyed without realizing they were writing and doing math both." What a wonderful way to use the strengths of both male and female brains! It allows the more spatially oriented brains to become excited, and it allows the more verbally oriented brains to enjoy the completion of the lesson.

For those students who need a little extra help with science conceptualization, Jan tried something similar: "When doing a third-grade science unit on simple machines, I actually brought in all types of simple machines for them to manipulate. I brought in materials for a lever, fulcrum, and load, and they had to create how to move the load, what made it easier or harder, what worked or didn't. We put them in groups of three. The group of three boys figured it out very quickly and knew why. The group of three girls struggled and never did figure it out until they were finally guided."

To teach music effectively, Rita Oglesby discovered what for her proved to be a fine way to teach the value of notes. She used the appropriate segments of a pie to indicate the notes (one-quarter of the pie equals quarter notes, half of the pie equals half notes). These manipulatives replaced the worksheets she previously used. The results were striking—especially, she found, for boys who had been bored and some-what difficult. These boys appreciated the physical activity involved with using the manipulatives, they showed pride in their accomplishment, and there was a competitive spirit involved in solving problems with the manipulatives. Using a spatial activity got to them and made them focus, since it played beautifully into the orientation of the spatial brain.

Jan Miller told us about another innovation using clocks in her third-grade classroom. "We are studying clocks and money. We have given the students clocks with movable hands and then also some bags of change. Throughout the day, we call for time checks or money checks, where students must write down the correct time or count the money, using the clock or the change bags." This has been a fun way for math and science to be learned together. "This hands-on activity has helped all the students. And it's not a difficult activity. It's a quick fill-in activity," in Jan's words. It breaks up the day, gives the students an immediate purpose, and teaches complex counting.

Denise Young has participated in this same activity. "We have been learning about money, and counting change all week," she reported. "This week, and into next, I decided to give each child a baggy [full] of change. Periodically, I put certain coins on the board and they must count them and record the correct amount. At the end of the week, they will turn in their answers for an extra recess or a special time to read."

This method is a wonderful combination of verbal and spatial. For girls who may need math taken off the blackboard and made concrete, this is concrete indeed! For boys who may be fighting boredom, this instant activity, interruptive but fun, breaks up the day.

Denise told us another story: "We have been doing a magnet unit with a lot of hands-on activities involved. The actual testing of the different objects has made a real difference in the level of understanding. Activities have also allowed more movement for the boys and that has kept interest high."

GROUP WORK. Denise has also found that working in student teams and groups helps math and science learning. "I have found not only that hands-on activities make abstract concepts much more clear, especially in math, but also that team activity helps a lot. For instance, we recently did an estimation unit, and used jars of items to predict accuracy. Using these jars and working in groups made both boys and girls have better results."

One of the finest experiential classrooms for teaching math and science is the Montessori classroom. A visit to one, and a look at the number rolls, number chains, and other manipulatives used there, is always edifying for any teacher wanting to help make the teaching of math and science very concrete and manipulative. Furthermore, Montessori's use of group learning and partnered learning is also quite successful.

Standardized Testing

In any discussion of elementary academic learning today, we must have the courage to confront what is happening nationwide regarding accountability testing for third, fourth, and sixth grades as well as middle school and high school. What is the place, in the ultimate classroom, for constant standardized testing, and testing that is beginning at ever younger ages?

In recent years, legislators have mandated accountability and skills testing in many grades. Teachers, students, and parents spend weeks preparing for these tests. School administrators and teachers have been fired or resigned because of cheating scandals. Students in Columbus, Ohio, admitted that adult tutors guided their pencils to correct answers; ironically, these students and this school had just been praised for its scores by then President Clinton. In Austin, Texas, a grand jury recently indicted eighteen school officials for altering student test results.

For people outside our public schools or who are childless, all this may seem crazy. But for any teacher, parent, or friend of a school, cheating teachers, cheating students, lessons not being taught so that test prep can be done instead, homework disturbed, social pressures exacerbated on parents and children, and most of all a painful sense that accountability is up but learning is down (an amazing paradox for educators to be in) permeates the new atmosphere of testing.

One of my own children's teachers said to me: "These constant accountability tests are one of the most disturbing things we've seen in
education in the twenty years I've been teaching." No one denies the
need to hold schools and teachers accountable, and no one likes
schools to constantly underperform, but is the present hysteria to test
students healthy for the learning brain?

Our research shows us that, for the most part, it is not. In this, we
are flying in the face of legislative wisdom at the highest levels. In the
summer of election year 2000, candidates Al Gore and George Bush
both proposed tying federal education dollars to states' test scores. As
the testing systems work now, they are more invasive of learning than
helpful to it. For accountability testing, in fourth grade for instance, to
be useful, its standardization would have to be more flexible than it
presently is. Legislators, fearing that America is behind other countries
in educational standards and rightfully impatient with low-performing
schools, have not consulted actual brain-development research in setting standards and passing laws. The sheer variety in brain development and capacity among ten-year-olds makes present modes of
standardization an impediment to learning, a terrible drain on teachers
and administrators, and an illusory standard of success for parents to
hold onto.

Linda McNeil, a professor of education at Rice University in
Houston and author of *Contradictions of School Reform: Educational Costs of
Standardized Testing,* studied the Texas version of state-mandated tests.
She concluded: "The enduring legacy of Ross Perot's school reforms in
Texas is not merely the strengthening of bureaucratic controls at the expense of teaching and learning. It is also the legitimating of a language
of accountability as the governing principle in public schools. Incipient in
the Perot reforms was the shifting of control over public schooling away
from 'the public' and away from the profession—and toward business-
controlled management accountability systems. . . . A very narrow set of
numerical indicators (student scores on statewide tests) has become the
only language of currency in education policy in the state."

Politicians and legislators have probably believed they held the best
of intentions in mandating accountability testing. Educators can work

now to instruct lawmakers on the realities of brain development. In the end, once a critical mass of testing problems is reached parents too will begin to rebel. Until then, educators are held hostage to fear in the spheres of politics and business that our nation's children are behind the rest of the world, and to a crisis response that (we hope) will not last for more than a few years in its present form. Hopefully, when the jury is fully in on mandated testing, we will find that the tests are only *one* of the standards used for teacher merit, state and federal funding, and student and parent self-esteem. Ultimately, we can hope that these tests are limited to two grades in elementary and one in middle school, augmented by the PSAT and SAT in high school.

Special Education, Learning Disabilities, and Behavioral Disabilities

The field of special education, learning disabilities, and behavioral disabilities is one of the fastest growing in the educational culture. The male brain has a greater tendency toward learning and behavioral disabilities, and most special education classrooms are filled with about three times as many boys as girls, but many disabilities girls experience—which show up less well on the radar because they are not as "neurologically serious"—go unnoticed. What we do know for sure is that the growing brain is developing numerous learning and behavioral disorders as it comes under great pressure in this generation, thanks to the breakdown of family and bonding systems, the lack of training for teachers and parents in how to "raise a brain," the increase in environmental overstimulation (from media and other cultural stimulants), and pressure to compete and learn earlier than the brain may be ready to do. Statistically, the majority of these disorders have been and will continue to be related to the male brain because it is not as good at self-development. Normal growth of the male brain typically requires additional external help.

In this section of each chapter, we cannot cover all aspects of the field. Hundreds of books are now doing that in the professional literature.

What we propose to do instead is offer teachers' stories and innovations that we hope fill in gaps in caring and teaching the disabled child. In this section you'll find references to these innovations italicized.

A veteran teacher who has a number of students with behavioral problems wrote us these poignant comments about her class:

> Today, I confiscated a diagram one student made. It was a map of our classroom. It plotted the war plan for throwing pencils. The map had all students' desks with their initials. He had drawn broken pencil pieces with their flight plans for each person he planned to bomb with his pencils. I think the thing that shocked me the most is the lack of bonding between him and the other students. The students are often disrespectful and rude to each other as well as to adults. These students are so caught up in impressing their peers, their good judgment sometimes flies out the window.

This teacher has applied a technique we have already seen, called the *sixty-second rule*. She wrote: "The sixty-second wait time has been helpful, especially in getting the students to give you things they play with. I ask for the pencil or other weapon, then wait sixty seconds. Usually before the sixty seconds, the child hands it over. Also, after this time, the kid will leave the room after being asked." When the brain is agitated, it requires time to self-stabilize. Behavioral problems may escalate if the teacher wants an immediate response. The student, on the other hand, needs to process issues of saving face, weighing consequences, and managing rage; this can take some time.

This teacher has used "taking away recess" in her discipline system, but she ended up with this to say: "I struggled for a while with recess. Some students would lose their recess privilege. They would have to sit against the wall and watch their peers play. They were the ones, however, who needed that active release. So I looked for other options. Yesterday, I decided that I would tally each student's daily violations. They owe me *a lap around the playground for each violation*. This seems to be working. They get to be active, but instead of them choosing how to be active they must run the laps they owe."

Elementary teacher Lois Hedge shared her innovations with us:

After making *stress balls* to be used by the class, I observe students who seem to most need them. It's not long before Jake, a boy who takes Ritalin for his hyperactivity, is tapping on his desk with his pencil. Two other boys who are on medication also have pens and tattered tissue paper on their desks. We are doing group work in my social studies class of fifth-graders. The boys outnumber the girls by five to one. The boys almost clamor to have certain boys in their group. They seem to need certain people in the group in order to feel secure in their ability to complete the assignment. I help them deal with these stresses.

One of my fifth-grade boys is a learning disabled student who loves math but usually pushes aside other assignments. I have found that giving him a different type of assignment makes a big difference. He likes *fewer words on a page.* Graphic organizers with *short answers or illustrations* get his attention. I prepare for this boy and other students differently. They are spending more time on tasks, completing more assignments, and are having better behavior with fewer class interruptions.

One of my male students is a qualified behavioral disorder student. His parents have refused to sign him into the program. As a result, he remains in my fifth-grade class. I find myself using many alternatives to get us through the day. The special education teachers also do the same. He responds well to *one-on-one help.* I make sure that *I am near his desk during work time.* Instead of writing his spelling words, he *types them on the computer.*

"I give him *an errand that takes a few minutes.* This also builds a trust and sense of responsibility for him. Sometimes we sit in the hallway for a time. I talk to him in a respectful, calm way. He seems to relish the time. He is not violent. With a student teacher, I have been able to spend a bit more time one-on-one with him and other students.

The variety of strategies Lois relies on with this BD student illustrate a key principle in the new brain-based special ed research: try numerous techniques and strategies to activate the whole brain.

Class Within a Class

In the innovative class-within-a-class program, students are not pulled out for their special education programs; instead the special ed teacher goes into the regular classroom and works with all the students, including those in special education. This way, classmates sometimes do not even realize who the special education students are. All the teachers and all the students get to take advantage of the extra training and experience of the special ed teachers. The special ed students don't have to try to reintegrate into classrooms and make up work because they never leave their assigned classrooms.

Jan Miller works in this program and finds it successful. It is a form of inclusion that falls short of full inclusion. Some critics say it doesn't give special education students enough additional help, which for very serious disabilities may be true. Yet for Jan it has led to some fine innovations. She wrote:

> The special education department had lined notebook paper for special education students who need notes, lists, messages that they cannot get down on paper. So a buddy can write his own down, tear the copies apart and give to another child to study, take home or whatever.
>
> This year, the special education department devised a *Cool Down Card* in triplicate form. Students who are sent to another room or having trouble can fill out the card. Then a copy can be sent home and to the principal for data to keep track of a child's time outs or problems. This helps to keep a record and also to keep others informed along with giving the child responsibility to own his problem and work through it.
>
> We do a lot of *group work* in our special education department. After reading a story and getting ready to answer comprehension questions from a rotating wheel that each child had made, one boy asked if he could work with a partner to answer the questions. This was a great idea which I allowed. It was amazing how eager he was to answer the questions when *working with another boy*. Also, the hands-on spinning wheel with six questions seemed to really keep them on track.

Jan's instinct about same-sex opportunities in special education is corroborated by teachers around the country. In mainstream classrooms there are many moments for single-sex group work, and with special ed students (whether mainstreamed or separated) same-sex partnerships can cut down on brain-learning distractions, making it easier for the child's brain to go right to the lesson and not spend time navigating gender difference.

Fast ForWord

Fast ForWord is a research-based program for students with learning disabilities (reading in particular), developed by neuroscientists Paula Tallal and Michael Merzenich. It consists of computer games that, consultant Ron Brandt reports, "first [teach] students to distinguish between similar sounds, using artificially slowed speech, and then [challenge] them gradually to increase their recognition speed." The largest national statistical group of learning disabilities involves reading and writing, and thus predominantly male deficiencies. Use of computer programs such as this one is invaluable. Phonemic awareness is crucial to handling reading and writing disabilities, and the computer enhances phonemic awareness through spatial stimulation, the virtual space of the computer itself.

Other Spatial Stimulants and Use of Movement

For all students, as we've established, using body movement as part of the learning process and using objects in space leads to greater success than when the head is bent constantly over paper. For special ed students, this can be even truer.

Our research indicates that when a teacher has a choice between putting material on *an overhead projector* or saying it verbally, the projector is more effective. It is a visual and spatial stimulant added to the verbal. For many special ed boys, this *multisensory approach* is not just useful but actually crucial, especially in first and second grade, where many boys have not developed verbal skills as well as girls have and need to see things better and try to occupy them spatially.

Acting out lessons is also very important for special ed. More of the brain is being used, so students better remember what they do. We are not exactly sure how this works neurologically—why movement enhances memory—but one theory is that perhaps hippocampal activity is involved when the child moves, and thus the child develops memory. Whether teaching evaporation, photosynthesis, landforms, dramatic scenes from stories, or even the spelling of certain words that students can make physically concrete by "becoming the letters," movement makes memory and memory makes for learning.

The Multisensory Approach to Reading Problems

Two well-known multisensory reading approaches are the Lindamood-Bell method and the Schinderling method. They work especially well with boys, who have decreased sensory processing anyway in comparison to girls. Many teachers are familiar with these methods, but parents and caregivers may not be.

When children—so often boys—have reading problems, it is often because the alphabets, phonemes, and other reading units are being taught only visually or only aurally. The multisensory approach asks the child to trace the letters on a letter form so he "feels" the letter in tactile fashion, then listen to it said, see it, say it, and finally talk about how it felt in his throat to say it. In this way, the teacher has gotten him to learn with more than one sense.

Cooperative and Competitive Learning

Humankind would certainly never have attained its place on the evolutionary ladder if it had not evolved through cooperative as well as competitive learning. Brain-based research indicates that the ultimate classroom be based in both.

Cooperative learning is, of course, something to be enjoyed and celebrated, and its praises cannot be sung enough for both male and female brains.

Third-and-fourth-grade teacher Julie Ogilvie uses it in many ways:

On Tuesday, we worked on defining the character traits that we are using as a school. The students were in cooperative groups and wrote down what they thought the words meant. Then we came back together and shared their ideas. Then we made core virtue posters that were hung around the room. We did a lot of cooperative group activities this week—community and relationship building.

We began to practice a play last week. The students decided to invite the multiple-handicapped class, other teachers, and our first-grade buddies. They had practiced, prepared, and they were ready to go. Three of the students were in charge of the production. All of the students did an awesome job.

These cooperative projects constitute the core of an elementary student's developmental experience. Their impact on difficult and behavioral problem students is often immeasurable. Julie continued:

Charlie (who is a constant discipline problem) was the lead in the play and this really helped him control his behavior. It was awesome to see him beam and feel good about the job he had done. Charlie gave me a hug the day of the play. It was special since he won't allow others to touch him. He has come a long way in four weeks. I am so proud of him!

One of the things that I think has helped us this year is that we are so open with each other. We, the kids and I, give each other feedback all of the time.

Quite often, teachers who receive training in brain-based research come to realize the importance of open classrooms and cooperative projects as stimulants to the growing brain. They also see how competition helps the brain. Linda Andrews, a fourth-grade teacher on Long Island, told us:

I was having some trouble with three or four of my boys. In fact, in my twenty-five years of teaching I often had a class where some of the

boys seemed bored, underachieving and outright discipline problems. I had been trained in cooperative learning and even though I
raised two sons, I still avoided competition in classrooms.

But then, after learning how natural competition is to the male
brain, I tried competitive games. They really worked. Some of the
bored and even belligerent boys really responded well. I discovered,
also, that this wasn't just good for the boys. Girls can use healthy
competitive learning too.

Linda's experience has been that of many teachers, trained well in
cooperative learning but not in the competitive variety, and now redis-
covering the use of games and contests as teachers seek innovations to
help boys.

A teacher in Texas who has taught first through fifth wrote us:

After discovering the new gender brain research I decided to use more
games in my third-grade class. In one math game, students have to
see who can do the problem fastest. We say "congratulations!" to the
winner. With math, it's generally a boy, although I have one girl who
is hard to beat. We also do the game with writing and spelling, and
here it's generally a girl who wins, although I have two boys who are
very good at spelling too. All the kids like the competition, especially
because it's part of "group spirit"—we're not interested in who's bad
at something, only at how everyone can have their moment in the
sun. I have some students who never win, and so I keep coming up
with games that I think they can win. By the end of the year everyone
has won at least a few times.

Everyone is less bored in class, class seems more fun, the rowdi-
ness that can happen is pretty manageable, and I'm noticing that kids
are learning about "fairness." I used to think fairness was taught by
no one ever losing and by everyone always feeling good. But I'm realizing how important it is for kids to notice that life isn't fair all the
time, and hard work is required for success. One girl, who doesn't
usually win, seemed sad one day and I talked to her. At one point I
asked her, "Are the games hurting your feelings? Would you rather we

didn't have them?" She surprised me. She said, "No. I think they're okay. I just have to work harder." She knew what she needed to do and took responsibility.

Sports and Athletics

Our classrooms can often use a few more contests, games, and other competitive exercises, but we generally think of elementary sports experiences as too competitive and wish they were more cooperative. Indeed, many coaches and parents have become obsessive about children's competitiveness in sports and athletics. Parents sometimes push kids into competitive sports too early for the child; and all too often parents and communities underuse sports.

In the ultimate classroom, we recommend a child not be placed in a competitive extracurricular sport until six to seven years old unless the child specifically requests the experience. Competitive, organized sports (outside of mandatory phys ed) are not crucial for healthy brain development before that age, so certainly any competitive pressure at all toward these sports is generally harmful. It overemphasizes competition and imprints competitive use of the body at a time when, developmentally, the child wants to enjoy his or her use of the body without external pressure to perform in a focused way. Gradually, after seven, competitive sports can be added to a child's daily or weekly curriculum. By fourth grade, many children, especially large groups of boys and the girls who are competitively inclined, actively seek out competitive sports. In early grades, however, it is essential for both teachers and parents to be vigilant about pressure to perform in competitive sports.

Not all children want to engage in team sports, but karate or tennis are good options for children in fourth grade and older. Sport activity—even if simply running and jogging—is especially important for boys after about age ten, which is when testosterone starts generating in the male body; we want to help involve them in some kind of daily and rigorous physical activity, generally of greater length than PE class. The male body needs physical activity to help it manage testosterone.

Organized sports for girls are also useful at these ages, not only to teach competition skills but to help girls increase their muscle-to-fat ratio.

In Spokane, Washington, a Junior Wrestling Association began a few years ago, with fifty participants age five through twelve. It now has eight hundred participants. It began because a group of fathers wanted to turn their children—mainly boys—on to the skills of wrestling. It flourishes because although it is competitive—when two kids wrestle, one wins and the other loses—every participant gets some sort of prize. Parents are trained by the association's staff not to bark orders at kids, but to call out support. This kind of sporting activity is an example of cooperative and competitive athletics in balance.

The Ultimate Elementary Classroom for Both Boys and Girls

As we have explored elementary school learning in this chapter, we see innovations, small and large, that help both boys and girls. To conclude this chapter, let's review briefly some key components for teachers and administrators of boy-friendly and girl-friendly classrooms, noticing that everything listed to help one sex is potentially good for the other.

For the Boys

- Support teacher training in male-brain development and the male learning pace, which is often different than the female's.
- Use boy-only groups when needed.
- Encourage close bonding between teacher and student.
- Enjoy and navigate normal Huck Finn male energy toward academic focus and good character.

- Pay special attention to the more sensitive, less competitive or aggressive males in the classroom.
- Advocate for boys' issues in the school and community.
- Allow physical movement, as well as engaging in physical activity, from hugs and touch when appropriate to getting down and dirty at recess once in a while.
- Be sure there are men in the boy's educational life, especially from fifth grade onward.
- Before third grade, never allow chairs to be kept in a row or nailed down, and always make available as much space as possible.
- Offer lots of storytelling and myth making in the classroom to help the male brain develop its imaginative and verbal skills through story making.
- Give boys lots of things to touch and otherwise sense, especially when reading and writing are being taught.

For the Girls

- Train teachers on how the female brain learns.
- Teach early elementary math by manipulatives and objects; teach higher levels of math not just on the blackboard, which requires abstraction and favors male brains, but also through graphs, charts, and written material on paper.
- Provide concrete manipulatives to touch and otherwise sense, especially when science is being taught.
- Tell stories and use images of girls and women who are competent, and who model varieties of mature female behavior.
- Offer girl-only groups when useful.
- Give special access to technology, computers, and the Internet and a little extra encouragement to use technology, master it, and lead with it (beginning around third grade, keeping in mind that intense computer use before about age nine may be hazardous to brain development).

- Match math and science lessons with journal writing expression so that girls can use their writing strengths to help them process math calculations and science data.
- Encourage healthy competitive learning as well so that girls do not end up disadvantaged compared to boys (who may naturally seek competitive activities in other parts of life).
- Provide healthy and constant feedback, so that girls get encouragement and have high expectations from teachers.

The ultimate classroom for both boys and girls is a gentle place during elementary school, but intense as well, and infused with the charge to teach not children but *boys* and *girls*. In American public education, this is generally a coeducational environment, in which boys and girls learn the bulk of their lessons from teachers and mentors—but also a great deal from each other. So our ultimate classroom can be a place where bonds run deep, conflicts are resolved, no child is left behind, any gender biases are noted, and teachers are trained to move beyond hidden prejudice against either boys or girls.

Among the elementary teachers in our institute, we found that of the many training innovations available to educators, training in how boys and girls learn differently was deemed one of the most useful. Schoolchildren come to school assuming teachers already have this training. They don't realize that their teachers, like their parents, are to a great extent shooting from the hip as they structure and teach classrooms. Fortunately, brain research is so advanced now that no teacher or parent need try to raise or teach a school-age child without available training.

Many of the innovations teachers are using in elementary school translate to middle school. As we enter the next phase of the child's learning experience, we ask you to carry forward the innovations in this chapter, and also to join us as we discover new ways to meet the needs of that crazy, confusing, and immensely rewarding time called middle school.

Before moving to middle school, however, let's again conclude with tips for parents and other caregivers.

Tips for Parents

- Support and advocate for structural innovations, such as year-round schooling, smaller schools, multigenerational classrooms, and a lower teacher-student ratio.
- Advocate and even help fund (privately and by public lobbying) teacher training in gender and brain differences.
- Get two to three professional opinions before putting a child on Ritalin, Prozac, or another psychotropic medication.
- Continue reading rituals in the home, but now augment them with writing rituals—making sure a child writes thank-you notes, birthday invitations, letters, e-mails, and perhaps a journal.
- Instill character education in the home, by example, didactic instruction, and spiritual storytelling.
- Be consistent with discipline systems in the home, learning what system the school is using and melding with that when possible.
- Use brain-based tricks of the trade, such as giving certain boys sixty seconds to fulfill a demand, and giving some of the girls extra verbal encouragement.
- Stay in constant contact with teachers, volunteer for school activities, and become a friend of the school.
- Plan computer, television, and other technology use to best augment brain development.
- Become more familiar with aggression nurturance and how it works, guiding it as well as we guide empathy nurturance.

In the end, the most important innovation for parents is to "be there." It is a cliché, but a true one. From a brain-based point of view, this means being trained in brain and gender material alongside teachers. Thus home and school are, together, the ultimate elementary school classroom.

The Ultimate
Middle School Classroom

"Rationality tied to moral decency is the most powerful joint instrument for good that our planet has ever known." For the life of me I can't remember who said it—Walt Whitman, Ralph Waldo Emerson, I don't know—but I read it years ago and as a middle school teacher it's always stuck in my head. It's what I'm about. I'm trying to teach these kids everything I can so they'll be reasoning, intelligent young people; and I emphasize character and behavior equally hard, so their intelligence is directed to a good life. Some people are scared of teaching middle school, but I'm not. I love the challenge of having to mold these young women and men.

—CLARENCE, MIDDLE SCHOOL TEACHER AND COACH

AN EIGHTH-GRADE GIRL AT A SCHOOL I WAS VISITING KNEW HOW much I enjoy hearing the jokes students like to tell, so she handed me a sheet of paper. It was the now-infamous story that's been around recently on the Internet. Turns out this "true story" is fictitious, but I was pleased by her gesture and reproduce it here for a purpose.

This is the transcript of an actual radio conversation between a U.S. naval ship and Canadian authorities off the coast of Newfoundland.

U.S. SHIP: Please divert your course 15 degrees to the south to avoid a collision.

CND REPLY: Recommend you divert your course 15 degrees to the south to avoid collision.

U.S. SHIP: This is the captain of a U.S. Navy ship. I say again, divert your course.

CND REPLY: No. I say again, you divert YOUR course.

U.S. SHIP: THIS IS THE AIRCRAFT CARRIER USS CORAL SEA. WE ARE A LARGE WARSHIP OF THE U.S. NAVY. DIVERT YOUR COURSE NOW!!

CND REPLY: This is a lighthouse . . . your call.

Its creator (not the U.S. Navy) certainly did not release this to create an analogy for middle school life, but isn't it just right? Jumping to conclusions, veiled threats, immense stubbornness, communication mess ups, feeling as though we and our students live in a world of constant and daily potential for stress and even (more often than we'd like) confrontation . . . if middle school is not exactly a battlefield, it is certainly a place of stress and strain. The brain is growing again, as it did in the first three years of life, with amazing speed and new potential.

To add to the massive growth of the cognitive and abstract skills in the neocortex, bodies are going through puberty too, moving along with the brain from childhood to adulthood, making middle school a time of great insights, great dreams, great pains, and lots of "Oops, I guess you're the lighthouse this time; maybe I'd better move aside."

Amid the obvious social changes that all early-adolescent kids endure, boys and girls go through their own sex- and gender-based brain restructurings too. Boys take a next step in acting and thinking even more like young men, and girls take a next step in acting and thinking even more like young women. The male-female similarities are very much present, but so are the differences.

What is the ultimate middle school classroom for both boys and girls? How does it best teach their intelligence and mature their character toward coeducational adulthood?

In our studies, teachers who come from all over the country help us answer this question.

Structural Innovations

Middle school includes a variety of configurations in grade level: sixth through eighth, seventh and eighth, fifth through eighth, sixth through ninth. Please apply our structural innovations to the particular configurations of the middle school you are involved with.

The first of these innovations is somewhat controversial.

Separate-Sex Education

Our young people are naturally inclined toward coeducation—toward finding time to spend with the other sex—but also toward separate-sex groupings and separate-sex education. In our culture there has been much debate about whether boys and girls should be educated in *either* group, when in fact their minds crave to be educated in *both* groups.

We see this from the very young, noticing the preschool boy's proclivity to do work and activity with other preschool boys and, at times, *not* with the girls. Similarly, we see preschool girls' desire to find one another and avoid boys in their games and work. This continues throughout K–12 education and indeed throughout adulthood. Men and women enjoy each other's company, but they often find it much easier to do things only with their own sex.

For educators, this commonsense observation is, hopefully, a liberating one, allowing all of us to look at separate-sex education as one of a number of possibilities for educational improvement—one of many plates served at the banquet before us. In employing this innovation, we are not in any way harming children, as they are already naturally inclined toward this way of being, and we are potentially helping millions of children who aren't learning as well as we'd like in the naturally gender-competitive environment that coeducation is.

For a number of years, we've been exposed to research showing improvements for girls in girls-only schools and classes, especially in areas of math and science learning. Recently, we've seen research coming out about similar improvements for boys in reading and writing and in discipline improvement. This research shouldn't surprise us, given that the human brain is sexualized and genderized—it is male and it is female. In an area such as verbals, where the female is strong, some males are lost, and vice versa with spatials and higher math or science skills.

Certain coed schools around the country are already experimenting with separate-sex education (and, of course, many traditionally single-sex schools remain so). The Williams School in Norfolk, Virginia, is presently separating sixth-graders. The Cranbrook Institute near Detroit, Michigan, has coeducational classrooms for first through fourth grade, then single sex for fifth through eighth and coed for ninth through twelfth. California public schools have been creating separate-sex schools and classrooms ever since former Governor Pete Wilson supported those efforts.

San Francisco's Marina Middle School uses separate-sex education. Principal John Michaelson reports that "parents and students have liked the program. It's more cohesive and less distracting," he feels, and he points to evidence that test scores and grades are rising for enrollees in the separate-sex classrooms and groupings. Virginia, which has had separate-sex classrooms since 1994, has seen students' grades rise, especially in math and science (their initial data-collecting base). Teachers also report fewer discipline problems in the separate-sex classes and more participation from students, very often girls, who remained hidden in the coed classrooms.

In the ultimate classroom and ultimate school, the brain's natural tendencies are respected not by forcing separate-sex innovations on a community but by pointing out their advantages and asking the community to test whether these advantages appear in the particular district.

Our research has concertedly directed teachers to experiment with separate-sex options, and you will read some of those results here. Separate-sex options can solve many problems at all grade levels, but we bring them up here, in this chapter on middle school, because we believe that a huge portion (perhaps at least half) of middle school learning and discipline problems would be curtailed or removed if middle schools were single-sex institutions.

Here's why.

THE LOGIC OF SEPARATE-SEX MIDDLE SCHOOLS. Middle school is the time of greatest hormonal upheaval in both males and females. Boys begin puberty with high doses of testosterone. Over just a few years, they need to learn to manage up to twenty times as much of this sex-and-aggression hormone as females. Middle school boys often find themselves in strange moods, angry, aggressive, clumsy and awkward, unable to verbalize feelings, focused on girls but scared of them, competing against boys for the attentions of girls, and relatively unable to verbally discern the complexities of their own developing nature.

Girls begin puberty with high does of progesterone, estrogen, and prolactin, finding themselves in an even more complicated hormonal picture than boys, and requiring their own stretch of years to learn to manage their new body and mind. They are faced with mood swings, vacillation of self-confidence, hyperattention to how they fit into the world of other girls, and competition with other girls for boys' attentions. They are often chagrined at how immature boys are in comparison to themselves; they mask their real selves in order to find romance. They are also harassed, quite often by boys, for their breast size, physical growth, weight, or other overt physical characteristics.

In all settings, children going through cognitive and physical transformations are likely to pick extreme behaviors as masking devices, whether hiding themselves as completely as possible or drawing attention to themselves with bluster and bravado. Their choice of extreme reaction—from pathology (eating disorders and violent behavior) to simple behavioral adjustment that affects learning (dumbing themselves down, not raising their hand or else making a point of raising their hand, dominating discussion and becoming undisciplined to get attention)—affects adolescent learning stress. Many boys and girls lose the highest level of academic learning that they are in reality capable of reaching. The adolescent community, especially in a classroom of thirty or thirty-five boys and girls age twelve or thirteen, focuses more of its verbal and nonverbal communication than we realize on the hidden psychosocial agendas of adolescent mating desires and psychosocial hierarchies, to the neglect of actual learning.

It is useful to remember that our present culture, through media imagery, forces early mating, romance, and sexualization on children.

Thus, normal adolescent confusions are heightened, making it even more essential that we pay attention to good options for early adolescents. Their lives are psychosocially more stressful than we realize. They live in one of the most gender-competitive cultures on earth, if not the most extreme.

Adults gear much of their lives toward competition with each other for resources and attention. Thus, boys and girls are pitted against each other as well, just as girls are pitted against girls and boys against boys. Peer pressure is used as a primary tool for the socialization of a vulnerable early-adolescent child into a competitive, toughened adult. Although peer pressure and social competitiveness have always existed, they have not been the way they are now, nor have they existed between genders with what we see as the present level of pressure.

If you think back to your great-grandparents' lives, you probably envision gender relationships in which males developed along a male path and females along female, especially in the areas of division of labor and romantic expectations. Codes were in place by which males worked mainly outside the home, females within; marriages were arranged or based more on survival and moral imperatives than on romance. Biologically speaking, males and females were raised to follow a clear masculine or feminine line, and mating practices themselves were based on social controls of hormones rather than the free flow of hormonal surges that are, biologically speaking, the basis of romance.

Presently, romantic expectations dominate the lives of young people, marriage is considered defective and even degrading unless it is based in romance, and division of labor between the genders (especially among youths) is to a great extent abandoned.

Is there anything inherently wrong with our present attitude toward romance, marriage, and work? We all have an opinion, but in this forum this is not our question to answer. We offer an historical perspective to demonstrate the increased pressure on early adolescents today. Many cultural, familial, and personal safeguards that used to exist for twelve-, thirteen-, and fourteen-year-olds learning to manage their self-transforming bodies and minds just do not exist any longer. Males and females are thrown together in large groups with little supervision and expected to try to figure out nearly everything—about how to mate, what work to develop toward, how to develop codes of conduct toward each other, how to accommodate the obvious and instinctual differences between males and females, how to compete with the other sex without offending the very person you may want to mate with. . . . There's an endless list of psychosocial challenges to early adolescents in our free-fall culture. These challenges take up far more of middle school classroom life than we've wanted to admit. Our classrooms are far less disciplined than they should be, and we are worried about learning quality and academic achievement within them.

Separate-sex options are, therefore, good ones. The psychosocial stresses are removed, to a great extent, from the learning process. Competition between the sexes is avoided. Girls who are not naturally proficient in math, physics, and chemistry do not need to fail in the face of proficient males. Boys whose brain systems are not verbal do not need to fail in the face of girls whose brains are quite verbal. As girls work with girls at this very difficult and vulnerable time, psychosocial self-confidence increases along with the academic; girls together, without hindrance from boys, learn to manage their own and each other's transformations. Similarly, boys learn self-management, and find safety in working with others who instinctively understand them. Not all competitions and problems are removed, by any means. But *unnecessary* stressors are removed, especially those not natural to boys and girls during puberty but instead culturally imposed.

Though our culture is perhaps the first to have to deal with these issues in free fall, the issue of removing early adolescents from unnecessary stressors and keeping them guided to natural human development is not new. For almost twenty years, along with many others, I have studied our own ancestral cultures and the still-extant tribal cultures around the world, among them the Shavante of Brazil; Australian aboriginal; and Native American tribes such as Ute, Hopi, Navaho, and Lakota Sioux, in search of clues for handling our present generation of children and adolescents. In the area of separate-sex education, there is a lot to learn from this research.

Many tribal cultures—as did our own ancestral cultures—separate boys and girls for a few years just before and during puberty. This is done to accommodate the natural transformations girls and boys go through, and specifically to create gender-safe and gender-mentored environments in which boys and girls can be taught how to live, how to relate to each other, how to mature, how to manage themselves, and how to be of service to the specific tribe as well as humanity as a whole. Tribal cultures do not have the luxury of allowing a five-to-ten-year adolescence, something quite new to humans (just a few decades old) and only possible in cultures like our own in which a large mass of the population does not have to reproduce or learn survival skills by middle adolescence. Our families and schools are primary places of adolescent development that extend growth time by giving students free-flowing adolescent stimulation, as opposed to highly restricted and gender-restricted growth structures more common to tribal cultures.

The inherent disadvantages of tribal culture are vast, especially the tendency to be parochial rather than inclusive. A tribe is not generally a melting pot, nor can it handle massive industrial growth. Our culture can't exist in its present ideals without being a melting pot, and it is the most effective industrial and postindustrial culture we know. Economically speaking, for adults in this society (and thus by extension for their offspring) our high-population, free-flowing, democratic system is an economic improvement over tribal life.

However, when it comes to the actual psychological care of early adolescents, it has some inherent disadvantages tribal cultures do not have. Because we toss these children into free-flowing existence before their very nature as developing beings is ready, too many of them live psychologically unprotected lives, experiencing gender confusion, sexual harassment, unnecessarily early teen pregnancy, loss of intellectual and academic opportunity, and increased psychosocial stress. In an ironic way, we have created a society that helps early adolescents remain innocent longer (they do not have to go to work at ten or twelve years old) but also destroys their innocence more quickly (they are exposed earlier to far more psychological instability and confusion than their grandparents knew, especially about perhaps the most important element of their adolescent transition: the other sex).

When all of these ideas and all the research is looked at together, a middle path reveals itself. Our culture can continue to teach middle school children about life coeducationally—in families, churches, the media, and elsewhere—but also offer them one gender-specific venue—the school—through which to learn the academic skills and technologies they need in order to flourish in later life. This one environment can be relatively free of the gender stresses that they encounter in the media, at home with siblings, on the street, on the Internet, and in other activities. It can be gender-safe; well mentored; and focused not on mating, romance, and psychosocial challenges related to hidden hormonal flows but instead on learning. Family and culture outside the separate-sex classroom or school can continue to be highly coeducational. The child thus has the best of both worlds.

HOW TEACHERS ARE USING SEPARATE-SEX EDUCATION.   All this would just be logic and theory, if teachers were not already using these ideas and benefiting from these innovations. To augment results that are in from Virginia and elsewhere as to separate-sex schools, classes, and clubs, we asked the teachers in Missouri to report on their experiments with separate-sex education at the basic classroom level. Given that there are often legal and administrative battles to fight in separating boys and girls at the macro level, we asked teachers to do it at the micro level, and see how it went. The results surpassed our expectations. Let us share some of them with you just as the teachers shared them with us.

Darla Novick, a middle school teacher in Kansas City, told us about a recent lesson on endangered species in which she used separate-sex groups:

> After some brief note taking, I divided the class into two groups (male/female) and started a cooperative learning activity. On this particular day, we decided the group of boys was supposed to be loggers and cut down trees. The girls were conservationists, trying to save the spotted owl and stop the loggers from cutting down the owl's habitat. The same-sex groups worked very well. The principal (who came to visit for a teacher observation) really enjoyed the separate-sex part of the day's lesson. Together we noticed that the boys had

similar ideas and so did the girls, yet they were different from each other, so if they were paired boys and girls mixed, the activity would not have been as successful.

Brenda Bock reported a similar ease in separate learning groups: "When we played our games we divided up into boy/girl teams. They worked better together when paired with same sex."

Ruth Whertvine, of Anderson Alternative Middle School in Kansas City, has noticed advantages for girls with this kind of setup: "This year our school separated girls into classes by themselves. It has helped the girls to concentrate. They seem more focused. I myself have noticed things about girls' behavior I never noticed before."

Jennifer, a teacher at Smith-Hale Middle School in Kansas City, has noticed a difference in the number of discipline referrals, which mainly affect boys: "I have found that putting boys in the position of working only with boys resulted in fewer discipline problems."

Linda, her colleague at Smith-Hale, corroborates this. She has one class of students that is only boys for a portion of the time. She finds that they work much better together than when girls are also in the class. "They help each other out more," she says. "Boys work better when they're with just boys; there are more conflicts when the genders are mixed. When the girls do come in, the class becomes totally different."

Ruth Whertvine agrees: "The boys work much better together and have less problems when there are only boys in the classroom."

These separate-sex groupings are action research that corroborates theoretical understanding of the male-female competition and psychosocial stressors that can invade learning. As many teachers have discovered on their own when they experiment with having boys and girls seat themselves, a natural segregation often occurs. Holla, a Hickman Mills Middle School teacher, allowed her students to choose their own seats. She found that the boys and girls segregated themselves anyway. You might try this experiment a few times in a month and see if you don't end up with similar results.

Shawna Middletree, of Smith-Hale Middle School, told us about her experiments along this line. She continues to have boys and girls separated in her class, with boys on one side of the room and girls on the other. During a particular week, the class was reading *Island of the Blue Dolphins*. She asked the students to raise their hand if they believed that it was better to seek risks in life than be safe. All but one male student immediately raised their hands in agreement with this statement. Not one girl raised a hand. This became a very interesting topic of conversation for the class, and it led to interesting gender and psychosocial teaching. It was available as a teaching opportunity because having separated the boys and girls manifested the gender difference so clearly in the room.

Shawna has seen such an improvement in her classroom that she set up seating charts to include boys on one side of the room and girls on the other. This requires that students work with others of their gender. She has found that she has fewer discipline problems when her boys work together in a group of boys. In fact, only two kids (both boys) even mentioned that the boys and girls had been separated by the new seating chart. The young people are not generally uncomfortable with the setup, and classroom behavior has improved.

Rose teaches music at Hickman Mills Middle School. Following training in brain and gender research, she decided to try segregating the boys and girls. She finds this works quite well. The boys tend to dance to the music (get up and twirl around) but the girls don't. She believes she is witnessing the greater need for movement that boys have, deriving from their lower serotonin and higher testosterone levels, and she finds them less self-conscious and even less potentially destructive in their physical movements when surrounded by the other boys.

Brenda Bock reported something very interesting to us that we hear elsewhere in the country. If any student is going to protest a teacher's attempt to separate boys and girls in the classroom, it is likely to be a girl. "The boys seem content," Brenda told us, "but the girls in my class protest being separate from the boys."

We have featured these teachers' stories in the hope of inspiring you to use separate-sex education techniques at the micro level of an assignment and a classroom, while you advocate (should you see reason to do so) for the larger, or macro-level, innovation of separate-sex education for all middle schoolers. Over a period of years, the anecdotal (and soon the statistical) results of separate-sex experiments will, we hope, not only help the millions of individual young people they touch but also build toward a larger social dialogue on this one innovation at the middle school level that has so much potential to help students learn, behave, and self-develop in a more orderly, comfortable, safe, and achieving fashion during this immensely vulnerable time in life.

Rites of Passage

In the next chapter, on innovations for high school, we also deal with this important structural component of the ultimate classroom: the school-based rite of passage. Middle schools are already benefiting from using the practice; given the hormonal and brain changes of the middle school era, a rite of passage is crucial. As the brain grows, it needs to mark its progress. A rite of passage, for both boys and girls, provides this marking, even if in somewhat differing ways for each gender.

Brandy Barnett, a Kansas City middle school teacher, told us of her school's reasoning in looking at rites of passage:

> Because many of the kids today don't have any type of ritual, whether it be spiritual or not, we decided maybe we could start some type of ritual in our school to initiate and recognize students in some way. Some of the ideas that we came up with were to give out letters for different accomplishments. Of course, right now we have recognition ceremonies, but they're for academics and attendance. Many of our students are unable to earn these honors, and the ones that are unable to earn these are the ones who need recognition the most.
>
> We decided we could come up with awards that each child could earn like academics, attendance, sports, and others. For earning these awards the students could receive a pin that would act something like a high school letter. No one would have to know if you earned yours for band or basketball or good attendance—everyone would fit in.

Brian Zipfel, also a Kansas City middle school teacher, reported on a rite he participated in with his students:

Last Friday, we took our team of students to Adventure Woods, which is a ropes challenge course. The different challenges or events are set up to encourage team-building values, cooperation, communication, and listening skills. Generally students are organized into groups with students they do not know. I served as a chaperone for a group of ten guys.

At first, the gentlemen were not very enthusiastic about the get-acquainted activities with the facilitator. They also were unsure of their fellow group members.

Over time, though, they built up trust and completed activities where a calculated risk was involved. I participated in these activities.

The students lifted me (all 215 lbs.) over their heads. One led me on a blind-folded trust walk, and others pulled and pushed me over a twelve-foot wall.

In written responses later the students were amazed that they could trust a teacher, and they were also amazed that a teacher trusted them. It was really a good bonding experience for students and teacher. It also was a positive risk-taking chance, a rite of passage, that the new brain research encourages.

For over a decade, I co-led ropes course events in the Pacific Northwest with parents, teachers, and young people. The ropes-course idea entails a well-structured opportunity for a rite of passage, and it is available throughout the country. With funding, schools can build their own. If such funding is not available, interested teachers and counselors can find the nearest ropes course.

There is a wonderful organization in Minden, Nevada, called Rite of Passage, which focuses on creating rites of passage for troubled youth. They have videos and other useful tools. High-risk youths are already prone to high-risk activities, and the rite of passage redirects their way of being toward organized risk-taking activities.

Every middle school classroom can incorporate an in-class rite of passage. Here are some rites we suggest:

- In the first month of the first year of middle school, have each student stand up with a picture. Have him or her talk about the boy or girl he or she was, wants to be during this school year, and hopes to be in the future. Have each student also discuss her or his definition of what a woman or man is. Make sure each student delineates the kind of help he or she thinks will be needed in this classroom this year in order to become a mature young man or woman.

• Do this again at the end of the year, directing the monologue now toward what has been accomplished, and what lies ahead.

• In the first month of the next middle school year, repeat the process. We say "in the first month" because it takes time for students to write their speeches, and time to feel comfortable with others in the class.

• At the end of middle school, each student shows a scrapbook of photos and other items, collected over the middle school years, and discusses them. Before the whole class, or in smaller groups, the rite of conversation takes place.

• At the end of middle school as well, each student writes a farewell letter to a classmate or staff member who has meant a great deal to him or her.

Lakeview Middle School, in the Park Hill School District of Kansas City, has each student prepare, in writing or other form such as art work, an autobiography of the child's family tree, philosophy of life, and future projections. During the first week of school, they have a "lunch sack" rite of passage: each student brings in a lunch sack filled with anything from his or her life that fits and presents himself or herself to the class by way of these objects. Debbie Henmao, one of the teachers there, told us she was amazed that the students always took this kind of thing seriously: "Kids *do* take it seriously, even problem kids." We have found this in all church, school, and home settings where young people set up, pursue, and then accomplish a rite of passage. They are so hungry for the experience of speaking their own truth, experiencing their own power, knowing themselves, and being noticed for who they are that they make a rite of passage a success for everyone.

Use of Uniforms

Our schools have a long history of assuming a child's freedom is sacrosanct. In neglecting brain-based research, our society has concomitantly assumed (as one of my own teachers in college put it) that "the more freedom a child has to control his life, the more he'll learn." For three decades, this assumption has translated into increased individual rights for children in all environments, from home to school, and that includes dress.

Surely none of us would argue against the idea that each child has the right to freedom from abuse and neglect, and no one would question the fact that free trial-and-error experiences for children lead to crucial learning. But it is also crucial to put the word *freedom* in the context of the *orderliness* that the brain also needs in order to learn. Although some students learn well in nearly any setting, many middle school students, moving through tumultuous changes, do not. If a child's individual freedom is not balanced by the brain's equally powerful desire for imposed order, the child thrives less well as an individual child and as a student.

The area of demeanor and dress is now under scrutiny nationwide because so many school districts are imposing dress and behavior codes again, with great success. Brain-based research supports this trend. The developing child's mind seeks an orderly learning environment, and many schools can better shape such an environment with a dress code. They are being imposed in small towns like Coeur d'Alene, Idaho, at Lakes Middle School; and in larger environments, such as Philadelphia's school districts. Fifth- and sixth-graders are wearing uniforms in the New York City school district, the largest in the country. The measure is being imposed there to restore discipline and a serious learning environment to schools and classrooms that are suffering from truancy and low achievement. The school board president, William C. Thompson Jr., said as the board unanimously passed the measure, "This policy is important to diminish peer pressure, promote school unity, and promote school pride."

As with single-sex classrooms, rites of passage, and all of the innovations we suggest, there is little downside to something like use of uniforms. The innovations can help create the order the mind needs, and though someone—whether parent or student—will always gripe, we highly recommend use of uniforms (even if just khakis and button-down shirts) for all students. Girls and boys alike benefit as they cut back on psychosocial attempts to impress each other, dress up, or dress down, and focus instead on learning.

Classroom Size and Other Innovations

We recommend a ratio of one middle school teacher to twenty students, though we know this is difficult for a larger school to attain. Especially when the ratio is higher, teacher's aides and voluntary second teachers keep discipline problems lower and academic achievement higher.

MULTIGENERATIONAL SCHOOLS. Teachers in Menlo Park, California, told us that area schools have experimented with having middle school and elementary school classrooms at the same location. This has, in the words of one teacher, "helped older kids stay younger and a little more innocent, in a good way, as well as helping them with building compassion." The sixth-, seventh-, and eighth-graders are constantly around younger children and have to be service-oriented and mentorlike toward them. The younger children, on the other hand, enjoy the mentoring by the older children, have role models, and are called by this daily contact to act maturely. The teachers we met were very happy with this model; they did not fear that the younger kids would be corrupted by the seventh- and eighth-graders. The schools have a lot of supervision. "Plus," said one teacher, "if they have a way to help others, most middle school kids really do want to help. They just need to be shown how, and given the opportunity."

In our work in Missouri, we have encouraged two innovations we want to call specific attention to here. These discussions follow.

TEAM TEACHING. The first is team teaching, which is effective and relatively simple. A team of teachers meet every morning, for a few moments, to talk about troubled students, what lessons they have planned, how they can support each other, and how they can weave a character lesson or something from a colleague's class into their own. The team bonds together, and so the students they teach are likely to feel themselves part of a community of teachers. Throughout Missouri, team teaching is being used and receives almost universally high marks from middle school teachers.

SINGLE-TEACHER EMPHASIS.   Some middle schools send students from classroom to classroom every hour. Our research suggests greater effectiveness with the presence of one teacher for the whole day: a homeroom teacher who teaches many of the day's classes, other teachers coming in and out of the classroom to teach specialties. Many middle schools use the one-class-every-hour method, which shuttles students from one teacher to another every forty-five to sixty minutes. Better is the single teacher's ongoing presence, which allows the student to be taught and also mentored. In other words, the homeroom teacher becomes a mentor from the outset, someone who knows the student well and commits to nurturing the child fully, rather than merely instructing in a lesson for forty-five minutes and hoping, over months, to bond with each student. This method depends heavily on the ability of the teacher to bond with the students present. The teacher cannot shuttle a child, with whom he or she is having problems, to another classroom after forty-five minutes. Teacher and student must work things out.

We feel that students in middle school are in such personal upheaval that having one mentoring teacher creates a possibility for trust building, access to a caring adult when the student is in crisis, easy classroom management from the teacher's point of view (because a new crew isn't coming in every forty-five minutes), good discipline, and full opportunity for bonding and conflict resolution activities throughout a school day (which fits the early adolescent's diurnal rhythm well).

Our research into how the early-adolescent brain system requires strong attachment indicates to us the need for middle schools to continue the elementary school tradition of the homeroom. By the time puberty and cognitive developments are about completed (around age fifteen), the student is able to handle hourly movement from classroom to classroom.

Models for this kind of middle school classroom exist in several spots around the country, for instance in Montessori middle schools, where students keep the same core teachers for two or three years in middle school. In St. Louis, a district is also experimenting with seventh-to-twelfth-grade classrooms being taught by one teacher, in all subjects. This is more difficult for later high school grades, when specialization is required in such subjects as math, physics, and chemistry, but it is not difficult for teacher training in middle school to focus on all subjects and give young people not just teachers but also well-bonded mentors built in.

Bonding and Attachment

In Lisbon, Ohio, a twelve-year-old boy held his sixth-grade class at gunpoint until a teacher, Linda Robb, whom he trusted, convinced him to relinquish the weapon. A student in the hall had seen what was going on in the classroom and run to get Mrs. Robb. She stood in the doorway, asking the boy if she could talk to him. He walked out to her, they hugged, and the boy handed the gun over to her. Authorities learned later that the boy had told a friend, with whom he'd done crossing duty that morning, "Goodbye, Katie. I won't be back." The twelve-year-old boy went to class with a gun he had taken from his father's locked gun cabinet, unsure of what to do but probably plotting suicide, in a severe state of depression because of a broken attachment with his mother (his biological mother had been put in prison). In the end, he returned to some stability because of attachment to a teacher he was able to embrace.

When I read this story, tears came to my eyes. For many years, as a family therapist, I have counseled families with children of this age. Over the last few years, I've been involved in nationwide efforts to understand school shootings in Littleton, Colorado; Springfield, Oregon; and Jonesboro, Arkansas. Every few months I face a child, or the story of a child, who pierces the armor any specialist has to create. This boy in

Ohio pierced mine, and as I think back I see why. His story is such a pure case of how deeply middle school children feel their attachments; how utterly disabling loss of attachment can be for them; and what a salvation a mentor's attachment (like that of a teacher) can be to the growing mind, body, and soul of a desperate child.

I remember being twelve, as you probably do. I remember how hard I took things, how sensitive I was, and how equally capable of both bravado and desperation. I remember how hungry I was for the stability of bonds.

The Early Adolescent's Drop in Self-Esteem

Most middle school children are not as desperate as the boy in Lisbon, but all are hungry—as he was, as I was, and as you were. We are hungry at this age (even as we push adults away) because we feel deeply that we must have attachments to survive, and this feeling confuses us as we strive to be independent of them. Middle school is the time for this particular life tension, and in the ultimate classroom we know that to a great extent the child's emotional well-being is a foundation of good daily learning. Thus we strive to understand well why our middle school children undergo a drop in what we popularly call self-esteem.

From a brain-based point of view, this is what we know:

- The brain and, of course, the body are growing at such a severe pace that natural psychological equilibria are thrown off course for a transition period of at least two to four years.
- Leaps in cognition and abstraction, especially in the top of the brain, show the growing child that he or she is very small indeed and the world very large; thus the child's earlier innocence falls away, leaving behind an ontological fear of not belonging, not being good enough, not having the capacity to really make it in the huge world.
- A cognitive leap invades emotional development by creating a state of overreaction in which even a small emotional hiccup can become a major production.

- The individuation process—the process of becoming independent of Mom and Dad—is a whole-brain experience that requires a large complex of neural networks. This upsets earlier equilibria at the very time when the upper brain must master difficult math, language, and other abstraction skills as well as learn new technologies. Furthermore (especially in our culture), other attachment safety nets such as extended family, religious community, and rite of passage have nowadays been stripped away from young people's lives, leaving the child of twelve, thirteen, or fourteen vulnerable to becoming overstimulated by the internal independence process but unprotected by external guidance systems.

- The brain often seeks independence in ways that alienate parents. They often say of a middle schooler "He wants to be on his own" or "She doesn't need me as much anymore," reading only the off-putting signal the mind is sending out (and at times reading it conveniently, for parents of middle schoolers are often very busy). This leaves the child, who is far needier of bonds than she appears, alienated from her primary caregiving system, the nuclear family.

In all of this, teachers play a far more crucial role than we have wanted to admit. We play it even more strongly than we did a generation ago, for the extended family, family, and other support systems are now generally shattered—fathers gone, mothers gone, grandparents gone, and so on. For many middle schoolers, the teacher is one of a bare handful of the most stable presences in the child's life. Even for those middle schoolers who have stability and networking through home, family, and other systems, the teacher is still a significant mentor. Middle schoolers of all kinds want attachment to the teacher. Some show it by anger, others by sadness, or silence, or attention-getting devices. There is no middle schooler who wants to learn language arts, math, science, or any other subject in the presence of an elder she or he does not trust or like. In fact, teachers constantly report how much easier it is to teach students who are bonded to them. This should come as no surprise to us. Whether we are infants or middle schoolers, we prefer to feel loved and cared for by those to whom we give our respect and trust.

Thus in our work with teachers we have responded to their desire to "help our students keep high self-esteem" and built a foundation in brain research about that very development of self during middle school. Teachers have themselves created innovations that help them bond and attach. Brain-based research, as well as teacher experience, alerts all of us to the fact that student self-esteem can be bolstered a little through external practices (for instance, making sure to call on everyone in the class every day so that no one feels left out, especially not a girl); yet these practices cannot satisfy the full mind of the child, who needs the kind of ritual we discussed in the last chapter (and some others we discuss here).

This is especially true of the students we are most worried about. Calling on them in class does not satisfy their deep need for help with emotional stress and the bonding process. For them, learning is difficult because the limbic system of the brain is clouded by emotional stress, including flow of the stress hormone, cortisol. The limbic system must also devote much of its energy to managing the emotional stress of bonding and attachment dilemmas, and as a result it can't let the rest of the brain, especially the four lobes on top, learn in the way the classroom demands.

Handling Students' Emotional Stresses

Teachers around the country have been able to identify specific emotional stressors middle school boys and girls experience. We asked teachers in Missouri to focus on ones they thought significantly invaded the learning experience. As we discussed in the previous chapter, among the absolute keys to solving these areas of bonding difficulty are one-on-one attention and other rituals. We will also find that another key in middle school is educating children about their own mental and emotional processes.

Let's look at some areas of emotional stress so that we can watch for them in our school settings, keeping to the forefront the fact that once we've identified them it becomes our job to integrate student education about them into all our classes. Our middle school students are capable of high abstraction and deep interpersonal observation. If we focus them on areas of difficulty and educate them on how to help themselves, they will.

PROBLEMS IN PRIMARY ATTACHMENT RELATIONSHIPS. As in the situation in Lisbon, Ohio, every school district knows of middle school children whose families are suffering upheaval: divorce, death, abandonment, trouble with the law, abuse. These students are living daily in attachment trauma, and the teacher's ability to teach is often hindered. Teachers profoundly touch students' lives when they understand and mentor their attachment traumas.

Brenda Bock told us: "When a classmate was killed in a car wreck, none of the parents took their kids to the funeral. I escorted a group to the funeral. I was so overwhelmed. The kids had so many questions about death. It was as if they had grown up without anyone to answer important questions." In becoming the mentor to the children's trauma, Brenda not only increased student trust and respect for her, making her teaching job easier, but also touched a child spiritually.

PEER HUMILIATION.   The level of girl-girl, boy-boy, and cross-sex humiliation has risen in the last generation. Our young people are very hard on each other, especially in the early to mid-teens.

From a biological point of view, adolescent peer humiliation is necessary and not altogether reprehensible. Human survival does depend on young people ferreting out each other's weakness—in the ideal, while they are under the supervision of elders and mentors. Youths help each other, sometimes through aggressive provocation, to resolve the area of personal flaw. All primates have their versions of peer pressure and peer humiliation, with humans practicing them on a wide spectrum of intensity and effectiveness. Some girls are very hard on other girls; some not. Some boys are very hard on other boys; some not. Some girls are forgiving of boys' foibles, some are not, and the same goes for forgiveness in boys.

In recent years, we have become increasingly sensitive to the effects of peer humiliation because of school shootings; thus we are striving toward zero-tolerance policies on any harassment or humiliation of each other at all. This goal will never be met because basic evolutionary biology resists it. But just as increasing one-on-one teacher presence is required to help with students under terrible stress at home, so too is it required to help educate students on what they are doing to each other, and why. Here are some key areas middle schoolers need to be taught more about.

THE CHILD WHO DOESN'T FIT HIS OR HER GENDER TYPE. During adolescence there is a biological pull toward the group, or the mass. The brain is already genderized at birth and continues to be so as it follows its natural male or female course; it is also socialized along its natural gender course. This can work fine for many, even most, children, but it is a profound emotional stress to those children whose brains are what we commonly call bridge brains—those in the center of the male-female brain continuum.

These young people are boys who feel as much girlish as boyish, and girls who feel as much boyish as girlish. These are, for instance, the sensitive boys and the aggressive girls. The mass of boys and girls pull themselves in masculine and feminine directions, because of biology and socialization, but we have many bridge brains in our classrooms who often don't fit the mass description. Attention to the needs of these students is critical.

Though brains often fit gender types, the nuancing of the human brain is perhaps the most complex of any species, and middle school is the very time when nuance becomes extremely important to the child; thus it must be important to us as we guide girls and boys beyond stereotypes, into nuance. The teachers in Missouri found it essential to talk about gender stereotypes in nearly every area of study, from science to gym class, from math to literature.

Many teachers find the visual media especially useful in this regard. They show video clips of movies, television shows, and commercials, leading students to understand how the culture is trying to create gender uniformity, and then leading children to see through the uniformity to individuality. This kind of ongoing middle school mentoring relieves a great deal of stress, especially for the bridge-brain boys who think Jean Claude Van Damme is silly or the bridge-brain girls who don't get much out of "being feminine."

INADEQUATE SOCIAL SKILLS AND MATURITY EXPECTATIONS. It is immensely stressful for a middle school student to understand inadequately what is expected of him or her by other boys, other girls, and elders. Early adolescent students ask, both verbally and nonverbally, crucial questions of themselves and their peers. The more we help them toward mature answers, the less distracted their learning brains are, and the more maturely they engage in bonding and learning. How can we help them, practically speaking?

"Peer dilemmas" are one way. Here are some peer-dilemma scenarios created by the teen magazine *REACT*. I've adapted them slightly here.

- Someone in the cool crowd has just asked your best friend to have lunch, but the two of you already had plans. What's the right thing in this situation?
- The class bully makes picking on you a priority. What should your friends do to help you?
- A friend begs you to borrow booze from your parents' liquor cabinet. When you say you won't, your friend trips out. What should you do?
- Your friend is having a party and you're not invited. What should you do?
- You accidentally tell your friend a secret about yourself and then discover she has told others. What should you do?
- Your friend has hurt your feelings. How long should you wait for an apology? If you don't get one, should you reach out? If so, how long do you wait?
- Should you always be honest with your friends?
- Is peer pressure always a part of your life, or should you expect to find someone who does not try to pressure you toward bad things?

Middle schools are challenged to find creative ways to help boys and girls with these and many other stresses. As our definitions of *teacher* and *school* expand, based on recent research into what the brain needs, and especially what boys and girls need in order to feel whole, then middle schools make adjustments toward handling student emotional stress. They start teaching classes in emotion, ethics, and social skills that take on peer dilemmas.

NEW COUNSELING APPROACHES. Brain and gender research begs the counseling profession to adjust how its members provide their services, both in schools and in the rest of the professional community, and to boys in particular. The counseling profession relies on words to a greater extent than many boys are comfortable with. It also regularly asks the boy to come to a counselor's office or sit down and talk, which, to many boys, indicates personal weakness from the start.

Another approach, which I've successfully employed in my own counseling practice, is what I call "peripatetic counseling." Based on the Socratic model of walking and teaching, this kind of counseling allows the mentor and student to do something physical together. This is, practically speaking, good for stimulation of the limbic system and emotional processing in any child, and for many males especially; it creates opportunity for objects and other people, along the way, to play a helpful role in the counseling process ("What does that guy over there remind you of?" "Look at her; what do you think she's feeling right now?"), and it takes counseling out of the small-space office and back into the larger world.

STRESS BALLS AND QUICK TENSION-RELEASE TECHNIQUES. Let's look at specific emotion-management innovations teachers are implementing. Many of them were developed specifically to help middle school boys, who are often hard to manage.

Middle school teacher Darla Novick reported: "I added stress balls to my class. The stress balls are working. During the time when my students need to calm down and talk to me, I allow them to use the stress ball to have something to do as they talk. I've found that this allows the boys to be able to actually talk and express their feelings better. I also allow the students to draw while they're talking. Just by giving them something to do they process better."

After learning about the effect of testosterone on boys' behavior, Brandy Barnett told us:

> I'm beginning to understand my boys in my class better. The testosterone level makes sense when I think about all of the acts that my students do in class. As I've taught the same group of boys for two years, I've tried to talk with them and bond with them. When they are angry or hurt I've tried to talk and comfort them. It has never worked as well as I'd like. Now I know why.
>
> I think much differently than them. My way of reacting to problems is to discuss them and problem solve. However, I've found that my boys would rather blame, yell, and shut down. All this time I've been thinking there was something really wrong with them. NOT. They are handling their anger the way they know and the way many boys do. So, I've changed the way I perceive the problem. Instead of thinking they aren't doing it correctly, I've begun to take what they have and work with it. I've begun teaching them appropriate ways to quick-release their testosterone. I've included such techniques as ripping paper, hitting a pillow, etc. These are techniques I'm using to get them calmed down. I've combined them with the stress balls and verbal processing, but *after* they have calmed down.

CARE TEAMS AND RITUALS.   Brandy told us about her school's use of care teams to increase bonding among both boys and girls: "In our training group, we've talked about the need for our boys and girls to have 'clans,' groups in which they feel very bonded. In our school, we have after-school activities set up as well as a care team to provide mentors and an excellent counseling staff. Since we're on teaching teams in middle school most of the time, each students bonds with at least one team member. We've done pretty well at setting up a system of referrals to connect students with at least one adult in the school."

Brandy has also instituted some of the in-class rituals we discussed in the preceding chapter. We asked how they worked with middle schoolers. She was enthusiastic: "I've created my first two days of lesson plans to center around creating a bond between the students by using a series of cooperative learning activities. Before we attempt anything academic, I want the students to be somewhat at ease with each other, as well as with me. We finished the first day of school and I am on cloud nine with the results! The students have really enjoyed the learning activities and we all seem to be creating a close bond with each other."

FOUR BONDING STEPS. There is a four-step method that works well in our efforts to increase (from a very practical point of view) the bonds we have with students:

1. Ask questions (for instance, about how they want to spend class time).
2. Listen to the answers carefully.
3. Find common ground.
4. Do something together (follow through on the action decision).

Bonding is a process so complex we cannot accomplish it by micromanagement; we just have to "be in the process." At the same time, asking questions, listening, finding common ground, and then working together are a foundation. These steps are good for adult-child relationships as well as between students. A number of the Missouri teachers are increasing bonds between pairs of students by letting them pair up and then training them in this process.

Convincing (or pressuring!) teachers to increase their bonds with students is certainly good for the students' brain and therefore holistic development, but it can feel like yet another pressure on the teacher. At all levels of school, community collaborators simply *must* help out.

Community Collaboration

Middle schools often desperately need the help of parents and friends of the school. Middle schools find that parents are willing to volunteer (and schools are set up to accept their service) during elementary school, but then by middle school both tacit and structural assumptions take hold: "The kids don't want parents around anymore, so we won't encourage it."

Though middle school students may posture as such, their physical, psychosocial, and cognitive brain development needs a wide variety of attachments and bonds. To discover just how much students want and need parental bonds as an active part of learning, the Hearst Foundation conducted a survey, asking students for their self-perception of their reasons for having achieved success. Respondents called parental support "the biggest factor" in their success. This reported outcome continued all the way through high school.

Community collaboration must begin, of course, during the early education years and go on through high school. In the St. Joseph's school district, an early education center run by Susan Colgan is available through which the school system facilitates parent participation in student learning.

In Southern California, the Canejo Valley Adult School is immensely successful at teaching not only elementary age children but also their parents, grandparents, and all other community collaborators who want to be involved in helping educate the preschool and elementary age child.

In Antioch, California, it was discovered that middle school African American boys lagged behind peers in academic and other areas, so Black Diamond Middle School Principal Barbara Ewing asked African American fathers in the community to help. They responded, working with students voluntarily in the library. The success of her program startles even her: "From time to time my teachers will go down and take a look, and they are amazed at the number of kids who are there who are focused and the number of people who come on a regular basis to work with them."

In communities where early parent participation programs are in place, middle school parent outreach is less difficult. The community is ready to supply the schools with mentors from faith communities and the elderly population, as well as moms and dads who volunteer time and energy. In middle school, it is easy to argue that the child's need for mentoring is as severe as in elementary school. As the brain grows in cognitive leaps, and as the body grows in physical leaps, the young man and woman desperately need a variety of elder, mentoring, and instructional personnel to guide and teach them.

Sex education is a specific area where help is needed. (We go into sex-education curricula in the next chapter.) However, in middle school, there are specific needs that elders, parents, and other collaborators can fill, easing the burden on the teacher. Marian Howard, a professor of obstetrics and gynecology at Emory University, asked more than one thousand teenage girls in Atlanta what they most wanted to learn in sex ed. Eighty-four percent answered, "How to say no without hurting the other person's feelings." Community collaborators, especially parents and other close elders, can help teach this skill, suggests Howard, by informal role playing. The community collaborator becomes the aggressive suitor and the pubescent girl practices comeback lines and other strategies.

To some extent, middle schools find themselves alone as they try to teach sensitive material. They know that many parents aren't teaching it, yet they don't get much on-campus commitment from parents. For middle schools to prosper as bonding communities, the school-parent gap must close. Sex education is only one area where collaboration can occur. At Ervin Middle School in Kansas City, there is a parent outreach center, run in part by the students. In one particular student activity, students interview parents for a rite-of-passage ceremony at the school. Parents and the school work together on rites of passage.

Middle school students do need more independence from parents than before, but not as much as we give them—not so much that the parent-school community acts like a separate entity rather than a community. The extent to which the middle school child doesn't want a father or mother in the school is also the extent to which grandparents and other elders—as well as business mentors, high school seniors, college students, and numerous other mentors—must step in.

How to Provide Discipline
in the Middle School Classroom

The BIST model, which we explored in the preceding chapter, is also used in middle school, as are many of the innovations already explored. Yet middle school discipline is its own particular creature, as any middle school teacher knows.

Ray McGowan, a middle school teacher in Kansas City, said jokingly, "Just listening to the kids in class, especially the boys . . . it seems like they have only one volume: loud. They are almost on top of each other, and they are still loud." For most middle school teachers, any historical idea of seventh or eighth graders all sitting quietly in their seats is exactly that—history. The middle school classroom is often a less disciplined place than we wish. In my study of thirty cultures, I've not seen another culture in which there is less middle school classroom quiet than in ours. Our middle school classrooms truly are loud! This can lead to great creativity—and to some real problems, as each of us knows.

Besides the general melee of many of our classrooms, there are individual discipline issues. Kimberly Walter told us a poignant story of a seventh grader in her class. "Tru is a darling boy. He sparkles with personality. However, as fall goes along, he is sleepy in class—droopy. He says football practice is getting him down. His performance is slipping and roughhousing behavior is becoming a daily occurrence, a real problem in class. At a parent conference, I learn from Mom that she and Dad are divorced and that in August Dad began refusing to see the kids. Now I get it: Tru is acting out. He is hurt and angry." Like so many boys and girls who disrupt class, Tru had a good reason, from a neurological and emotional point of view. His brain had to prioritize gaining attention above the learning process, and his body followed the brain, going for negative actions, sacrificing learning, and asking for love and discipline that would quiet the hurt.

Strategies for Providing Discipline

Every school has its discipline modalities. We hope these ideas and practical applications add to those you already enjoy or are familiar with. If you have not read the section "How to Provide Discipline in the Elementary School" in Chapter Four, this would be a good time to do so.

COMMUNITY COLLABORATION. When asked what she thought was most needed to help middle school discipline, Brenda Bock surprised us by saying, "Actually, if I were ever to do an educational study I would do it on the following: to show that there is a direct relationship between chores and responsibilities carried out at home and discipline and completion of work at school." Teachers naturally tend to try to solve, in school, all the discipline and motivation issues that present themselves at school. It is useful to remind ourselves constantly that if there isn't discipline at home, our job is harder. Community collaboration in the area of discipline management is crucial. Developing a parent education coordinator (Chapter Three) can aid in this effort, since the coordinator educates parents in effective discipline techniques.

THE EVER-ESSENTIAL CONTEXT OF BONDING. Brandy Barnett told us:

> Things have been going fairly smoothly in my room until today. One of my boys did something: he got angry at another student and flipped the desk over, striking my foot. This was a typical male reaction—immediate and explosive without thinking first. The instant he realized that it had hit me he felt terrible and then shut himself into the recovery room [see the BIST model]. We couldn't get him out for two hours, until his mom came. He was so embarrassed he couldn't even look at me.
>
> When he came back to school after his suspension, I made sure that I let him know that I still cared about him. This was so important to him, me, and everyone.

A middle school principal in Cape Cod who had twenty-five years of education experience told me he tries "to love the most behaviorally deficient kids the most." By this he does not mean favoritism; he means that he senses the reality of how much bonding they need in order to improve undisciplined behavior. He practices a Saturday detention schedule, taking the young people into the school yard to rake leaves, or into the community to do chores elsewhere. He reports that the kids enjoy it; in his words, "most of them love it. I think they are getting love and attention that they don't get at home, especially with most of them having no dads."

WHEN IN DOUBT, BECOME AN ALPHA. A few years ago, the "60 Minutes" television magazine show did a segment on young elephants in Africa that had been brought up without parents. When their testosterone came in, the males began killing rhinoceroses (a very unusual behavior for an elephant) and trying to mate inappropriately. The park wardens had to put some of the young males to sleep. Then one insightful ranger realized that these young adolescents were like juvenile delinquents who had no alphas or role models. They were following their hormonal pressures without guidance from elders. So a number of communities worked together to bring in alpha male elephants from another part of Africa.

The amazing outcome? Within one week, the juvenile elephants had come into line. The inappropriate mating ceased, and the violence ceased—no more rhinoceroses were harassed or killed.

A middle school student is not an elephant, but the analogy is a useful one, especially when you are faced with a student who is trying, however subtly, to dominate and destroy. Sometimes, there is nothing to do but become an alpha: strict, no second chances, rapport based on strong authority. If you can't do it, then you must enlist the aid of a potential alpha you know.

Some districts are bringing fathers into school as volunteers. Others provide mentors, as does the very successful Big Brothers Big Sisters of America program School-Based Mentoring. Still others have gone to faith communities and even nursing homes to increase the presence of elders in the school community. In Montgomery County, Maryland, the BROTHERS program (Brothers Reaching Out to Help Each Other Reach Success) provides strong mentors for minority and at-risk males, coaching college students to mentor high school students, who in turn mentor middle schoolers.

In my own district in Spokane, one of the middle school transportation routes was plagued by discipline problems on the morning bus. The female bus driver enlisted the help of a grandfather who now rides the route, sitting in the front seat—an elder presence that has erased undisciplined behavior.

ANTIBULLYING CAMPAIGNS. Formal safe schools and antibullying campaigns are a necessity in many districts. We want to call special attention to an effective one with which we are familiar (and which we described in Chapter Four): On Target to Stop Bullying, a program guide for addressing bullying and violence in schools. It is, as we pointed out, a project of the STOP Violence Coalition and the Missouri Safe Schools Coalition.

JOURNALING. Rita Whertvine has her students keep journals, and those with greater discipline issues sometimes write on their issues. Occasionally she asks the whole class to participate in their own emotional education by writing on an emotion-based theme.

She recounts: "Today the students' journal entry was 'feeling frustrated.' When did they feel it and what did they do about it? One remarked that he got violent when he got frustrated, but he knew that was not the best. The other boys said they did different activities, but they were all related to physical activities. That fits in with what we're learning about boys being action oriented. These boys were more comfortable getting into movement rather that trying to talk it out."

REMEMBER THE SIXTY-SECOND RULE. Rita writes: "I tell students what to do and give them sixty seconds to do it. If they start to question and argue, I go on to something else. They almost always do what they have been told to do if they cannot engage you in a verbal battle and if you take the focus of the classroom off of them. So many of these boys are competing for manhood and who wants everyone to notice they are controlled by a woman!"

Rita's insight is compelling. Middle school boys are generally involved in psychological separation from their mothers, and caught up in battles of pride and hierarchy with classmates. Allowing sixty seconds for compliance, and turning away from a conflict, can stave off a lot of misbehavior.

THE BOYS TOWN SOCIAL-SKILLS MODEL. Sharon Fisher, as assistant principal in Missouri, has found this model (from Omaha-based Boys Town) quite effective. She advises her teachers to "go over number five of the *Boys Town Classroom Social Skills* every day, if necessary, with students: 'Number five: getting the teacher's attention: (1) Look at the teacher. (2) Raise your hand. Stay calm. (3) Wait until the teacher says your name. (4) Ask your question.'" She finds that, especially with frequent review, most students cooperate.

SEPARATE-SEX GROUPINGS. Earlier in this chapter, we explored the logic of separate-sex groupings, especially in middle school, and the potential decrease in discipline problems any school can enjoy through this means. In Sharon Fisher's school, boys and girls are separated in the lunchroom, which cuts down on discipline problems. Ray, a teacher at Anderson Alternative School, is in charge of in-school suspension. He separates the students by cubicles and finds that it cuts down greatly on discipline problems. The boys accomplish more when their cubicles are next to other boys. In his words, "They have no need to show off."

We have presented some small things we can all do to improve discipline. We would also like to call attention to systemic changes schools can make.

Mandatory Sports

Like character education (to be discussed in a moment), and like focusing on school bonding systems, mandatory athletics can help with proactive and preventive approaches to cutting down on discipline problems.

Middle school is a time of enormous physical upheaval, so we suggest that middle schools engage all students in a sport or athletic activity. Through directed physical activity, the brain learns to manage the body. For boys generally, this is crucial to learn to self-manage testosterone; thus it is even more vital for high-testosterone males. For girls, mandatory sports are useful in helping develop the skills that pertain to healthy physical competition. Studies show that both male and female students who have to develop self-discipline in sports are less likely to engage in drugs and other high-risk adolescent behavior.

In this context, then, we recommend mandatory sports for middle school students. Some students just don't like team sports. They can be directed to martial arts.

The Landon School in Bethesda, Maryland, is one of a handful around the country we have heard about that mandate a sport for all students. Headmaster Damon Bradley believes it is a major aspect of a Landon education, and especially critical for teaching self-discipline.

In high school, student choice can return—certainly by tenth grade, which is customarily the time at which physical and hormonal upheaval eases. Between around sixth and ninth grades, however, some extracurricular athletic activity ought to be mandatory. It is essential, of course, that if sports become mandatory, schools be vigilant in training coaches how to bond with and mentor, in healthy ways, the energy of youth.

Even further, since athletics is a primary human way of developing character, coaches need good training in how to impart character education. Our brain research directs us to go even further than this and note that in middle school especially, athletic attainment and physical success should be considered secondary to character education. What do we mean?

Historically, sports and athletics (ancient Greek culture comes to mind) were the training ground for moral character. Actual physical success and winning were important, but first and foremost the culture used athletics to train its young men for life missions and self-management of personal energy that would be required if the young person is to be capable of sacrificing the self for the society.

Present-day male and female athletics are obsessed with winning, and it's difficult to dissuade any community from this obsession. Yet it's also worth remembering our recent past, and slowing down our competitive mania. Our young people need athletics for their souls as much as for their bodies.

Character Education

The CHARACTER*plus* model described in Chapter Four is useful in middle school and beyond. It focuses on community agreement regarding certain key character traits, and absorption of training in these traits into all aspects of schooling.

This model has been applied extensively in Missouri and elsewhere, in communities large and small. Although the traits and their definitions vary with the community, the similarities are greater than the differences. For example, practically all communities address the character traits of honesty, respect, and responsibility.

Darryl Cobb, principal at Smith-Hale Middle School, was a member of the community committee that identified and defined the traits to be used in the Hickman Mills School District. He began to implement character education immediately after the successful community meeting. His goal for implementation was that this process should change the culture of his school, and he reports that it has.

The decision to infuse character traits into the day-to-day curriculum has become an important element for Smith-Hale Middle School, in many interesting ways. Teachers were reporting to Darryl, for instance, that students would come into class between periods needing time to settle down during the transition. What a terrific time to emphasize character traits! Smith-Hale decided to spend five minutes at the beginning of each class presenting and reviewing character traits and their definitions. To guarantee that all the character traits chosen by the Hickman Mills School District would be taught and reinforced, the staff decided to emphasize a trait a month in this period at the beginning of each class.

At Smith-Hale, another opportunity to emphasize character traits came about as a result of a student poll. The staff asked students what they would most like to be able to do while they were attending school. The three most common responses were requests for greater freedom: (1)

to go to the restroom when they needed to without having to get a hall pass, (2) to visit the vending machines after lunch periods, and (3) to wear badges as the adults did. The staff tied this information with their character-education program. Students who exhibit good citizenship (meaning they consistently model the good character traits) or who exhibit an outstanding act of character that ties to one of the Hickman Mills character traits are now selected as VIPs. Once selected, these students remain VIPs unless they lose their badges (on account of three infractions of any character trait). Darryl says no one has yet lost a badge.

Before implementing the character-education process, the principal reported that an average of twenty to thirty students were referred to the office each day for unacceptable behavior. After only two years with the program, that average has dropped to no more than seven or eight. The principal credits character education as a major source of this dramatic difference.

According to Darryl, improved student behavior carries outside the schools walls as well. He has seen an increase in reports (from establishments that students visit on field trips) saying that Smith-Hale students exhibit good behavior.

In talking about character education and the difference it has made at Smith-Hale, Darryl says "character education was a group decision and the entire staff must get the credit for the ownership and implementation of the process." He also says that a major factor in the success of character education throughout the Hickman Mills School District was the decision of the district to make it a component of the performance-based teacher evaluation process: "An unexpected side effect of the program is that staff behavior now consistently models the character traits." When we interviewed middle school teachers about the program, there was nearly unanimous agreement about its usefulness and relative ease of implementation.

Parents as well have responded positively to the character-education process in place at Hickman Mills in general, and in the Smith-Hale Middle School in particular. Penny Mizener, a parent of a Smith-Hale student, says, "I feel the character-education program at Smith-Hale is 100 percent successful. I have seen firsthand how my children demonstrate the traits and how it has been successful for all the students at Smith-Hale. I also know it is very successful because I compare how students act in other schools who don't have character education." To expand Smith-Hale's character education beyond the classroom, it was decided that parents would be encouraged to reinforce the character traits, and a special plea was made in a parents' meeting. The parents asked that the traits be included in the student handbook so they would have easy access to them. School and home share credit for Smith-Hale's success.

The superintendent of schools, Jerry Cooper, described a recent visit to Smith-Hale Middle School. All of the approximately nine hundred students were in the gymnasium for a school assembly. Cooper noted that the students were somewhat noisy as he entered with Darryl Cobb. The principal immediately reminded the students that one of their character traits was *respect*. He told them that there were visitors in the building and their commitment to respect meant that they would be orderly and quiet so that they could hear what was being said. Cooper proudly reported later that the students were quiet and respectful throughout the assembly—quite a feat for a school that had been considered unruly just a couple of years before!

Such comments speak volumes about what we hope will soon become an integral part of every school's academic year. The advantage in providing discipline to children is clear, as is development of a strong core self in each student. A hidden by-product of character education is its ability, in the long run, to improve academic learning. A student who feels strong in character is better motivated to perform well when the going gets tough, as it always does at some point for students struggling to attain academic success.

Innovations for Teaching Language Arts and Math and Science

When we think of gender and the brain in the context of learning vulnerability, we probably immediately pair up boys with language arts and girls with math and science. In middle school, teachers have been vigilant in helping in these areas. Let's move now from middle school discipline to middle school academics.

Innovations for Teaching Language Arts

Carol Jago, a teacher at Santa Monica High School, has led classrooms of boys and girls through the classics. She trains her students in "the rules of scholarly discourse," something she learned from Yvonne Hutchinson, a master teacher at one of the most challenging middle schools in the Los Angeles Unified School District.

The rules of scholarly discourse are that

1. Students must talk to one another, not just the teacher or the air.
2. Students must listen to one another. To ensure this happens, they must either address the previous speaker or offer a reason for changing the subject.
3. Students must all be prepared to participate. (Says Carol, "If I call on someone and he or she has nothing to say, the appropriate response is, 'I'm not sure what I think about that, but please come back to me.' ")

Carol's rules of scholarly discourse fit well with another innovation she practices: the "seminar." She explains: "The word itself seems to lend an air of importance to our discussion." Indeed, many of us remember being electrified in English or social studies or history class when a seminar-style classroom circle was formed; we not only discussed, we debated. Carol follows a method grounded in these rules:

- She tells students everyone must participate at least once during the seminar.
- No student needs to raise a hand to be called on, but they all have to look around and take notice of the shy classmates ("Luke, you look as though you disagree. What are you thinking?").

- She teaches students how to manage the compulsive talkers. One method: "Just when the motor mouth inhales, insert your comment!"
- Silence is allowed. While someone's thinking, silence is fine. This is a time for a student to open the book and find a passage to ponder, rather than just jump into another person's thinking silence.

Carol tells the students she won't be involved unless necessary, and not until the last five minutes of class.

Regarding her involvement, she also says she won't correct students' content during their discussion of, say, *Beowulf,* but she might comment on their conduct. Her job in seminar is mainly to teach them the skills of scholarly discussion.

Carol talks about her methods in her book *With Rigor for All: Teaching the Classics to Contemporary Students.* Teachers, especially in language arts, benefit from her work. Her methods lead to a maturity of discussion that helps leave no one out, does not punish the attention seekers (many of whom are loud males) but instead reigns them in, allows the class itself be responsible for helping shy peers (who are usually girls), and meanwhile teaches some of history's finest literature to minds starved for primal stories. Certainly Carol's rules and seminar can also be used for any related subject, not just the classics.

CONNECTING LANGUAGE ARTS TO OTHER EXPERIENTIAL PROCESSES. Middle school teacher Sharon Fisher told us that she now connects language arts to her girls' rite-of-passage group. The connection of language arts to rite of passage has given the girls a deep, even spiritual connection with some of the material they are reading. This is useful, of course, for boys as well.

In language arts, both boys and girls can find some subject matter boring. Darla Novick has found subject matter, in unusual places, that has not bored the students: "A judge used to call me to let me know of items coming up in court that would be good for the kids (especially the boys) to observe. We visited court often." Many class assignments grew from these visits—experience coupled with language arts, and grueling boredom a rarer thing.

MORE MOVEMENT! Given the reality of what is happening to middle school students' bodies and brains, it is essential we consider increasing physical movement during the school day. Movement helps release pent-up energy, cut down on discipline problems, and stimulate the bored or zoning-out brain.

Brandy Barnett allows more physicality in her classrooms now, after receiving brain-based training. "One of the first things I noticed in my class," she related, "is that boys like to move around and be active. My lessons now involve more movement and getting up to do things. This has really invigorated our learning."

NOTE-TAKING INNOVATIONS. An area where both girls and boys can have difficulty with language arts is note taking. Girls sometimes get preoccupied taking down everything a teacher says, or everything other students say. Boys might not keep up with quick discussion or instructions, and their note taking is shoddy. Of course, these deficiencies cross gender boundaries too.

Brenda Bock's teaching team has focused on this problem with incoming sixth graders. This team has decided to actually train the students in how to take notes: "In all subject areas, we first give out a full copy of notes and go over them orally step by step. Then we make a skeletal outline with spaces for students to fill in. Finally, they take the notes themselves." Note taking is, for this teaching team, a fundamental skill that must be taught before actual curricula can begin.

Brenda also connects note-taking innovations to multisensory learning: "The brain-based research has convinced me that classes should be multisensory. We've adapted this to our note-taking strategies, using the visual on the overhead and hard copy, auditory in the class lecture and discussion, and the kinesthetic sense in writing the notes." By combining eyes, ears, and hands, Brenda and her team see better learning taking place.

TOPICAL PROJECTS BY GENDER. Brian Zipfel, of Park Hill, told us:

> I teach social studies, specifically American history. This subject is often
> not a favorite of students, especially females. To appeal to and use the
> different learning styles of females I assign different topical projects. The
> students can pick a historical topic from the unit we are studying.
> The students can also select a mode or medium to present their project.
> The topics often include women in history. That often appeals to girls'
> interest. The way of presenting the topic (mode or medium) includes
> several ideas which can lean towards strengths of the girls. They often
> are more verbally and linguistically inclined. They often perform and
> create dramatic presentations. Often I also use small group situations
> which allow students to verbalize responses in ordinary class settings.

We readily think of girls being at an advantage in language arts, and certainly the female brain in general shows that advantage; but how often have we lost our girls to boredom because they are reading yet another book about males and men? Vigilance on this problem, especially in teaching social sciences and history, is essential for girls' learning.

In general, Manzo and Manzo's *Teaching Children to Be Literate* is one of the finest practical resources a teacher can consult to improve ability to teach language arts and literacy. The Manzos are brain-based researchers, and also trained in numerous other areas of literacy learning; they have written a valuable book, one that anyone dealing with language arts might enjoy reading.

Innovations for Teaching Math and Science

The teaching of math and science has been well researched, especially the ways in which these subjects usually give girls trouble. According to the federal education department, girls have nearly caught up to boys in math and science scores, and in fact they now take more math and science than boys do. At the top end of the scales (highest math and physics) boys still dominate, and given the configuration of the male brain—more focus on the right hemisphere, greater tendency toward high abstraction and design—we will probably always see a statistical advantage for males in the stratosphere of math and science. The fact, however, that within about fifteen years we have helped so many girls find parity is a testament to what a society, especially its teachers, can do to solve a brain-based and gender-based disparity in schools.

Boys are about a year and a half behind girls, according to the Department of Education, in reading and writing skills. Some literacy disparity favoring girls will probably always exist, owing to the female's left-hemisphere focus and development, but within ten to fifteen years, if we do for reading and writing disparities what we've done for math and science, we should bring the disparity down significantly. Our math and science success with girls is truly inspirational.

Girls are, of course, not alone in having math and science problems (many boys do as well). So even though many of the innovations we share here have grown from teacher training in brain-based responses to math-and-science learning problems for girls, they are often equally applicable to helping boys.

COOPERATIVE LEARNING GROUPS AND PAIRS. Sheryl Sullivan, of Ervin Middle School, wrote in her journal: "I form cooperative groups so that the girls will feel comfortable being participants and leaders. I try to put girls who may lack confidence in math into groups with other girls. At the sixth grade, girls seem to become very self-conscious about themselves with boys. I also try to put girls who have strong math skills with boys who will allow them full participation and/or leadership. As their confidence builds, the group they're in becomes less of a concern."

CALL-ON RATIOS. It was fascinating to read about a visit, in the spring of 2000, that then Vice President Al Gore made to a middle school outside Detroit. He himself has daughters and is well aware of the research that shows how boys can often dominate discussion in middle school, a problem many teachers find in math and science classes. Despite Gore's best efforts, while he led a discussion, three boys dominated the dialogue and he did not draw out the girls.

Any of us who are well-trained and sensitive to this disparity can still find ourselves passionately leading a discussion and forgetful of the need to make sure we find some parity in how many times we call on shyer students, many of whom, in our middle school math and science classes, are girls.

SHOWCASING GIRLS.   Anthony Becker, a middle school teacher in the Kansas City, Missouri, school district, frankly notes the importance of what we call "showcasing" girls in math classes: "Being a math teacher, I'm very much aware of the bias against girls in math. I try to always point out their talents in math, and encourage them to pursue math. I also try to make sure I call on girls an appropriate number of times to answer questions. I showcase them by asking them to take leadership positions. I showcase my girls to make them comfortable in their mathematical achievement."

USING A VARIETY OF APPROACHES.   Ray McGowan, one of Anthony's middle school colleagues in Kansas City, summed up some of the best approaches to teaching girls math and science:

- When needed, separate girls from boys.
- Pick field trips to places where females are in a position of dealing with math or science, thus providing role models.
- Give directions over and over.
- Emphasize hands-on work.

Tanya Wittleson, a middle school teacher in Kansas City, adds another key element: "Use visuals, like an overhead. This captures their attention. It is more like watching TV for them."

Given how quickly the brain is growing during these years, variety is in itself quite useful for engaging boys' and girls' brains. Where a child has a disadvantage, for instance some girls in math, variety is even more important. Combining clear instruction—giving directions completely and repeatedly—with overhead visuals and hands-on work visuals is multisensory and engages more of the brain in learning.

BOYS AND GIRLS NEED SOME OF THE SAME THINGS. Patricia Campbell, an educational consultant in Massachusetts, decided to study key classroom characteristics that helped *both* boys and girls in math and science. She discovered that effective classrooms:

- Allow no disrespect, whether teacher put downs of students or students or each other
- Use more than one instruction method (lecture, small group, diagrams, peer tutors); students learn best, as we know, when they have variety
- Do not allow one small group of attention seekers to dominate

This is basic wisdom all of us can use, both common sense and a confirmation of the brain-based innovations we have been discussing.

Girls and Computer Science

The female brain is not so naturally inclined toward the kind of quick, right-hemisphere stimulation that computer games (especially fast-moving ones) generate. We just don't see girls playing these games as frequently as boys, and probably, from a statistical standpoint, never will. Similarly, girls are more inclined, if in a social situation, to choose a verbalizing activity or relationship activity over zoning-out time in front of a computer screen. (The exceptions are chat-room use and Internet buying. Girls and boys, according to recent surveys, pursue these two for about the same amount of time, with girls slightly more likely to stay longer in a single chat room and boys more likely to roam, and boys and girls, of course, buying different kinds of products.)

Boys and girls will probably always differ somewhat in computer use. We must be watchful, however, of thinking the computer gap has been closed. We might say, "Well, it's OK that girls don't play the video games—they're not worth much to the brain anyway," and "Girls are using computers as much as boys; look at the Internet." Actually, there is a marked disparity between girls and boys in some essential computer technology education, especially development of those skills that translate into workplace success.

According to a new study by the AAUW, only 17 percent of high school students who take the advance placement tests in computer science are girls. Women earn only 28 percent of the bachelor's degrees in computer science and constitute just 20 percent of information technology professionals. Some of this disparity is natural, and girls will probably never want to stare into a screen and design very abstract computer programs as much as boys, on average. Even so, the disparity is frightening, especially in an era such as ours when knowing fluency in the language and use of computers is crucial.

It's in middle school that we can begin dealing clearly with this disparity. As much as possible, teachers need to help girls deal with computer phobia; make sure boys don't dominate computer use; and make sure girls get the opportunity to deal, as concretely as possible, with learning computer languages.

Sometimes, no matter what we do to support a child's academic development, it feels as if it is not enough. A middle school teacher told us about one student who ended up with all A's on his report card. He was praised accordingly. However, he told his teachers he didn't want any more A's. His behavior and classwork began to suffer after receiving this great report card. He was suspended shortly afterward. This student could not handle the success and positive remarks he received. He couldn't live up to the high expectation. The student did get back on track, with help from his teacher and his parents. But even the most seemingly accomplished kid can be fragile.

This young man got back on track pretty quickly. What happens to the students who don't? What can we do better for them?

Special Education

An e-mail recently informed me of a school district in Dallas in which 20 percent of the twelve hundred students are labeled "special education. The *Diagnostic and Statistical Manual* says 5 percent of the population ought to be so diagnosed. Can you tell me what is going on?" the author of the letter asked.

In our survey data at the Missouri schools, we asked teachers to tell us some of the things they had seen change the most in their middle school classrooms over the years (we asked teachers with a decade or more of experience to answer this question). The most repeated answer was "The number of learning or behaviorally disabled has shot up." Many teachers recalled having one to three disruptive students per year during the 1980s but now have more than ten. The male-female ratio is about three to one in diagnoses of learning disorder—and about ten to one in behavioral diagnoses.

Nearly all the teachers agreed that although it is essential to separate learning-disability diagnoses from many so-called behavioral ones, in reality a lot of behavioral problems correlate with children (mainly males) who become behavioral problems as part of their ego reaction to their learning vulnerability.

What, indeed, is happening to our students? Why are school districts all over the country reporting so many disabilities and problems? Part of the answer, brain research tells us, lies in these factors:

- The human brain is formatted for preindustrial life, not the over-stimulation of today. Many, even most, brains can adapt to the constant and intense stimulation of modern life, but some cannot.
- The male brain is especially fragile in this regard because it does not naturally multitask as well and is not as flexible; if either gender's brain system is going to be more vulnerable to a learning disability, it will tend to be the male.
- The male brain and male hormones mix to drive vulnerable and disabled males toward aggressive, uncontrolled, and inappropriate behavior more than females, which adds to the frequency of male BD diagnosis.
- Classrooms and schools have not focused on male brain systems and favor the female brain in terms of daily classroom functioning, so some males who are what we would recognize as normal don't fit and are diagnosed LD or BD.

If these are some reasons, from a brain-based point of view, for the recent increase in LD and BD diagnosis, what are some solutions? First, our research shows us how critical it is that schools revisit the problems they are having.

Rethinking Special Education Through the Lens of Gender and the Brain

A teacher wrote two things in her journal, juxtaposed, that are a basis for arguing that we must rethink special education to fully incorporate the new brain and gender research:

> I taught behavior disordered seventh- and eighth-graders for eight years and I can't think of a single boy I ever had that had a good male role model with any consistency. It was painful to see how desperate they were for a male to pay attention to them.
> [and]
> There are about 145 to 150 students in my building identified as having some sort of handicap. About two-thirds of them are males. Our educational system has been focusing on equal education for females since I started teaching twenty years ago. I have never been trained to focus on the male.

Our anecdotal research keeps bringing us to this kind of juxtaposition in the thinking of special education teachers, especially those focusing on the behaviorally disordered kids: young males lack male role models, develop disorders, and are put in the care of specialists who have been trained in behavior and in disorders, but not in "maleness" or male psychology.

We believe that, along with other innovations, special education must now focus on questions of masculinity, male role models, male brains, and male culture in order to fully progress to the next level of assisting young people.

Ruth Whertvine has noticed the second area of revision that is necessary: bonding. BD kids crave love. "At Anderson Alternative School," she says, "we have five girls enrolled and over fifty boys. All of them seem to be searching for love, respect, acceptance, a feeling of being OK. How does a school environment supply that, and can it be enough for them if it does?" Ruth also notes that the boys especially "respond to guidelines that are set and then enforced," but she wonders how to go further into the heart of what ails these boys.

Linda, a teacher from the Hickman Mills School District, told us about using Beanie Babies in her middle school special ed classroom, allowing students to pick one up and keep it on their desk during class. She finds that the male students take a Beanie Baby and keep it on their desk as much as the girl students. It's something they can touch. They can listen better if they have something to touch, she has noticed. Could it also be that they are starved for affection, both to receive and to give it?

With her severely disabled kids, Ruth has noticed that "boys enjoy crawling under cabinets to read. They have a need for security that we sometimes forget these boys still need." She goes on to notice the intense need of all the BD students to be noticed.

In her alternative ed program, this innovation has been effective: "Our students put up their own bulletin boards. Because they take ownership in their work, they do not tear them down. For the first time, many of these at-risk students have something displayed in school that is *theirs.*" These children, prone to calling negative attention to themselves in the hope of getting any at all, enjoy feeling cared about positively. Again we must wonder, since the vast majority of these students are male, are we at present a human culture that systematically withholds from boys the love they need? Have we methodically cut out of our care of the masculine a deep understanding and acceptance of its brain, body, heart, and soul? Are these boys trying to get us to notice how unloved males presently feel?

Randall, a middle school teacher, told us: "I see many of these boys who are not connected with a peer group. Some walk around, dejected looking, hoping to blend in with a wall, looking at groups of boys. I see loners and outcasts who seek the attention of these groups through aggressive acts. In the in-school suspension room, I see a pack of kids (boys) whose main way of group connection is misbehavior. They cheer each other's presence and rally together in suspension!" Randall practices "the idea of devising a mission—giving a boy a series of tasks or a sacrifice in order to complete a bigger picture." This works for girls as well, he finds, yet he also notices how hungry males are for a direction and a cause, something to which they can attach their own vast resources of love.

My two decades of research has convinced me that the male brain and the masculine approach to life is vastly undernurtured in our culture. Certain male imagery—often very macho—gets a lot of attention. Certain individual men hold great political and social power—highly visible CEOs of companies and politicians. Certain other male models—what have been called the "feminized" males—also crop up in a great deal of discussion. But most boys are developing along a masculine path at neither extreme, and 99.9 percent of males will never be CEO of a company. The "normal Joes" who constitute the vast majority of males have little voice. In this sense, boys and girls are in the same boat: so many girls, too, feeling unloved for their authentic voices.

As we begin now to focus on the problem among our males with similar vigor to the focus on our females, we will see the number of disabled students decrease. Masculinity does not need to act out so much to get noticed and loved, and its neurological weaknesses can be better cared for, especially in early school years, so that many of the weaknesses don't become disorders.

Innovations for Dealing with Behavioral Elements of Special Ed

Let us share some practical innovations from the Missouri schools with you.

CLASS WITHIN A CLASS. Brenda Bock describes a program that works well in her school. She is in the unusual position of having more girls in it this year than boys: "Our team of sixth-grade students is the class-within-a-class learning disability team, with myself as the LD teacher. My caseload is unusual this year, five boys and eight girls. This is my sixteenth year teaching LD, behavior-disordered, or mentally handicapped students. In the past, the boys have always outnumbered the girls. I am happy to see a particular girl, whom you can barely understand, stand in front of our team and give a short speech." Brenda has found that having the LD students within other classes helps to build confidence in taking learning risks.

Anne Walker confirms Brenda's success stories about class within a class, and the use of teams. This year twelve of the three-teacher-team's seventy-six students are on IEPs, and the program handles those numbers well.

SEPARATE-SEX LEARNING.   Once introduced to the idea of separate-sex education in special ed, and once trained in brain differences, many teachers opt for this method. Sara, a teacher at Anderson Alternative Middle School, recalled to us her attendance at single-sex schools. She believes in general in the advantages of this education but finds it particularly applicable at work now: "My single-sex groups work better with each other, get more done, and create fewer distractions."

Shari, also at Anderson, now generally prefers single-sex groups. She works mainly with boys. She sees advantages not only in the academic and behavioral learning process but also in the deep bonds that can form in single-sex classes. She told us about one of her students who was acting out. He told her that he was acting this way because her class was so boring. An hour later, he returned to her room from his next class and asked if he could come back to her class. She asked him why he would want to return since her class was so boring. He said that the other class was even more boring. She feels that he really wanted just to bond with her—be with her—but didn't know how to express that. In her class she felt there were fewer distractions, hence greater ability for him to bond. From that bond came fewer behavioral problems.

The advantages of single-sex classes outlined earlier in the chapter double or triple in special education settings.

CHARACTER EDUCATION. Rita Whertvine has discovered that integrating character education into her special education classes cuts down on behavioral issues. She ritualizes character education into *morning mentoring*, describing in this journal entry how she does it and why:

> Morning mentoring [a set period in the first hour of the day] is an interesting time. One morning they had to write about respect. They could all define it and give examples of how to show it. But there was disrespect shown to each other before they got out of the room. There was pushing and name calling. When I asked how their behavior was different than what they had written, they each blamed the other. So I am increasing this work.
>
> We will focus on one skill a week during mentoring. After the mentoring, the teachers will also try to reinforce the skills during regular classes. The life skill for next week will be honesty. When I talk to the students in the hallway and cafeteria today, I will reinforce how important it is to be honest.

STRUCTURE AND ORDER. Any special ed teacher knows how important structure and order are. Rita told us about the coming of ROTC to her alternative school: "The ROTC program was started in our school—at first the kids did not like it. Now, for the most part, they take it seriously. A male student who tried to commit suicide last year is now a leader in ROTC. The group was also invited to be in the Veteran's Day Parade—they took this very seriously and received many compliments from other schools—they were the only middle school in the parade, and we're an alternative school!"

Rita feels that this program gives the students structure, order, boundaries, and identity. All these she finds especially important for the male students, who make up the lion's share. Given that many of her students are African American boys, Rita believes the ROTC program has the good fortune of having a positive African American role model (the ROTC teacher). Like all of us, Rita has noticed the dearth of positive role models for middle school boys in general and African American boys in particular. She believes some of ROTC's success with these boys lies in this role model's presence, and Rita reported how proud she felt to watch some of her students achieve success in the parade. For some of them, she realized, it was their first real taste of this kind of social success.

The Underachiever as a Special Ed Category

I received an e-mail from a mother of a son who had been diagnosed "gifted" at one time in his school career and "learning disabled" at another He had been an underachiever who clearly possessed immense intellectual ability, but could not, from the mother's point of view, land in a school community that fit him. She wrote:

> I do a lot of networking with other parents like me. I am the president of our local Parents Group for Gifted Children. One of our concerns is that a disproportionate number of boys are underachievers. My sense is that a large part of it is related to instructional approach, especially in middle school. So many gifted boys and learning disabled boys are right-brain dominant, and have difficulty in school. It seems to me, if gifted children who are right-brain dominant have difficulty in school, imagine the difficulty a child of average or below-average intelligence, who is also right-brain dominant, would experience if the curriculum and instruction were not suited to his learning style.

This is a crucial point. There is definitely right-brain dominance in many gifted (and many disabled) kids, and we suspect there is also this link in underachievers. With the vast increase in underachievers—many of them males who tend by natural brain formatting toward right-brain dominance—we hope underachievement becomes a focus of study for researchers in the field of special education, especially in the context of brain patterns. Middle school classrooms are very verbal (meaning, left-brain) places. This simply does not complement many of the brains in the classroom. Throughout history this has been true, but the level of verbal skill now required far surpasses that of a century ago, when so much learning was experiential—on a farm, in a marketplace, in a home environment, in a church activity.

We do not want to say that underachievement is not also caused by depression, learning disabilities, bad time management, excessive time spent with mass media, lack of support for learning at home, and boredom with the whole process of learning—all of which may grow as much from external factors as the child's brain and its lack of fit with the verbal environment. At the same time, underachievement is becoming a great concern for middle school teachers. We suggest brain research as a primary area of inquiry.

Teachers who have worked with underachievers were almost unanimous in telling us that team learning and group work, even pair work, is a crucial step toward raising underachievers' performance, as is continuous and intense contact between the school and home. Teacher-student bonding is also crucial. Some teachers have also had success by increasing the competitive aspects of learning; games, contests, puzzles, and debates motivate some students, especially boys, who are underachieving. Finally, more physical movement and experiential learning, coupled with greater attention to emotional needs, has increased success.

"Mr. Daba": The Power of Bonding

Paula Dee Rogers, a sixth-grade teacher at Ervin Middle School, told us about her experiences with a particularly difficult behavioral problem. Hers is a powerful story we want to share with you.

> I began this year by choosing one boy I would really get to know. I decided this would be a boy who was at risk and would be difficult to get close to. The first day of school, I spotted a boy who had on a shirt with *DABA* written on it. He was in and out of his seat. He made loud comments such as "Shut up," "I don't care," "So?" "So what?" "You don't know nuthin," and "Get outta my business." I decided to observe this boy and see if he was the boy I wanted to try to get close to. Before the day was over, I was calling him "Mr. Daba." He laughed and/or smiled each time I reminded him to be nice, talk softer, or raise his hand, all the while calling him by Mr. Daba instead of his first or last name. He [appeared] to be tough and mean, but seemed to enjoy the attention.

Mr. Daba came to class the next day complaining about being called Mr. Daba, but he smiled every time he said, "That's not my name." I still didn't learn his real name since he seemed to be enjoying the attention he got from his peers when he was called Mr. Daba. The students laughed, but they thought it was a fun game. They were not laughing *at* him.

As the days passed, whenever he acted mad I cautioned him, along with calling him Mr. Daba. He would smile and calm down right away. I learned his name, of course, but stayed with calling him Mr. Daba.

One day he was running around the room when I came into the room. I said, "Mr. Daba" and he sat down.

On another occasion, I worked with Mr. Daba as a partner. He didn't want me as a partner, but he didn't choose a partner within the allotted time, so he was odd man out. That means he was stuck with the teacher. We were giving ideas for our play, each student developing a story line. All were also supposed to discuss the types of characters they wanted to write into their plays. Mr. Daba was reluctant to work. He sat with his arms folded.

I decided to tell him a story about a boy who had run away from home so he could live in the country. He went fishing the first day in the country and he caught three very large trout. He was very excited, but when he turned to tell his father, he remembered that his father wasn't there. He decided he could have fun without any family or friends, falling asleep under a large tree. The next morning, he caught some more fish because he was hungry. Fishing didn't seem as much fun. He began walking along the river to find the nearest town.

With this story beginning in mind, I told Mr. Daba that we could create two additional characters at the next town. Then we could incorporate a mom and dad at the very end when this lost and lonely boy returned to two very joyous parents.

Mr. Daba made little remarks throughout my telling of the story beginning. At first, he acted bored, but as we continued, he began adding details to the story. Then he began mentioning other ways the story line could go. I didn't make him talk, I just began talking and he began jumping in throughout the story. He wasn't as tough as he wanted to appear.

On another day, Mr. Daba came in angry, complaining about another teacher. I asked him what he did wrong. He said, "Nuthin.'" I asked why he appeared to be upset at this other teacher. He said she sent him out of the room. I asked him why she sent him out of the room. He said he didn't know. I told him that saying "I don't know" wouldn't get him back into her room. He finally admitted to "talking." I told him talking in itself did not constitute a problem. He insisted that talking was all he'd done wrong. I asked if he talked at home, and he said, "Yeah."

I asked if he got in trouble for talking at home. He said, "Sometimes." I asked him when he got in trouble for talking at home. He said when he got an attitude. So I asked if he had an attitude with this teacher. He said, "Not until after she got mad at me for talking." I went back to my original question: why would he get in trouble for talking? He began mumbling. I replied that he didn't have to tell me any more if he didn't want to. He said louder, "She was talking. I was talking." From there, he was able to admit he had some responsibility in it.

I believe he has come a long way. He still smiles when I call him Mr. Daba. I believe we have bonded. I also believe that he would be treating me with anger as he does . . . the other teachers if I didn't search for reasons without showing any anger.

A last incident. I heard a student yelling in the hallway. I went out into the hallway in order to see what was going on. Mr. Daba was kicking out, yelling out, and stomping around.

I went over to the pacing Mr. Daba. I introduced myself to him as if he didn't know me. I let him know that it was me. I was hoping that would get through his anger. He stopped pacing, but wouldn't look at me. I asked if he was OK. He wouldn't answer. I said, "If you aren't OK, follow me into my room. If you are OK, stay out here in the hall." I turned around and walked into my room. Mr. Daba followed. He came into my room and stood. I continued teaching. He was allowed to calm down without any pressure. After class, I just looked at him.

He hadn't left the room. I waited expectantly. He finally offered a reason for his outburst. He was able to go back to his teacher and offer an apology since they had both calmed down.

Paula's patience and insight in working with "Mr. Daba" are inspiring to all of us who have students we initially believe no one can get through to. Paula never gave up on the idea that the key to helping a child is to bond. Her hard work was rewarded by the small, everyday successes of guiding this child toward incremental improvements that, taken individually, might not seem like much; yet, taken as a whole, they may mean the difference between a child who is lost and one who comes to love learning.

The Ultimate Middle School Classroom for Both Boys and Girls

In middle school and high school, our vigilance about making sure classrooms serve the hidden needs of boys and girls is one of our primary concerns, even if we never think it aloud. Here is a summary of key ways to ensure a school classroom that is friendly to early adolescent learners of both genders.

For the Boys

- Make sure every middle school teacher is trained in male hormonal and adolescent brain development.
- Use separate-sex groups and classes whenever possible.
- Increase group work and pair work.
- Increase character education and absorb it into *all* classes.
- Have high expectations, both in academic areas and in social maturity.
- Talk about and model "heroic" behavior, ideas, and stories that show adolescents what it means to truly "be a man,"

that is, an adult male who is essential to his community's care and development.

- Offer boys rite-of-passage experiences.
- Provide boys with quick tension-release strategies, both within and outside the classroom.
- Teach and integrate emotional literacy and emotional development curricula in *all* courses, not just human growth and development class.
- Teach sexual ethics curricula in all applicable courses, including gym (where boys, especially after physical movement, can often be honest and attentive about links between emotional and sexual feelings).
- Teach media literacy in all applicable courses, and help train parents to know the effects of prolonged exposure to video games and television on the developing brain of the adolescent child.
- Carry out consistently applied discipline systems in all classes, with teachers and administrators working as a discipline team, rather than as isolated authorities.
- Bring in mentors from the community for every young person who needs one, and match every middle school student who is capable with an elementary or preschool student; consider making mentoring a homework assignment.

For the Girls

- Use separate-sex groups and classes whenever possible.
- Call on young men and women equally in class, when possible; if a few kids dominate—often a few attention-seeking boys—discuss with the whole class what is happening, and allow the class to help develop solutions.
- Teach all subjects with the use of field trips, physical movement, and multisensory strategies.

- Be very careful about technology; use fairness, being aware that girls need computer time equal to that given to spatially prone boys.
- Make sure every girl has at least one female role model in the school to bond with and look up to.
- Offer girls rite-of-passage experiences.
- Give girls hands-on methods for learning math.
- Teach character education with universal principles of character; also pay attention to what a girl might mean by good character, and how this might be similar to or different from what boys might mean by it.
- Have high expectations, both in academic areas and also for social maturity.
- Bring in mentors from the community for every young person who needs one, and match every middle school student who is capable with an elementary or preschool student; consider making mentoring a homework assignment.

Tips for Parents

- Stay *very* involved in the life of middle schoolers; this includes attending parent-teacher conferences, volunteering, mentoring, and conducting advocacy for and with the school.
- Carry out rites of passage at home, within the extended family and its spiritual community, and with the school.
- Gain training in all aspects of adolescent biological development, especially brain and gender material, to aid the middle schooler's gender-based learning experiences.
- Teach empathy nurturance through example, didactic conversation, and story.
- Become familiar with aggression nurturance, and help direct it in early adolescents so as to increase strength, focus, attentiveness, and hierarchical success.

- Give special attention to alternative strategies for those girls and boys who don't fit the gender type for their age group or class.
- Provide consistent discipline, especially including rewards and consequences for all actions.
- Instill constant character development, in liaison with the school.
- Help the child balance sedentary (computer and study) activities with active (sport and athletic) ones so as to maximize brain development.
- Watch the children's carbohydrate and other food intake carefully, on the assumption that whatever they take in affects pubescent physical and brain development; pay special attention to junk foods and sugars.
- Develop and consistently apply a media plan with the early-adolescent child.
- Offer regular training on sexual ethics and social intimacy.
- Spend more time with the child than he or she seems to ask for, especially in intergenerational pairs (special mother-child time, special father-child time, special grandparent-child time, and so on).
- Advocate for smaller middle school classrooms, and above all for separate-sex education in middle school.

Once when I was doing a middle school training recently in a school district, a teacher handed to everyone a small slip of paper. On it was written: "You can't get to the mountaintop if you don't climb." She said she had spent the first two days of class with her eighth-graders making a collage with this saying at the top. Every student had put something on. Some brought photos; some brought pictures cut out of magazines; and others did their own artwork, both written and visual. The theme of everyone's offering had to be the theme of this quote.

"Quite often during a school year," she confided, "I don't just repeat the theme to students, I say it to myself, to give myself inspiration through the hard days. To me, being a middle school teacher is like going to the mountaintop—what's up there is probably well worth the climb, but I don't think I ever quite get there. The year is over, the kids move on to high school, and I have to just be proud that I made the climb with them."

Middle school can be very much a difficult journey, especially for certain classrooms and teachers. If each of us could think back to our own middle school years, we would certainly remember that the sixth, seventh, eighth, or ninth grade (or more than one!) was very difficult indeed. Middle school lives up quite accurately to its name. We feel we are in the middle of so many developmental challenges.

Brain-based research and brain-based gender research are of particular interest to middle schools because children at this age are so much in their bodies and so much in their minds. Every moment, we are dealing with some sort of biological energy. The teachers in our Missouri research found that the more deeply schools explore available knowledge about the *nature* of our adolescent students, the less difficult the climb becomes.

6

The Ultimate High School
Classroom

High school can make or break us. It seems like life depends on how
we do in high school.

—CARRIE, NINETEEN, RECENT HIGH SCHOOL GRADUATE

IN A FOCUS GROUP OF RECENT HIGH SCHOOL GRADUATES, WE ASKED
for recollections and suggestions for high school teachers and high
school culture in general. Terry, a very poised young man of nineteen,
said: "I lived in Japan for two years and there the teachers are considered like doctors or very high level government officials. They're respected. I came back to the United States for ninth grade and was
amazed at how the teachers were treated, especially by the guys. After a
while I fell in with some guys who were always dissing teachers. I'm
ashamed of myself now. I wish my friends and I paid more respect. I
think everyone would learn better if we respected teachers like they do
in Japan."

Jan, a young woman of eighteen, said, "I remember a math teacher,
Mr. Velt. He was really wealthy and didn't need to teach but he did so
because he wanted to give something to the next generation. We respected him because it got around, you know, that he didn't have to be
here. He did it because he cared. And he cared about all of us, not just

the boys. He was really into teaching, really good at it. We had to do something in Calc II and I remember he brought in an old song, and lip synced it. I don't remember the song, but I remember we laughed and we learned. He really got into our minds, you know."

Many of the recent graduates talked about good high school teachers as those who, in Jan's words, got into their minds, and bad ones as those who didn't. Some of the students said their gender had no real influence on their high school learning experience, but the majority felt it had a great deal to do with it. The idea of the teacher "getting into our minds" was not just "teaching the student's growing brain," but also the young woman's or young man's. As one twenty-year-old woman reminisced:

> We were girls and boys in high school trying to be women and men. The two teachers I respect most now, Mr. Cantlyn and Ms. Sylvester, knew how to talk to us as women and men, not just kids. Mr. Cantlyn, our chem teacher, was popular with a lot of the guys. He talked their talk. Ms. Sylvester, who taught English, was a great role model for us girls. Until I just started learning about how boys and girls think differently, I didn't think of them in this way. But now I see why the boys went for Mr. Cantlyn and the girls were really into Ms. Sylvester. We were looking for help with chemistry and English, sure, but also we were looking for help with how to relate to the other sex. I think boy/girl stuff is really the most popular course in high school!

In brain-based and gender literature, high school is usually treated as a lesser subject because so much of a student's learning pattern has been set in middle, elementary, and preschool. Although it's true that the high school student is "mostly formed," it is also true that he or she is not at all finished. High school is a time of refinement for all students, in both brain and gender development.

In the brain, for instance, myelination of cells continues through the early college years. Development in the prefrontal cortex continues at least till the young person is of college age, female prefrontal growth moving a little more quickly than male. For the physical or psychological late-maturer (in both body and mind), the first two years of high school are developmental years like middle school. These students are especially tender. For nearly all high school students, the last two years of high school are when intense mentoring in "gender symbiosis" (how females and males can relate in society harmoniously) is required.

A great deal of what we've said about middle school learning carries forward to high school in this chapter, but we also make many new discoveries.

Bonding and Attachment

We generally use the terms *bonding* and *attachment* for young children, but brain-based research shows us that to limit these needs to early or even middle childhood is to rob our growing children. The brain is still growing in adolescence; it needs bonding and attachment from caregivers to grow, and as before, the primary intergenerational bonding groups for the growing brain are family (parents, extended family, and nonblood kin) and educators.

It goes without saying that by high school, peer bonding groups have an even more profound effect on brain development than they did when the child was, say, seven years old. The seven-year-old relied mainly on adults for brain stimulation; the seventeen-year-old relies heavily on peer interactions. Nonetheless, this same adolescent still relies—more than perhaps we've admitted for some years now—on our parenting and educational models.

Patricia Henley recalls:

> It's often true that the teachers whom students credit later with having a major influence on their lives are high school teachers. I not only credit one of my high school teachers with whatever success I have made of my life, I also sometimes think of the high school teacher who was very nearly responsible for what easily could have been my downfall.
>
> I had a high school English teacher who consistently found promise in me. She seemed to understand that I did not respond well to

negative criticism and consistently looked for ways to make positive remarks. It was fairly common for her to say, "I really liked the way you described the main character in your essay. Perhaps, you could use some of the same kind of words and length to describe the plot of the story, as well." She knew that if she said I had done a poor job of describing the plot of the story before finding something positive she could say that I would inwardly chastise myself for not being able to do the work well. Moreover, I would never have spent the time I did spend rewriting the description of the plot. While I think boys and girls both were hypersensitive like me, I was very "female" in the way I reacted to criticism. This teacher seemed to sense my and some of the other girls' vulnerability.

Patricia poignantly remembers another teacher:

Another high school teacher of mine consistently found fault with my work, my behavior, and even my appearance. She didn't have a very insightful read on me as a girl, or as an individual. I think the more she criticized me, the more I became the "bad" person she expected me to be. Finally, an event occurred which almost resulted in my being re-moved from school. After some discussion about the incorrect use of a verb and my poor accent (foreign language class), she told me I was "stupid." I responded by throwing down my book and walking out of class. Only because my dad brought me back to school and visited at length with the principal was I allowed to reenter school.

This teacher did not support me, as a girl, in taking risks. She wanted me in a little feminine box. Interesting to me in retrospect is the fact that she was far less hard on the boys. Their risks were all right to her, and she supported them.

Gender does not have everything to do with bonding and learning in high school, but our research shows us that it has more to do than we may admit. Patricia's experiences are not uncommon; she was not appreciated when she stepped out of a box. In the language of bonding, we would say that the teacher withheld love and attachment because

Patricia was not "the girl she wanted her to be." The teacher who saw promise in Patricia became a mentor to her.

How we learn is not always dependent on how we feel about our teachers, but just as often, it is. Studies show us that memory, for instance, is enhanced if an adolescent learner feels emotionally cared for by the instructor. We do not often use the language of love when speaking of high school instruction, yet what the adolescent's brain wants from instructors is myriad kinds of love, not just instruction. The adolescent's learning brain receives that love in various forms of nurturance, many of which are useful when attention is paid to gender.

Communication and Conflict Resolution

High school is a time when students need very badly to look good in front of their peers. According to Gail, a Hickman Mills teacher, "If you call a boy down in front of his peers, his posse, his homies, you need to be prepared for the war." That is certainly true of girls, too. Studies show us that when a teacher and student enter a conflict, the boy tends to use a louder voice and fewer words, while the girl favors more words. The intention of the hurt student, whether male or female, is the same: to return the self to a position of respect in the face of lowered peer respect, and to do so by attempting to dominate or defy the instructor, who is perceived as the betrayer of the respect and the bond.

When ego conflicts emerge between teacher and student for which the teacher can apologize, sometimes eliciting a student apology, an immense teaching moment occurs. This is especially true if the teacher has the trust and respect of the students. If the teacher does not, increased teaching training and bonding activities are important. In previous chapters we have looked at numerous possibilities for bonding activities. One that has been used by some high schools is the ropes course. Both in wilderness and urban settings, trained ropes-course supervisors help build student-and-teacher teams through a combination of exercises on ropes and poles and group-trust rituals (Chapter Five).

When conflicts emerge between students, peer mediation is very useful. This is a mentored program in which students are selected and trained to become mediators in other students' conflicts. Many high schools in our Missouri research have had success with it.

THE STORY OF GERALD. Gerald transferred to Washington High School from a high school out of state. He didn't want to move from his previous city of residence and brought an attitude with him to Missouri. From the time he enrolled, the assistant principal noted that he was argumentative and apparently looking for reasons to get into conflict even if none was obvious. But the assistant principal also noticed that Gerald was intelligent and could be an effective leader. This assistant principal told us, "He was like many young high school males who have to be tough and defiant to try to fit in."

The assistant principal was a person of vision who had become intrigued, in brain-based training, with adolescent male biology—especially the natural internal conflict between a high level of male aggression and the equally high need in males to develop self-management of that aggression. He decided to try something with Gerald: he chose to trust his potential rather than disregard him because of his presenting attitude. The assistant principal asked the counselor who was in charge of the school's peer-mediation program to consider Gerald for peer-mediation training.

Although the process was not without its ups and downs, Gerald did become a successful mediator. We might say, using the language of brain science, he learned to balance the abilities in the top of the brain (facilitating safety and relational harmony to promote the self) with those in the middle and lower brain (use of aggression and ego to promote the self). The peer-mediation sponsor collected information from Gerald's teachers that indicated he was increasingly using his conflict-resolution skills in many settings, not just in mediation. The assistant principal knew that his plan had been successful when Gerald's mother reported that the boy was serving as both a facilitator and a mentor for successful conflict resolution at home.

As a result of Gerald's abilities in the area of conflict resolution, he ultimately emerged as a leader with positive skills he could model for other students. He balanced his own brain functions—thereby achieving one of the primary directives of adolescence. Gerald saw that he had an outlet to use his skills, and he felt respected. This undoubtedly contributed to his success in other classes. His behavior improved, as well. He continued to spend time with the counselor who sponsored the peer-mediation program, gaining new skills, a new attitude, a new mission, and also a new mentor.

In Toledo, Ohio, the Catholic high schools practice a similar six-step peer-mediation process, led in part by Frank DiLallo, of Catholic Youth and School Services. Frank has reported amazing results: "The students [who are] engaged in peer mediation not only act better and live better, but they even look forward to participating." In his program, high school students go into the feeder middle schools and train sixth through eighth graders in peer mediation. While training the younger students, they mediate middle school conflicts, and the middle schoolers in turn gain training to help mediate conflicts among younger children. Through the feeder school interactions, early bonds form that carry through later grades. Frank has found this program to be of great value for both girls and boys. The girls, he told us, often use highly verbal strategies and the boys few words, but the outcome is equally powerful for both.

The Art of Mentoring

Because of training in brain-based attachment research, Anthony, a music teacher, decided to spend more time with students he believed needed some additional teacher support and mentoring. Many of these were young men who had neither father nor mentor. One of the ways Anthony began to let students know he was interested in them and their success was to use some of his planning time to visit other classes these students were attending. He reported that the visits really made an impression on students, and before he knew it, Anthony became known as a mentor.

On one occasion, a colleague reported to Anthony that one of her students was disrupting class. Anthony visited with the student. The student at first seemed recalcitrant and wanted to know what business it was of his. Anthony responded that he was concerned that this student be successful in all his classes. Anthony and the student talked for some time. Later, the teacher who had been having trouble with the student informed Anthony that his discussion with the student resulted in improvement. The student had bonded with Anthony and would listen to him. Even though he was at first oppositional toward his mentor, he ended up restabilizing.

Mentoring is a an art for which many teachers and parents have natural skills, and in which every adult can be trained. But "teachers" are not necessarily mentors. A teacher instructs numerous students in information and skill building. A mentor bonds with a group of students, is a primary role model, and treats them as a grandparent or aunt or uncle would, pushing them, prodding them, listening to them, and—only when appropriate—letting them go.

Big Brothers Big Sisters, which has a well-known family-mentoring process, is less renowned for its school-based mentoring. If a school is looking for a model for teaching the art of mentoring, the local Big Brothers Big Sisters agency is always available. High school students are matched with elementary students under the tutorship of adults.

In Michigan there is an exemplary mentoring program called KUDOS, sponsored by Phi Delta Kappa, a professional service organization of African American educators. Students from ninth to twelfth grade who maintain a 2.0 GPA are eligible. The Kudos club meets weekly for ten months, beginning in September and ending in June. The group leader, an adult, facilitates activities that build social and academic skills, character development discussions, and recreational opportunities. John Rhymes, the principal of Flint (Michigan) Elementary School, is a Kudos facilitator who has led young people through personal issues as simple as setting goals and as complex as sexual responsibility.

Miami-based reporter Leonard Pitts recently shared the story of one Jermaine Barnes, who was "trouble-prone, sullen and sometimes violent, shipped off to a last-chance school for bad kids. Jermaine was so difficult that his new teachers were given a two-word warning: 'He's hell.' "

Art teacher Janis Klein-Young became his mentor. It happened by accident. She gave him a picture of wildflowers cut from a magazine and asked him to paint them. He turned out to have immense talent (his art sells now). Jermaine is still a problem, and still behind—eighteen years old and only in tenth grade. But he has been and is being mentored, and his life—and therefore the life of his classmates and community—is rewarded with less hell and more stability.

A number of mentors are receiving clear guidance on how to mentor and what to mentor by using an "assets inventory," which we highly recommend. H. Stephen Glenn, an innovator and founder of Capabilities, Inc., has authored *Skills for Adolescence*; he is a good resource for anyone struggling to ground the art of mentoring in specific asset-building activities and theories.

Peer Leadership, Not Peer Pressure

A key asset is leadership; one bold new innovation in high school education is the peer-leadership program. This innovation is partially born of concern in the medical community, which has recently found in brain-based research an understanding of the neurological and psychosocial need to reduce student stress and increase psychological health. As we have been discussing in earlier chapters, teachers have long noted how difficult it is for students to learn and maintain behavioral standards when under intense emotional stress. Studies on adolescents have confirmed teachers' instincts.

Adrian Raine's studies at the University of Southern California are an example. He has recorded how fifteen-year-olds' heart rates, EEGs (a measure of brain activity), and other internal stress monitors change in response to stressors. New technology makes it possible to measure increased heart rate, increased activity to certain parts of the brain, and decreased activity to others. The picture we gain from all this is of students feeling pressure on all fronts and needing continuous support and assistance in order to "learn through" the pressure. Peer-leadership programs help students support each other so as to diminish education-numbing stresses that lead to high-risk behavior, violence, and dropping out of school.

The Medical Foundation, an organization specializing in health training innovations, has devised peer-leadership programs that schools

ıunities can access through the foundation, in Boston. Schools
ıers, as well as students, can be trained in this model for learn-
ion making, conflict resolution, negotiation, and even confi-
oral presentation. Public schools in Boston are using this
ınd experiencing, in trainer Laurie Jo Wallace's words, "a
l climate: young people are heard better on public health issues
ool reform. Pressures and stresses are decreasing."

line Systems

An immense stressor on both high school teachers and students is lack
of discipline. Teacher-student and peer bonds can be built or broken by
discipline issues in the classroom and on school grounds. High school
is similar to middle school in this way, though there is generally more
maturity and a somewhat less serious breakdown of discipline.

Much of what we've said in earlier chapters is applicable to high
school discipline. For it to be the rule in the ultimate classroom, rather
than hit-and-miss, high school students need:

- A firm and loving teacher, who genuinely cares about each student and shows it
- One who sets strict rules and reinforces them verbally and non-verbally
- One who sets expectations high and helps each student rise to meet them
- A classroom environment that provides equal educational and technological opportunity to every student
- A team-learning environment where students' emotional stress management is an integral part of the learning process
- Openness to discipline innovations as needed—as opposed to a single set of strategies that may, in some cases, just not work
- Support from other teachers and administration as needed for giving help to problem students
- Conflict-resolution standards and practices that, when needed, take precedent over academic learning

- Access to alternative education when a student needs it
- Consistent support for discipline from home and family
- A schoolwide character-education program
- Mandatory service programs

Discipline of the high school student is a holistic process of adulthood maturation. It is crucial to the making of an adult. The high school student's brain craves discipline as much as it craves free individual expression. High school is the last chance to develop the limits and self-management (self-discipline) the mind needs to succeed in the adult world.

USING DISCIPLINE COUNCILS. In the ultimate school, discipline councils, made up of students and teachers (and, at times, an administrator and a parent representative), become part of the fabric of the school discipline system. At a number of schools, we have seen discipline councils made up of ten or more students and three or more faculty.

In this model, offenses at the school are promulgated as level one, two, or three, depending on severity. Level one offenses are corrected on the spot by a teacher, level two offenses may go to the vice principal or other disciplinarian, but level three offenses—such as hazing, vandalism, cheating, repeated failure to attend class, recurrent defiance of authority—go before the council. The student's conduct is analyzed, and all the people involved in an incident—including teachers—find their behavior scrutinized. Generally the student is required by a vote of peers to make redress (and is sometimes suspended). Occasionally a teacher's behavior is found wanting and the incident is seen in this light. St. Mark's School of Texas has a model discipline council in place and practices the three-level discipline system very effectively, providing a model for all schools.

Healthy brain development requires a healthy team environment, which in turn requires a clear and well-enforced discipline system. Peer mediation, peer conflict resolution, and peer-driven discipline councils are good innovations for making more of the responsibility for self-discipline a peer-directed experience, while ensuring that adults supervise and teach methodology and care of the growing child.

Character Education and Service Projects

School and communitywide processes for character education have been described in previous chapters. As students approach adulthood, these character-education traits continue to be important in building strong character in both boys and girls. Our youth not only benefit from character education but welcome it and its challenges.

Fr. John Sanders, headmaster of St. Augustine's High School in San Diego, recently discussed some of his school's policies: "We have forty-eight rules in the handbook, random drug testing every eight to ten days, and one hundred hours of mandatory community service a year. The kids and parents know these things are not impositions—they are part of youth education."

When I randomly polled students at St. Augustine's, especially about the drug testing, I generally heard positive feedback. One young man said: "Sometimes I meet up with some guys from other schools who do a little weed and I think, 'Can I get away with it?' But I know I can't. I'm glad the school has the policy. It keeps me healthy." Adolescents, especially adolescent males, are set up for high-risk behavior and beg the community to impose limits. As high-risk behavior increases among our adolescent girls—especially regarding drugs and alcohol—rules of this kind are good for all teens. Drug testing in public schools cannot (at present and in most places) survive court challenges. But we believe it is possible, after perhaps a decade or more of character education in core curricula in public schools, that it may well survive challenges in the future.

Many schools, like St. Augustine's in the private sector and some Chicago and Missouri schools in the public, require some form of "service" as a prerequisite for graduation from high school as a part of their character-education program. This service component has been challenged by critics who say that students fulfill this requirement only because something is required of them, not because they really want to perform a service for their communities. Motivation is certainly an element of service, but it is not the only one. The service itself still teaches the reluctant.

This was true for John, a sixteen-year-old Missouri high school student who performed his community service according to how he could best fit his service activity into his schedule. He dutifully counted his hours so that he could document them and complete the requirement. This was his choice, and inasmuch as he fulfilled the requirements, he was credited and benefited from the experience.

Shelley, seventeen, went to a Missouri high school where she had a homeroom arrangement. In her homeroom, students discussed options for suggested community service possibilities. Shelley's grandmother was in a nursing home. Although she managed to visit her grandmother a couple of times a year, she knew that probably wasn't enough. She shared this information with her homeroom class, and the teacher helped her design a service program of work that met her schedule and fit into the area of service in which she wanted to participate: longer hours of nursing home volunteer time. Her community service project really meant something to her, she felt she learned a great deal about the nursing home situation, and she felt good about what she was able to accomplish. In fact, the time she spent in her project exceeded her required hours of service, and she was happy to donate her time.

We highly recommend mandatory service hours for all high school students for all years.

Structural Innovations

Many of the structural innovations suggested in earlier chapters, especially the preceding one on middle school, can apply to high school. Let us look at some other elements that may call for innovation in high school.

Class and School Size

We consistently read and hear about the problems associated with large schools and large class size. Although in America we sometimes think we are alone in these worries, other industrial countries share our problems. Recently in France, hundreds of thousands of high school students took to the streets to protest large class size. The situation there has gotten so difficult that education minister Claude Allegre unveiled a plan for high school reform that must be carried out within months, not years.

It goes without saying that the smaller the class size the higher the potential for deep bonding with peers and with teachers, and the lower the potential for discipline problems. Especially in early to middle adolescence, discipline is more easily accomplished if the potentially undisciplined student can't hide in a big school (or even a big classroom). In neurological terms, the seriously undisciplined student is often the bored and underachieving student who has decided to act out in order to call attention to his or her unstimulated brain growth. In smaller classrooms and schools, this student need not act out so severely to be noticed. The teacher and his peers—to the extent they are trained to be helpful—tend to see the problem a priori, before the problem emerges.

Furthermore, the daily sense of general classroom discipline is often dependent on everyone in the class being able to shine and excel at some moment. True, a well-disciplined classroom is led by an able adult leader, but it also consists of student learners who feel they get a chance to succeed. Especially during puberty (in which males must learn to manage themselves in the face of testosterone, the aggression and dominance hormone), boys are likely to show more extreme behaviors of acting out (undisciplined behavior) and opting out (dropping out of class and school) than do females.

For the particular care of boys, it's especially important to lower class size to one teacher for twenty to twenty-five students, especially in classes that require a great deal of discussion (English and social studies classes, for instance). Many of the boys feel inept at their verbal skills in comparison to higher-alpha males and adept females. The lower the class size, the easier for the lower-verbal males to compete and cooperate in the group.

Regarding care of girls, it is especially important to reduce size in classes that require high spatial and abstract intellect (physics, for example). Lower-spatial girls often recede and lose personal power in an environment where they feel less capable and are dominated by a few high-abstract girls and many high-abstract, loud boys. Lower class size allows these girls more latitude to find their voice and place.

What if small class size is not possible? Regarding this case (and even if it is possible), Patricia Henley draws upon her thirty years in all aspects of school life, from teacher to district superintendent, to say that

> a teamlike atmosphere is the key in whatever the class size. A teamlike atmosphere can be achieved even in large schools. The Hickman Mills Middle Schools have been organized with this in mind. Even though these schools have large populations of students, teams of teachers are assigned to work with teams of students. These students feel the teachers have a special interest in them, and they get to know their teachers and the students within their teams very well. It is essential that students feel that they have a group to which they can relate at the high school level. Some high schools have begun addressing this need through home rooms where students have an opportunity to deal with issues, whether academic or social, through instruction and discussion. These home rooms are small enough in [population] for all students to interact on more than a superficial level.

We suggest homerooms for all high schools, even through senior year. The brain learns best in a group or team that cares. In large schools, lowering class size may not be possible, but creating homerooms is, along with use of team teaching (as we've described it earlier) in high school classrooms.

Uniforms

Both boys and girls dress in ways that we might consider inappropriate for developing a cohesive team-learning environment. Girls' dress is often sexually provocative (high skirts, low-cut blouses), and boys routinely dress toward dominance strategies (gang or hip hop, faking gang affiliations in some cases, or displaying genuine affiliations in others).

It is natural for adolescents to seek identity-attention ("This is who I am; pay attention!") and use clothing for individuation ("I'm an individual and can take care of myself"), dominance ("I demand respect and can outcompete"), and mating strategies ("Look at how cool I am; you should like me"). The more individualizing, competitive, and romance-oriented the culture—and ours is one of the most intense at pushing children to seek individual expression, rebel, compete, and sexualize early—the more the adolescent uses the colors of clothing, hairstyle, tattooing and jewelry styles, and other personal innovations to call attention to growing sexual, social, and personal identity.

If this individualizing, dominance, and mating behavior hits a critical mass in high school adolescent culture, the school can suffer. Academic team learning and psychosocial maturity enhancement are what high school is really supposed to be about, not "I'm better than you," or "I don't care about anyone else," or "I came to high school to get laid." We all know this, but we are afraid of crushing students' individuality and so we are likely to avoid dealing with this whole panoply of issues.

There is a better way of looking at all this, and brain-based research helps us. From the viewpoint of the developing brain, learning and maturity are most important; thus any critical mass of other behaviors that impedes the brain's ability to increase knowledge of social and academic technologies that enhance success and personal maturity must be made a lower priority. The issue of "students' rights" is relatively low on the priority list because we come to realize that students' rights are better safeguarded by the protection of solid learning and maturity enhancement than by superficial attention to individualizing, dominance, and mating behaviors.

Many schools are using school uniforms as a way of ensuring true students' rights and letting go of superficial ones. Some schools require all-out uniforms for all students; others simply enforce dress codes. Generally, jeans, T-shirts, and any gang or hip hop clothing are disallowed in dress codes. Enforcement is firm. A first offense may be let go with a warning—and an increase in individual and schoolwide promulgation of the new code. A second offense may lead to a minor infraction notice. But a third offense can lead to a one-day suspension.

In Ashland, Oregon, peek-a-boo clothing (that is, female low-cut attire) is not allowed. Principal Julie Reynolds explains, "Things you can see through or [that] don't leave much to imagination—that's been the greatest concern among teachers and kids. One student told me, 'I don't know where to look when I'm working with my lab partner. At the ceiling?'"

Pius X High School in Lincoln, Nebraska, has gone further than dress codes; it requires uniforms. Principal Tom Seib reports: "A lot of people are actually excited about it. It's actually been a very positive thing." The move to uniforms followed a period of dress codes that were hard to enforce. For instance, the no-jeans, no-T-shirts policy just wasn't enforceable without a great deal of interruption in learning. The school, like many others around the country, weighed risks and benefits and ended up opting for all-out uniforms.

We suggest at least a dress code for all schools. If after a year of dress code use enforcement becomes tedious, uniforms can become the policy. Some students and even some parents will object to clothing policies. Andrea, a senior at Pius, was unhappy with the dress code. "High school should prepare you for college," she argued. "Wearing uniforms doesn't prepare you for college." Other student objections generally range from "lack of individuality" to "You don't trust us." It is important to hold an assembly to explain the reasons for a policy, as well as promulgate it in homeroom, and integrate it into discussion in a class like social studies.

Fitting this kind of policy into character-education curricula is also helpful. In the end, students manage to adapt to dress codes and often find the policy to be a new way of bonding at school. Laurie Behne, a parent of a high school girl and a teacher for sixteen years, said, "Putting on the uniform isn't going to make or break who [students] are, inside. But putting on a uniform in a way represents putting on a commitment to your school. It says, 'I support Pius.'"

Especially in a school that is losing males to interruptive dominance behavior and females to overly sexualized self-image, and especially in a class wherein sexual and romantic selection of mates becomes as important as learning, uniforms can be a panacea. We highly recommend it for high school, and hope schools will try it for earlier grades as well.

We hope also that high school teachers and innovators think of the issue of dress codes and uniforms as a kind of lens on other issues. Whenever teachers and administrators brainstorm school policies, we hope they will conclude on the side of protecting bonding and maturity of higher-order brain development (that is, academic and social learning in the top of the brain) for both males and females, rather than protection of student rights of individuality, dominance, and mating behavior. In making this distinction, they will notice that adolescence is a different developmental time for the brain than, say, late elementary school, in this specific way: for the most part, especially before puberty, great variety of stimulation is the best brain food (variety enhanced, that is, by focus). As puberty hits, and as abstract cognitive development explodes in the developing brain (around eleven to sixteen), the brain self-generates variety at an exponential rate and asks the defining culture to help it limit that variety when the variety overwhelms development. Uniforms and other structural innovations that temper external psychosocial variety are immensely helpful to the adolescent brain in a paradoxical way that is nevertheless similar to the effect of variety in the early years of life.

Perhaps it is also helpful to realize that, historically, adolescent individuality has been a privilege and not a right. Our ancestors were raised and educated in groups that learned respect for the group first and respect for the individual second. We have always put dominance behavior lower on the maturity index than group and team development. We have always treated sexual mating as a private matter. From a brain-based standpoint, we've kept these limits on adolescents in order to protect healthy development of the widest variety of brain systems. We don't want only the dominant brains to flourish; we don't want individuals to put themselves above the group; we don't want promiscuous mating to distract healthy social development for all. In the last generation or two, our high schools have experimented with freer adolescent development than was traditional, and it has been fruitful. But limits are innovative too, especially as the modern brain strives to manage all the social technologies it now confronts so overwhelmingly.

Time and Time-of-Day Innovations

A great deal of wonderful brain-based research has come out recently regarding teen sleep and waking habits, and the relationship between these sleep cycles and learning. The National Academy of Science recently held a forum to deliberate on the best time-of-day innovations for teaching teens. The forum noted that a generation ago, high school starting times ranged from about 7:45 A.M. to 8:15 A.M. The average is now from 7:15 A.M. to 7:45 A.M. Most midteens need nine hours of sleep a night. Earlier starting times are cutting down on this sleep.

Michele Kipke, director of the academy's Board of Children, Youth, and Families, put it bluntly: "Sleep experts feel strongly that high school timings are out of sync with the natural circadian rhythms of adolescents." Our research corroborates this finding. Teachers constantly tell us how difficult it is to teach teens in the early morning, how out-of-rhythm so many teens become for a few hours in the morning, and how difficult the already-tough teaching areas become (as with the verbals for many boys and the high math and physics for many girls). William Dement, director of the Sleep Disorders Center of Stanford University and a sleep researcher for forty-eight years, says bluntly: "Since the amount of sleep a student gets correlates strongly with academic performance and social behavior, it is important for high schools to have later start times." Some school districts are already heeding this advice; we hope that soon all will do so.

Detractors from this brain-based research might say, "It's not the school's fault that the kid doesn't sleep enough. The parents should make them go to bed earlier." Our response: we must realize that the adolescent stays up later, *by nature,* than he or she did earlier in life. One primary reason is hormonal self-management: the adolescent's circadian cycle is dominated during these years by the need to learn management of personal energy—hormones and brain chemicals that are just now assaulting the system. A second reason is structural brain development itself. Certain parts of the brain—especially in the limbic system and prefrontal areas—are experiencing accelerated growth that is natural to late evening. Forcing the adolescent to go to sleep is not only a bad battle to pick (among the many battles adults have to pick with their adolescent children) but in most cases an unnatural solution imposed on a child to fix a problem in a social structure. As schools start later, they find increased learning and fewer discipline problems. We encourage all schools to innovate in this direction.

Another time-of-day innovation schools can try has to do with the timing of certain subjects during the school day. Spatial learning is, for instance, easier when the testosterone level is high, as at midmorning. This is a good time for math learning. Verbal learning can improve with estrogen increases. Though these are less diurnally cyclic than testosterone, teachers can certainly watch when girls' minds seem "electric" with learning; they may be seeing estrogen surges in the girls' bodies. In coming years, research into these hormonal-cycle learning advantages should expand. At a minimum, band and art—which involve movement and whole-brain activity—should be taught early in the day, as they stimulate the sleepy brain by making demands on the body.

On a final note, extending school hours and holding Saturday classes (six days a week) should be considered if a high school is thinking about innovations for handling greater demand from the larger culture for more student learning and better use of student leisure time. Certainly for students with learning or behavioral problems, going to school on Saturday and extending school hours should be considered. The more time the brain spends in learning and practicing its knowledge, the greater the chance of learning success. Schools are already increasing tutorial and teaching time on Saturday. Soon, successful results will be demonstrable.

The Innovations Students Are Asking for

A two-day student-teacher "summit" (the Mead Education Summit) was recently held in which hundreds of high school students brainstormed their most important requests of our school systems. They genuinely touched the educators present, and there were few surprises. Students want what the brain wants for good learning. This is what most affected us as we analyzed the results:

- At the top of the students' list was *smaller class size.* Students instinctively know their need for closer bonds and team learning environments.

- Students want more emphasis on *technology.* Especially in the present competitive technological marketplace, high school students need more access and learning. High school is the perfect time to emphasize the influence of external technologies on the brain.

- Students need our support of *AP and honors* classes. They want greater options to increase learning at the highest levels, especially those that prepare them for college.

- *Focus on the arts.* This category may surprise some administrators and teachers. Students at the summit felt that a great deal of emphasis went to sports and too little to band, drama, pottery, painting, choir, photography, and other arts. Both male and female students instinctively understand the importance of these brain-expanding, interactive learning forms. There may be a stereotype in our culture that only girls want an arts focus, but adolescent boys supported this category at the summit. Our own research has shown us that throughout K–12, boys want and need drama and other arts. A father told us about his sixteen-year-old son and the school setup in Oakland, California. His son wanted to do football, track, and wrestling—he was a big, high-testosterone male—but also was musically talented and wanted to focus on French horn. This particular school appreciated the fact that, more often than we realize, a high-testosterone child, male or female, may also be musically and or spatially talented as well. Hence the school taught band in the morning rather than in the afternoon, when it might compete with athletic practice.

- *More field trips.* Both adolescent boys and girls were adamant in wanting more field trips, especially for science learning. Planetariums, zoos, doctors' offices, government agencies—whatever the lesson, the students want to experience it in the world. They know their brains learn better when the learning takes place in space-and-time stimulants that mirror the lesson. Field trips are essential, we feel, in helping those girls who may not abstract the scientific material as well as some science-dominant males.

Counterinnovations

Brain-based research is showing us that we may have to be counterinnovative as well as proactively innovative in today's high school. This means throwing out some practices that were once thought, for political or other reasons, to be innovative not so very long ago. As school districts focus next on what shall be deemed innovative, we hope that brain-based reasoning (including hormonal assessments) are considered as important as any political end. We believe this was not the case when schools were forced, or voluntarily moved, toward mixed-gender sports activities, especially those that require high schoolers to engage in prolonged and intimate tactile contact. Wrestling is a prime example.

Barbara Carton wrote a story for the *Wall Street Journal,* from Weymouth, Massachusetts. It began: "Tiffany Fagioli, a 17 year old junior from Durfee High School in Fall River, strides onto the wrestling mat, her muscles rippling. She seems not at all concerned that her opponent in the 112 pound weight class is a boy—a sophomore from a Boston high school. A minute ago he was nervously chewing gum. Now, crouched before Ms. Fagioli in a skimpy yellow one-piece uniform, he looks scared to death. He can't win. If he beats her, he beats a girl. And if she beats him, how will he face his friends?"

In 1998, nineteen hundred girls wrestled in organized high school events. Many of them wrestle in girls-only systems. Colleges are starting female wrestling clubs and teams. Women's wrestling will be included in the 2004 Olympics. Giving girls the opportunity to enjoy this ancient sport, and to develop themselves through it, is clearly essential. But like so many other areas of cultural innovation, wrestling has become embroiled in gender warfare, and is creating far more strife than health for growing young people.

For the most part, gender innovations become counterintuitive when the social principle that "girls must do everything boys do and do it with boys" takes over cultural progress. Wrestling is a good example because it involves embarrassing tactile contact, which in turn makes full accomplishment of the sport between males and females needlessly difficult. Furthermore, adolescent embarrassment about girl-boy contact is developmentally appropriate and useful in cutting down premature sexual behavior; it is not something we want to systematically decrease by trying to force this contact on high school boys and girls.

Jim Giunta, a former wrestling official, points especially to moves that require grabbing the lower midsection as difficult for males and females to do with each other. David, a wrestler at Norwood High School, recalls losing to an older girl during his freshman year. During the match, his mother noted, "he was closer to a girl than he'd ever been in his whole life. When he grabbed her on the mat, he apologized to her. He lost concentration." The boy has difficulty expressing how he felt about the match.

A Massachusetts tournament official, David Breen, says this is not uncommon. He points out that boys often do not indicate to him how they truly feel. "Boys are conditioned even in school to a sexual-harassment type of mentality . . . to never, ever say anything against women—to never put any woman down, and never say she can't do something." He has seen boys wrestling against girls become "a wreck" before their match: "People don't understand when they talk about high school kids—they're children. They still have fragile egos."

To ensure gender equity for girls in areas such as athletics where equity has not traditionally existed, the ultimate school promotes girls' wrestling. It promotes physical and psychosocial safety by separating girls and boys in this sport, as well as in other high-contact sports such as football and basketball. Gender tension in the school community is lessened, and individual emotional stress is diminished. Ultimately, the school environment is more successful at its primary goal: protecting and encouraging developmentally appropriate human learning.

Rites of Passage

Brain development, and therefore psychosocial maturity, exists not only on an everyday continuum of experience but also in the context of "minicrises" that are created organically by the brain's attention to its environment, and by the community's attention to the brain. A child grows up by force of nature and environmental stimulants, but some of these stimulants need to be planned by the leaders and teachers in the environment.

We know this—it's basic and intuitive—and we attend to it relatively well when we think within the box, that is, about how to teach math, science, reading, English, social studies, and all academic subjects. But somehow we forget that the teacher must stimulate psychosocial learning in specific ways, outside the box.

Perhaps the most lost art in our service to teen development today is the rite of passage. We require our high school students to grow up by self-creating such a ritual, which then takes a form that may be high-risk and unnecessarily chaotic, from driving too fast to having sex for the first time. Unlike our own ancestral cultures—whether European, Asian, African, Native American—we do not *organize* the adolescent journey into a set of minicrises called rites of passage.

I have offered detailed structures for family-, community-, and school-based rites of passage in *The Good Son* and *A Fine Young Man*. I hope you will refer to them. Let me now feature two excellent programs that schools and communities can access.

At St. Mark's School of Texas, ninth-grade students go on the Pecos Wilderness Trip during the first two weeks of August each year. No student is allowed to be excused except by certified medical waiver. The students, faculty, and community at St. Mark's consider this one of the most essential features of high school.

Near Los Angeles, the Millennium Oaks Institute holds a voluntary rite of passage in the fall of each year. Boys from thirteen to nineteen, along with fathers and mentors, engage in a series of half-day preparatory weekend gatherings that culminate in a retreat on a November weekend in the mountains of Ojai. The whole three-month rite-of-passage program focuses on self-expression, confidence, self-esteem, and leadership skill building.

These models and others like them are crucial, in our view, to full development of the adolescent boy or girl. Without a rite of passage in which the community provides healthy crises to encourage psychosocial stimulation of the maturation process, we believe certain areas of the brain (the prefrontal lobe and areas of the temporal lobe, which control moral and other psychosocial decision making) may not develop on schedule. This is especially true, we find, with high-risk youth.

Full Psychosocial Education, Not Just Sex Education

Terry Trueman and I were talking one evening with his sixteen-year-old son, Jesse. We wanted to know what he wished schools would teach more of, especially in human growth and development and sex-education classes. A direct and honest young man, Jesse said, "Just about everything they *don't* teach."

"What do you mean?" we asked. "Specifically."

"How to talk to girls, especially because they call and e-mail all the time. What they want from a guy. What's the best way to act with them. That stuff."

"What about the sex ed itself?" Terry asked. "What about the human development stuff?"

"Oh that," Jesse retorted. "That's kind of a joke."

Jesse's cynicism (and his need for different information than he was getting) is a reality among high school students, both boys and girls. One girl told us, "They teach you mostly things you know already or don't need, and they don't teach you what you really want to know."

We hear this kind of thing all over the country. Students certainly have to know more about the mysteries of sex, but they need other knowledge as well. *Parade* magazine polled students, asking them to focus on "what life skills high schools should teach." Their responses are revealing:

- Teach more about people of all cultures.
- Teach social success skills.
- Teach manners.
- Teach how to fix things.
- Teach success theory—how to find a job.

- Teach how to protect yourself.
- Teach us how to care for each other.

Recently I spoke to a group of youths at a teen pregnancy prevention conference. One girl noted, "How come hardly any boys take the human growth and development classes?" A boy said, "They're for girls. And women teach them." Another girl said: "I don't think boys know what's hurtful. We tell them we feel harassed and they don't get it." A boy said, "It's the girls who don't get it. They don't know when to let up. They find a weakness in a guy and they never quit." Another boy said, "Girls always expect you to know what they're feeling even when they tell you everything's fine." A girl said, "All you need is a group of guys together and they'll look at you and either make you feel like you're meat, or just ignore you. What's up with that?"

Few conversations are livelier than those with teens who decide to trust you. They talked and talked and talked about the psychosocial areas that confuse them. I listened.

Ten years of this kind of conversation has shown me and my colleagues that these young people feel unmentored, untaught, unaided in their psychosocial education. Their sex education not enough, in many cases, and their formal education about each other—which is perhaps one of the three most important things on their minds in high school (along with "Will I make it in life?" and "Who am I?") is nearly nonexistent.

The ultimate classroom aims to redress this.

Improving Sex Education

A recent national survey of adolescent males pointed out that television and school appear to be the primary sources of contraceptive information for young men; fewer than half get information from their families. More than half of males age fifteen to nineteen have had intercourse. This is a huge pool of young males engaging in sex without getting information from home and family units.

Surveys of males are a relatively recent phenomenon. Surveys of females have been showing how important school-based sex ed is for years.

Females and males alike need more of it; in some states teens can go through all of high school with no sex ed at all, or maybe one hour of it. Adolescents don't just need more sex ed in order to know more about human sexuality; they need it because so much is at risk for them.

Teenagers must take risks; most will take risks they consider (later in life) slightly or seriously immoral, and certainly quite dangerous. It has always been the job of mentors and educators to help young people through their risk behaviors. The Centers for Disease Control and Prevention report that the only age group our culture has *not* been able to affect significantly with campaigns to reduce risky behavior is our adolescents—the statistical group from ten to twenty-four.

Until recently, sex-education support material emphasized female involvement more than male. Fortunately, there is now more emphasis on male involvement. Freya Sonenstein's *Involving Males in Preventing Teen Pregnancy: A Guide for Program Planners,* is very useful and makes the point that male involvement is not just about pregnancy prevention but also about helping young men become responsible husbands and fathers later in life.

Hablando Claro (Plain Talk) is a San Diego–based example of a male involvement program for the Barrio Logan area of that city. It reaches more than a thousand young males a year.

Abstinence curricula are now part of the sex-education field in many states. Alone they are not enough to meet the needs of most already sexually active teens, but such a curriculum can be a worthy addition to an already existing program, especially in late middle school or early high school. Most sex educators, of course, seek a middle ground between straight abstinence and contraception: focused sex education.

Anne de la Sota, a Los Angeles sex-education trainer with more than two decades of experience, has added parent-training innovations to normal sex ed packages, providing sex ed to students and also showing parents how to teach and talk about it with teens. Like many trainers, Anne favors separating boys and girls for some portions of sex ed. "We need lots more men involved in sex ed training," she laments. "Women can't do this alone, or by dragging men in to help. Men have to start wanting to do it."

In the ultimate classroom and school, we suggest these innovations for sex education:

- Human growth and development classes should be team-taught, by a female teacher and a male (counselor, coach, male teacher, father, or other male volunteer).
- If a school is not going to make this course mandatory, parts of it should be taught in gym and in other classes where boys are already found.
- Same-sex and separate-sex groupings should both be used, so that sensitive and difficult areas can be covered without members of either sex shutting down or resorting to attention-getting devices with the other sex.
- In all sex education, fathers and other elder males should be conscripted to volunteer to talk about a man's responsibilities and adolescent male feelings and experiences from their own memories.
- Sex-education classes in some form should be taught in *all* years of high school, becoming more sophisticated and oriented to student questions as the teens get older.

Sex is one of life's most confusing and crucial activities; it is in no way merely the responsibility of the family. It has never, in fact, been only the family's responsibility. Grandfathers, grandmothers, uncles, aunts, and other people with whom adolescents were bonded have always taught children and adolescents about sexuality. In a school that bonds teachers and students, sex education is a responsible area for discourse and greater wisdom.

Gender Education

Sex education is only a piece of the male-female puzzle, and our students know it. As the students at the teen pregnancy conference indicated, they want far more "gender education" than we give them. They want us to help them know what makes the other tick.

The brain-based research we adults are just now learning can be taught to boys and girls. My own guidebooks for this kind of teaching, one for boys (*From Boys to Men*) and one for girls (*Understanding Guys*), hope to join other books written for young people themselves in this endeavor.

Ric Stuecker, a trainer for National Training Associates, has cowritten a curriculum called *Reviving the Wonder,* which is targeted to both boys and girls and exists specifically to help teachers and students facilitate dialogue between young males and females. He told me about creative ways he has found to involve young people and elders in his project, which combines material from *Reviving Ophelia,* Mary Pipher's book on adolescent girls, and my own *The Wonder of Boys.*

Ric recruits off-duty and retired firemen and other males already oriented to service, as well as grandfathers and retired men, to help mentor the gatherings of young men and women. He and his colleagues find that recruiting elder women takes less effort.

He and his cowriter and cotrainer, Suze Rutherford, train women and men ("the elders") in the kind of honest, compassionate gender dialogue they hope to create with young people. Then these trained adults help young people, in both separate-sex and same-sex groups, prepare to dialogue, have the dialogue, and process it. *Reviving the Wonder* helps young people ask such hard questions as "What is it about me as a woman (or man) that I want the other to know?" "How do I define a woman (or man)?" "What are the things about the other I need to know to be a good man (or woman)?"

Ric, Suze, and their trainees use a powerful technique with which some teachers are already familiar: the fishbowl. Young men sit in a circle around young women sitting in an inside circle. Deep questions are asked and answered in the interior female community, with the males sitting silently. The outer circle is not allowed to talk but learns by observing and listening. The circles are then switched, young men moving into the inner circle and young women to the outer, and the questions and issues are covered by the males (the females now not interrupting). For many young men and women, this is a life-altering experience. If the elders do the same, joining each gender group and speaking their stories along with the youths, it can be even more fruitful.

This full curriculum can be carried out by any interested counselor, teacher, or teaching team, though like all cutting-edge material it helps to receive the training initially or some form of similar training in gender group dynamics. Ric, Suze, and their colleagues combine this gender training with asset-building curricula that already are used in some school systems.

Another easy technique for dialogue I have used with success is simply to divide the classroom into two sides, males on one, females on the other. Questions are asked that are answered by first one sex group, then the other. After both groups have talked uninterrupted, the groups ask each other the deep questions. The teacher facilitates mainly by making sure silent youths get a chance to be heard, since predictably a few dominant boys and girls will do all the talking.

Whether it is math, social studies, English, gym, or any other classroom, teaching young people how to understand who they are and who their eventual life partners are is a crucial part of the ultimate school. It is highly respectful of the developmental paths of young people, for whom learning literature and math is certainly important but is not, in the growing brain, compartmentalized away from psychosocial development.

Some areas of specific concern for each gender cannot really be handled by school systems unless the whole school, in many classes, embraces the importance of gender dialogue. They include

- Sexual harassment, which is a terrible problem in high-density, high-population high schools, to say nothing of its potential for difficulty in any coeducational setting
- Gay bashing and lack of understanding of those people who develop homosexually
- Sexual involvement, from flirting to intercourse, which is being set up nonverbally in classrooms and schools even when it appears students are completely focused only on the math, science, or other lesson
- The high extent to which young women feel they are dissed, objectified, and dominated by male nonverbal (as well as verbal) communication

- The great extent to which young men feel overwhelmed by the relating styles of young women

A hundred years ago, schools did not have to do much of this kind of training; it could be left to the family (though many families were certainly reticent to do it and negligent in practice). Nuclear families were cognizant of nature's rhythms, and extended families did much of the training. Young people were trained by the larger culture to stay away from the other gender except in sanctioned (or surreptitious) activities. Many schools were not coed, so there was less need for constant gender training.

Now, the school is quite often the extended family. Nuclear families are deficient in parenting teens (whether due to divorce, parent workload, or parenting style), schools are vigorously coeducational, and culture and media go out of their way to push males and females at each other in order (among other things) to create the kind of gender tension that sells products (perfume, movies, and the like) to the wealthy young-adult demographic group. Principal Bill Callahan of Minuteman Regional High School in Lexington, Massachusetts, put today's situation very well: "Some people wish we could just teach reading, writing, and arithmetic like the old days. But it's a fact of life that we are now responsible for helping our kids to grow and develop as people." In the past, many teachers and schools made helping kids develop as people an interwoven, community priority with academics coming first and religious training second. Today, it must become an overt secondary priority, secondary only to academic learning itself.

Innovations to Improve Academic Learning

When there is schoolwide improvement in bonding and attachment, psychosocial learning, and brain-based structural innovations, the ultimate classroom becomes an easy place to teach math, science, English, social studies, and other academic subjects. Classrooms are emotionally stable; discipline and student core-self security (self-esteem) are high, which in turn leads to good brain development. Improvements in emotional and social areas of the life of the teen's mind bestow neural gifts on the other areas, such as memory storage and critical thinking.

Having said that, I'll add that there are also direct neural pathways to improving high school academic learning. Let's explore these now. In the high school classroom, most if not all the recommendations for middle school again apply, but we make some additions to them.

Teaching Mathematics, Science, and Technology

Amy, a recent college graduate, struck up a conversation with me on an airplane, having recognized me from a television appearance. She said something like this:

> You know, when I heard you talking about how different the male and female brain were, I didn't want to believe it at first. But when you were talking about how much harder math and science can be for girls, especially when a male teacher teaches it, I really got it. I just couldn't get physics in high school. I was bored by calculus. I tried and tried, but I couldn't get it. The boys around me, they would make fun of me and I felt dumb. I really thought I was dumb. But this thing about the blackboard—that's what I remember. Everything was always up on the blackboard, and the guys and the teacher were going so fast figuring things out, and I couldn't quite get it.

In the same way that males are often at a disadvantage throughout school (from a statistical point of view) because they are male brains in a female-brain classroom, girls taking math and science in high school can find themselves female brains in a male-brain classroom (with exceptions, of course, for the math-and-science-talented girls). Male math and science teachers quite logically teach their subject to fit their own brain system. Many girls, and some nonspatial boys, can have difficulty with that.

The changes we have made in the last decade in helping girls reach parity in math education is stunning and inspiring. Girls now take as much math and science in high school as boys and test out nearly at par (with the male brain advantage still showing up clearly at the highest and most abstract ends of math, as well as physics). Some of the new statistical parity is due to the fact that more girls finish school than boys, so male numbers are down and female up. But a lot of it is due to our culture's hard work toward training teachers to seek male-female parity.

Many high school math teachers, like middle school teachers, have recently experienced some training in how to help girls reach parity in math and science. Nevertheless, we'd like to mention some new material, based on direct brain research and gender-based brain research, that is compelling.

Girls have great difficulty in learning certain aspects of math, perhaps because they are not called on as much by teachers, but also for some biological reasons. One involves testosterone: surges of the hormone, which males receive during adolescence between five and seven times a day, can increase spatial skills. Heightened presence of estrogen during the menstrual cycle increases female performance on all skills, including spatials, but the female cycle is not as diurnal as the male. Thus the adolescent girl may have a few days a month when she performs very well on any sort of test, including math, but the male may have certain times *every day* when he might perform better at spatials, such as higher math.

Another basic male-female brain difference is the male proclivity toward high abstraction, which a great deal of higher math learning is predicated upon. Statistically, males are going to be able to master math a little better than females (especially as it becomes more abstract in the high school years) by enjoying it on a two-dimensional blackboard.

We cannot affect testosterone-estrogen dynamics, but we can innovate in math as a result of our new knowledge of the strengths of the female brain. Teachers are using some interesting, commonsense strategies with success. Some are increasing the aural quality of math teaching—in other words, putting the math on the blackboard or on paper but also talking math with the girls (and boys). "Talking it" uses more verbals and relies less on the single-sense visual blackboard teaching strategy.

All the way through school, the more tactile and concrete the math and science teaching, the easier it is for the widest variety of students. Visual, aural, *and* tactile is a three-sense approach. See it, hear it, and touch it. Washington state has established, and promulgated to teachers, essential academic learning requirements for science, one of which states that "science and technology are human endeavors, interrelated to each other, to society and to the workplace." In order to fulfill the spirit of this requirement, teachers are being trained to integrate science and technology with real-world tactile applications. In some cases, the integration can go as far as to include another essential aspect of high school learning: multicultural education. Here is a wonderful example.

Teacher Jeri Buckley tells this story. One summer, a friend from the Blackfoot tribe, Long Standing Bear Chief, taught her how to erect a tepee. She confesses: "I had always wondered, 'How do they balance all those poles together? And how do they get the canvas up around that tall cone?'" The solutions her friend showed her, solutions to complex spatial questions that were quite ancient, inspired her to bring this experiential, tactile process to her science class.

> If I could get my students to consider the tepee as a solution to an engineering challenge, they might come to understand that the way in which Blackfoot people solved that tough survival problem was scientific. . . . So I posed a question that Blackfoot people had confronted and resolved over time. Erecting a tepee was traditionally women's work, so the question was "How could two Blackfoot women erect a tepee three times as tall as they were without using a ladder?" The students used dowels, string, and rectangles of cloth to plan their solution.
>
> As the small groups began working on their models, they soon figured out that they needed to tie the dowels together near the tops to get them to balance against one another when they were upright. (Blackfoot people traditionally begin with four poles to represent the four directions.) A greater challenge was to imagine how they would get the poles upright.

And so went the experiment, from first question to group work to trial-and-error to solution. Jeri didn't allow the students to be satisfied only with physically working the models. They also had to imagine how shorter people could wrap the full-size tepee cover in place two to three feet above them.

Jeri's innovation has many obvious advantages, from using effective group brainstorming, to making a multisensory science experience. Especially after it was united with mythology and spirituality from the Blackfoot tribe, the experience became both science and history—a potentially wonderful way of creating group bonds early in the fall semester as class begins and students are just getting to know each other.

Math and science teachers may need no experiential innovations like Jeri's if all the students are learning well. Yet the whole-brain kind of experience that her exercise constitutes should be done for its own sake, many times during the science year. It is what we call integrated curriculum, the blending of many disciplines. As the adolescent brain increases its abstract abilities, it seeks these integrative experiential elements in science curricula. Through integrative and experiential activities, the abstracting mind makes even larger intuitive leaps than it can in a "read the problem, now write the solution" kind of exercise.

Technology and Gender

In the same way that girls have traditionally been at a disadvantage in math and science, some research shows that girls are at a disadvantage in acquiring technology skills. Despite male-female parity in Internet activity at home, parity in the classroom can be trickier to accomplish. Although some thinkers have argued that females are technologically behind because of inherent sexism in patriarchal school cultures— males encouraged to use computers and females discouraged—we have found little concerted sexism. We have found, however, that males aggressively seek out the computers, and are loud about wanting to use them. Females easily step aside, allowing the aggressive user to dominate time on the computer, especially in the majority of school districts where it is not possible to have one computer for each student.

Constant teacher vigilance in this area is important for our girls. Some simply do not gravitate toward the spatial stimulant of the computer screen as vehemently as a male does. Once the male-female psychosocial dynamics are added in, some girls who need to learn computer technologies will not do so, and our culture as a whole ultimately suffers for leaving the child behind, as it does in any area where it robs a child of a chance to succeed. Furthermore, some girls do not push themselves into the most sophisticated computer programming technologies. For some young women, the spatial and abstract computation elements of the brain are not naturally as developed as for many males. The girls must be encouraged to use computers generally, but also, if needed, to seek tutorial help for sophisticated uses.

Teaching Reading and Literacy

Judy Greene, a reading specialist in Kansas City, shared the story of a nineteen-year-old who had "a lot of self-pride, machismo and natural leadership, but is reading at around the sixth-grade level. He has become vociferous in his defiance about the reading class he is in. On bad days you'll hear, 'I don't need this class. This is baby stuff. I know how to read. This is for LD kids and I ain't no LD student. Why don't we do something different besides read in this class! I hate reading!'"

Typical of many students in this situation, he started skipping class and Judy feared he would drop out of school. He needed to read at an eighth-grade level in order to graduate from de la Salle, which it appeared he would be unable to do; he was getting angrier and more isolated, and Judy and others felt unable to reach him.

Judy concluded: "His reading issues have caught up to him and are hitting him hard. We've lost others due to similar situations and I want very much to prevent it from happening again. I know it's not within my or a few people's power to remedy an entire school history of negative reading experiences and attitudes, but I want to do what I can. Anybody got anything to offer?" she asked her colleagues on a university listserv set up to help support reading specialists.

She and her colleagues around the country are constantly faced with students like this one, whose core-self development has been damaged by reading trauma. As brain-based research assumes power in educational culture, and as brain-based gender research increases its usefulness, we generally notice what so many reading specialists already know: the vast majority of reading-traumatized and reading-deficient high school students are young men.

What can we do for them (and for girls who are reading-deficient as well)?

CUT REPETITIVE AURAL STIMULATION. A mother recently told me about her fifteen-year-old son's very frustrated comment: "Mom, Mrs. Diehl [the English teacher] talks too much. She reads the poems over and over. It's so boring." Her mother brought this up to me because her teacher had diagnosed the boy as having "trouble reading, being a problem in general, and being defiant." From the mother's point of view, the problem was in the teacher's approach to teaching English. Her son had no problems in other classes (his grades were B's and A's), but in English he received C's and D's. He liked school but despised this class. His frustration grew and grew.

It is the teacher's perfect right to say, "So what? I teach English the way I teach it," but it is also the student's right to relay to the teacher, both verbally and through nonverbal behavior, his distress at her teaching style. The student is following his own brain and seeking left-hemisphere stimulation that fits him. Being read the poem over and over is not working for him. He is probably unable to handle the complex vocabulary and subtextual material as easily as most of his female classmates and many of his male classmates when the words are "just words."

He had difficulty grasping and decoding the text of the poem when it was aurally presented. He became frustrated, his pride was hurt; he controlled himself but couldn't perform well. He was on his way to an LD diagnosis.

ENHANCING AURAL STIMULATION. A similar situation regularly faces some young men (and young women) who, instead of finding aural presentation of complex word sequences difficult, in fact *need* it to help them compensate for visual difficulties in learning how to decode complex texts. In this fifteen-year-old's case, he needed less sound stimulation, but another boy might need less staring at words on the page and more group aural reading or partnered aural reading.

Whether he needs more or less of either, he almost certainly requires parsing of text into discrete units that can be analyzed separately. He would probably also benefit from having concrete manipulative experiences interspersed with reading experiences, physical learning that integrates reading with other parts of education.

Gail, a high school teacher in Kansas City, finds that her boys learn better if hands-on activities become part of the literary lesson. Recently she described to us two particularly successful language arts lessons for young people with reading difficulties that were wonderfully integrative of the arts, geography, social studies, and even math.

In one, she assigned continents for the students in her class to research, asking students to research facts about countries in a continent, its area and size, and so on. "I used large cardboard sheets and had them draw the continents. The next step was to paint them. Then, they used papier mâché to build the mountains and waterways. My students have to research and make notebooks on their particular continent. This was very effective for low readers paired with better readers."

In another lesson, Gail was teaching parts of Homer's work—*Odyssey* and *Iliad*—and it led to a research project concerning the Trojan War. She first set a reading assignment. Then students made Trojan horses. "One of my boys, a particularly moody kid," she said, "did some extra credit research and decided to build the Greek Parthenon. He meticulously built it." Engaged by the physical task, he learned more about the literature being read by the class. His brain could attach scenes, words, and other content to objects so as to enhance literacy learning.

A PROMISING LANGUAGE PROGRAM. An immensely promising program for helping deficient high school–age readers has been developed by Jane Fell Greene, a literacy consultant to school districts nationwide. It is called Language! and its success is stunning. Jane made them available to *American Educator* in the summer of 1998, which is where we learned of her program. We recommend it for many reasons, especially because it is a practical, already developed literacy program teachers can be trained in and use right away. Its innovative three-tiered approach fits what we know of brain development in adolescence and also concurs with what we know about areas of reading trouble that we specifically denote as male-brain deficiencies.

Based on the premise that high school learners need a literacy program that fits their phase of development, and also on the idea that "literature" is not "literacy" for those with literacy difficulties, Language! teaches essential phonemics on three levels: basic literacy, testing the student along the way, and finally "literature learning."

At level one, the high school student learns phonemic awareness, decoding, encoding, fluency in passage reading, increased vocabulary, comprehension, and basic grammar. Writing and editing, even if rudimentary, are foundational. The student is tested until he reaches a level of mastery sufficient for progress. These essential developmental skills are not interrupted by expectations of mastery of higher-level skills or texts. In other words, the student doesn't learn phonemic awareness one day and then face the teacher's expectation to be able to read *To Kill a Mockingbird* the next. He can read *To Kill a Mockingbird* if he wishes, but it is accepted that he won't get a lot of it.

On level two, students are introduced to new strands, such as more sophisticated syllabication (polysyllabic words and the like), greater vocabulary, morphology (Latin roots), and syntactically more complex sentences. Expository writing, appropriate for this level, is emphasized. Again, the student is encouraged to read harder, "higher-up" texts than he is able to fully decode at this level, but competence for this level does not include the expectation of level-three mastery.

In the level-three material, literature enters the picture. Metaphor, theme, point of view, plot development, and myriad other elements of sophisticated literacy are now taught, along with Greek morphology. Over many months, these three levels build; sometimes it takes years. At level three, the teacher can start testing the student on *To Kill a Mockingbird.*

Jane's program comes with computer software and other technologies. It is the kind of multitasking, brain-based, and developmental program that can work not only in the schools for which she has shown positive results, but in far more as well.

Like most successful academic achievement support programs, the effectiveness of Language! stretches beyond academic success. Jane tells this story of Anthony:

He was an eighteen-year-old tenth-grader who had spent three years in grade nine but still couldn't read or write beyond a basic second-grade level. Frustrated and angry, this minority youth was ready to drop out and head for L.A., where there were "real gangs." But between Anthony's ninth- and tenth-grade years, middle and high school teachers in his south Alabama district received intensive training in our literacy curriculum. Assigned to a two-hour literacy class in grade ten, this youngster, once destined for a life on the margins of society, started back at the beginning: phonemic awareness, phoneme-grapheme correspondence, writing words and sentences, reading decodable connected text, and expanding his vocabulary. By the end of the second year, he was writing sophisticated, syntactically varied sentences, paraphrasing content area text, and reading for pleasure. He stayed in school for a senior year during which his elective course was journalism.

Jane ends her story with Anthony's personal observation as he looked back on his experience: "I always knew there must be some kind of secret to reading, but nobody ever taught me the code."

Our research shows us that reading and writing difficulties, throughout school, are a primary reason for male dysfunction in school culture. If by high school a young man (or young woman) is having reading difficulty, self-esteem plummets, core-self and identity development are more difficult, and the future becomes academically frightening. Not to read in this culture is to be lame. Anthony's success is not just reading success, but the turning of a young person back to the bonds, attachments, and other social supports that he needs to develop as a healthy man. In this sense, literacy in high school can be a secret to decoding texts, to be sure—but also to decoding adulthood.

Standardized Testing

Teachers and students gear up for the SATs and other tests at different times depending on the school. In middle school, the students have probably taken PSATs (see Chapter Four, on the elementary school, for analysis of statewide standardized testing). Some high schools already start ninth-graders talking about "getting ready for the SATs," while most wait until the junior year.

The gender literature of the last decade has had much to say about standardized tests, mainly that in high school females generally test lower than males. Let's look at brain-based reasons for this—and let's ask, "What is the place of standardized testing in the ultimate classroom?"

There are two important things to know about test scores. First, students are getting higher grades in high school today without similar increases in SAT scores. In 1997, the average GPA of students taking the SAT was 3.22, up from 3.07 in 1987. The SAT scores themselves, however, remained relatively constant (the clearest exception being that girls' math scores have risen since the early 1990s). Second, males outscore females by 7 points on the verbal and 35 points on math.

Brain-based research is helpful in understanding why it is that males, who get 70 percent of the D's and F's in our schools and only about 40 percent of the A's, end up outscoring females in standardized tests. The adolescent who naturally favors deductive and quick abstract reasoning tends to do well in a multiple-choice format. The adolescent who tends to quickly single out information rather than thinking out a larger variety of possibilities also does better. The adolescent who tends toward high risk taking is likely to quickly answer questions under pressure and risk guesses. This student could be male or female, but there is a high statistical probability that the student is male. There is also a high statistical advantage for males in math because of male-brain math advantage.

As standardized tests come to include more essay formats, females do better, bringing the male-female scores nearly to parity. The math scores become even closer as math questions are invested with more essay features.

GRADE INFLATION AND ACADEMIC FAILURE.   The rise in student test scores nationally is not commensurate with rising student grades. Student grade inflation is rampant, and there are many reasons for it; some are revealed by brain-based research and reasoning.

Quite simply, the brains of our young people are stressed increasingly in academic areas but not supported enough to meet the expectations that new social and intellectual technologies put on all of us—especially the young, who live in the throes of constantly expanding innovation. Our students' minds are having trouble keeping up with everything we want and need them to learn. They require extra help from teachers, something teachers often can't give in total time spent or one-on-one attention. But they grasp that they *can* give it by inflating grades. Grade inflation creates the illusion that the educational system is stable because it mitigates excessive student failure; thus teachers and schools do not have to look at the reality of potential failure.

As schools and students are under ever greater performance pressure and thus experience greater anxiety, teachers continue to compensate by inflating grades; they also inflate grades in proportion to the organic pressures on the school system (classes growing larger, students receiving less discipline, academic education becoming consistently harder to ensure). Like any organic system, the educational system tries to keep failure from becoming disaster.

The academic failures hit more boys than girls, and although boys outnumber girls as the "beneficiaries" of grade inflation (teachers compensating for boys' weakness by inflating their grades) this is a double-edged sword. It also means these boys are not getting the real help they need. All in all, both male and female failures cannot be compensated for by statistically higher test scores. Though boys get slightly higher scores, they do not look as good statistically to colleges. Colleges know what is happening with grade inflation in high school, and they know there are gender elements at work.

Echoing the comments of her colleagues around the country, Delsie Phillips, director of admissions for Haverford College, put it this way: "Girls mature sooner, so they get more serious about their schoolwork. It really shows when you start reading applications. Girls have followed through and done all the things they are supposed to do, while boys are still trying to find themselves."

She is, of course, generalizing, but high school teachers echo her experience. Given that most college admissions officials give grades, class rank, and activities more weight than standardized tests scores, high schools are now challenged to deal with the various ways that males and male brain systems are not getting the mentoring, challenge, bonding, direction, and academic education they need. Judith Kleinfeld, a professor of psychology at the University of Alaska-Fairbanks, completed one of the most comprehensive educational surveys in history. She concluded that "males are more apt than females to believe that the school climate is hostile to them, that teachers do not expect as much from them and give them less encouragement to do their best."

The decline in college admissions among young males has become so frightening that some officials, according to Margaret Miller, president of the American Association for Higher Education, are giving males a slight break: "Colleges and universities are dipping down deeper into their male pool than their female pool." In this regard, standardized test scores, which slightly favor males, are not affecting the overall outcome of college admissions. We are losing more and more males, and this is ominous because college is a prime determinant of earning power and adult success later in young people's lives.

As the ultimate classroom takes shape throughout the country, we will see standardized test scores become less important. The research into gender and the brain will be used to improve academic teaching of males as much as political advocacy research has improved girls' chances.

Given how the standarized tests are administered now, brain-based gender research asks us to be cautious about using these scores as the prime forecaster of the present or future of a high school student's intellectual life. I myself recall scoring higher on both the SATs and the GREs in math ability than in verbal, yet I did less well in math than in English classes, and the only extent to which I have used math ability in my decades of professional life is in statistical work. Otherwise, I have spent the bulk of my life in verbals. My test scores, like so many young people's, did not reflect my brain's reality. Certainly the many girls who have gotten high grades (well deserved) but tested out on the SAT lower than less-intelligent boys have had their own version of my experience. It can happen to anyone.

Special Education

The federal Education of the Handicapped Act in 1977 guaranteed that students with disabilities get a "free appropriate education and related services which are provided at public expense, under public supervision and direction, and without charge; meet the standards of the State Education Agencies; include preschool, elementary school, and secondary school students; and are provided in conformity with an individualized education program." The concept of free, appropriate public education (FAPE) began in 1975 with the passage of P.L.94-142 and in 1997 was revised by the Individuals with Disabilities Education Act.

We have looked in detail in earlier chapters at techniques for improving special education. It is worth reminding ourselves that in high school the majority of students who are classified as special education are boys. Statistically, high school students who express themselves well through spoken and written communication are less likely to be classified as special education.

As part of their training in brain-based gender research, special ed teachers in Missouri are using a number of techniques:

- Increasing the teaching of conflict-resolution skills
- Decreasing verbal instruction and increasing problem-solving approaches
- Increasing one-on-one mentoring in all classes, especially alternative-education settings
- Increasing the use of bonding activities between teachers and students, and among students themselves
- Allowing more response time for questions

On this last point, high school students often don't need the sixty-second rule, but males and females alike in special ed benefit from increased answering time (a technique developed from observing the greater male need). According to teachers in Missouri, waiting at least ten to twenty seconds before encouraging an answer or calling on someone else makes a major difference in the number and quality of responses from male students.

Another area of innovation being used effectively in high school special education is integrating curricula with the arts. The arts are such a whole-brain activity they can work with reading-disabled, the learning disabled in general, and behaviorally disabled. The arts are useful not simply with diagnosed students, but with all difficult students.

Frances, a Missouri high school teacher, described an especially inspiring experience she had when teaching Shakespeare in an urban high school.

> To my surprise, one of the toughest, most-difficult-to-teach boys in the school auditioned for Romeo when I held a festival of Shakespeare's plays. He requested to write a special soliloquy and present it before the play began. I agreed and proofed it. It went something like this: "Classmates, teachers and countrymen—women, too. You need to hustle and lend me your ears. Today, I come to court, you know, date this chick. Now, you know me as Terry. You shall not see me as me, but ye shall see me as but handsome Romeo, the love of the eyes of fair Juliet. She waits in yonder window, pining for my love."
>
> With this, he began his stage entrance, but not before he added, "Oh, by the way, when you first see me, get your giggles and laughing out. Once I begin as Romeo, I do not want to have to stop and deal with you about my outfit. My costume is from the era of the time and it has tights with these short blossom pants. It is best that you do not disturb the lover Romeo with catcalls, laughing, or tomfoolery . . . you dig?"
>
> With this, he stepped out on stage and made a grand gesture with his hat to the audience. Much to our surprise, no one laughed and he immediately became the character Romeo. His performance was wonderful. Each time he performed, he got standing ovations

and no one laughed. His mother even cried when she saw him. He was given his chance in the limelight, and he was a star. His behavior changed after that. He graduated and went on to life.

This young man, a special ed "problem" student, became a success story—inspired to enjoy literature by becoming a part of it through a blending of arts with literature, words with drama.

Frances concludes: "I know, from this experience and other similar ones, that what these difficult kids want is a fair chance. They love the opportunity to be respected and recognized. Through the arts, I think many of these difficult kids can be saved."

Alan Wells, an innovator with the municipal government in Kansas City, agrees. He has succeeded in obtaining funding for a program called Sentenced to the Arts. The program allows juveniles who commit crimes to be ordered to participate in an arts program run by a participating school or agency. Although the program is still in its infancy, early results are promising. This program is funded by a Juvenile Accountability Incentive Block Grant from the U.S. Department of Justice.

In order to prove her point that "Romeo" was not an isolated event, Frances described another. She taught theater to a high school class in Texas. She was working in an urban school where students were considered low-achieving because test scores were low:

At the end of my first season, I directed *The Wiz*. There were some three hundred students involved in the project. It involved members of the jazz band, majorettes, flag line, choir, ROTC, television production class, and theater arts students. After the opening show, several teachers confronted me and asked, "How in the world did you get [name of student] under control long enough for him to perform?" I answered that I taught him to focus by offering him something he wanted—attention. I used a creative teaching opportunity for him to shine. Everyone wants a chance in life to be a star.

The Ultimate High School Classroom for Both Boys and Girls

High school gender innovations are, as we've mentioned earlier, consistent with those geared for middle school. But let's highlight some here.

For the Boys

- Make sure each student has participated, as needed, in conflict-resolution and communication training.
- Know enough about "male nature" that it can be taught to males and that, in teaching them who they are, they can gain insight into how to find personal worth and meaning in what they do.
- Encourage teachers to carry powerful authority, whether in personal charisma or simply in consistency, academic quality, and intuition of teenagers' needs.
- Allow movement in the classroom, especially for those students who think better when they're moving around. Help the teenager refine future options by giving him a mentor's vision of what his strengths and weaknesses are (let no high school student graduate without having experienced mentoring).
- Bring fathers and other males into school to tell their story and mentor males into healthy manhood.
- Use separate-sex education whenever necessary, and advocate for it politically.
- Offer character education and service projects as an integral part of learning (that is, nonelective).
- Teach boys how to understand girls, through frank discussion.
- Teach media literacy, including the effects of media imagery on male character development.

- Provide rite-of-passage experiences.
- Allow check-in and talk time in human growth and development, social studies, psychology, and other applicable classes, in which students have a chance to verbalize issues they face, including harassment, depression, and bullying.

For the Girls

- Train girls, like boys, in their "nature," giving them training and material similar to what teachers get regarding gender-brain differences and similarities. Make this information part of classroom discussion. (In high school, both girls and boys are mature enough to read Chapters One and Two of this book and discuss them.)
- Pay special attention to innovation that makes high-level math accessible to girls, such as manipulatives, field trips, journaling, and note taking.
- Use separate-sex classrooms and clubs whenever necessary, and advocate for separate-sex education politically.
- Carry high expectations, and offer even more encouragement than appears necessary.
- Do not shy away from competition (as in games) in learning, especially in math and science learning.
- Make available to girls equal computer access time and female role models (from within the school and from the community) who know computers well and can build girls' interest in computer technology.
- Team-teach and provide group learning frameworks as much as possible.
- Make sure every girl leaves high school having spent time with a female role model and mentor.
- Pay close attention to special education needs of girls whose disabilities are often not as marked as boys' and thus can be missed.

- Extend gender-specific support to female athletics, without infringing on developmentally appropriate boy-girl separation in sports.
- Train girls on the effects of media imagery on their self-concept and character development.
- Bring mothers, grandmothers, and other females into school to help girls learn sexual and social ethics, and hear stories of the female life span.
- Hold check-in and talk time in human growth and development, social studies, psychology, and other applicable classes, in which students have a chance to verbalize issues they face, including harassment, depression, and bullying.

Tips for Parents

- Do not give up your "star" position in the child's unfolding life drama; but when you do have to relinquish it, remain the most important supporting character.
- Be an active listener, by asking important questions and not judging answers.
- Let no topic of conversation be off-limits, though rules of discourse ("no cursing in front of younger siblings") can always apply.
- Conduct extended family and familial rites of passage (sometimes connected to church or other spiritual communities), and support school rite-of-passage experiences.
- Make older siblings responsible for the character education of younger ones (if a film is bad for younger brother or sister, the teen does not view it in the younger sibling's presence).
- Give new freedom and responsibility to teens, in equal proportion; if you give a new freedom (say, staying out past midnight), the teen gets a concomitant new responsibility (perhaps a new set of chores).

- Make sure the teen knows that homework and school activities are more important than leisure activities.
- Instruct a child to treat teachers and school officials with respect, even when disagreeing with their policies or positions.
- Remain a friend of the school through involvement in school sports, volunteering, and school rite-of-passage experiences.

What High School Students Are Saying: Their Fears

Kay Chatterton, a clinical social worker, former schoolteacher, and director of professional development for the Utah Education Association, co-led focus groups of high school students that asked them to identify their deepest fears. She was surprised to learn that the source of their fears was the perceived inability to compete during (and once they leave) school. The teenage students spoke openly about their fear of not meeting the demands of their parents, and then the marketplace. They felt immense pressure to compete both in school and out "in the world." Many were sure of their own failure.

Kay's research corroborates our own. We have led focus groups asking youths the exact same question and getting very similar responses. We began our research expecting to discover that girls would have greater fear of failure than boys, but we discovered in many cases just the opposite. The federal Department of Education has corroborated this finding. In surveys of both eighth- and twelfth-graders, the department discovered that girls had higher aspirations than boys and higher confidence that they could reach their aspirations. Recently I was involved in filming a PBS education special in which a group of high school boys were asked how they felt about their lives, their schools, and their futures. From ninth to twelfth grade, the similarity in answers revolved around fear of failure. Nearly every boy was afraid he would not meet expectations, whether his parents' or his own.

Our boys and girls become men and women in perhaps the most competitive social atmosphere in the world. Both genders have profound fear of failure, which we are called on to help them process, and master. A high school education is certainly about academic preparation for college and for the workplace. It is also about the deeper elements of human consciousness on which academic preparation soulfully depends.

We end the final chapter with this mention of high school students' fears because we have found teachers, parents, and others to be surprised by the extent of the fear young men and young women feel today. It is well-masked fear, an undercurrent to be expected in a society that pushes the minds of boys and girls without fully understanding the minds themselves. If our research in the field of adolescent education has taught us anything, it is this: teen girls and boys want to be female and male, while learning the social and academic technologies that the other gender learns. It is still up to the high school teacher to help them achieve a balance between being young people to whom only intelligence—not gender—matters, and young *men* or *women* for whom being masculine or feminine is a worthy ideal, and essential to adult life.

EPILOGUE

A ship is safe in the harbor, but is the harbor where a ship should be?

—ANONYMOUS

Our educational culture is struggling today not only with clear problems of undisciplined children, pressure from legislators to raise test scores, lack of funding, parental fears for students' safety, and overwhelmed teachers; it is also struggling for an identity. Students, teachers and administrators, school boards and parents, policy makers, and seemingly every political commentator weigh in constantly these days on what educators should do and who they should be. We, too, have weighed in with the strong belief that to carry on a discussion about our schools without basing it on clear understanding of the brain (and on the differences between how boys' and girls' brains work) is to leave out a key component of what education needs. We hope that as our culture embarks on deciding what kind of training teachers need, it will realize how essential education in brain and gender differences is.

Our research has taken us to schools that are doing and being wonderful things. We have been involved in teaching, inspiring, and discovering innovations regarding how boys and girls are taught that have knocked our socks off. As we began our research, we wondered, *Is our teachers' lack of training in brain biology and in gender biology a missing piece of educational identity?* Now, as we present some of our research to the public, we have our answer. We've tested the question with school districts, and they've answered with a resounding "Yes! This training is a next step for us."

Every generation, committed to children and to the nobility of learning, searches for the tools and models that allow it to find a safe harbor and settle there. Perhaps what brain research has taught best is that there is no safe harbor. Just as the brain is a living, changing organism, we are always having to adapt and change, take on new tools, and then go out to sea again.

My coauthors and I hope you will seek deeper understanding into the brains of both boys and girls. Through such effort, we can make our children's classrooms and schools even finer places of bonding, attachment, love, and learning. The educational structures we've all worked in the last few decades are adapting and changing, along with everything else in human society. Educators and parents are not secondary figures in cultural progress; they lead the way. Despite any indication to the contrary, everyone in the culture wants (in differing degree) to trust teachers. Every parent of a boy or girl has an instinct toward making the teacher central to that child's development—and, through him or her, to human progress.

Consequently, it's our belief that the ultimate classroom must have teachers, supported by administrators and parents, who are both trained and committed to gender-based education. Now that we have the scientific knowledge and empirical evidence to document the major differences in anatomical structure, neurological development, and the chemical and hormonal climate in developing boys and girls, we can innovate and sustain gender-appropriate educational techniques that bring the greatest benefit to all of our children, with all of their unique and personal strengths and needs.

NOTES

PART ONE

HOW BOYS AND GIRLS
LEARN DIFFERENTLY

I **HOW THE BRAIN LEARNS:**
INHERENT DIFFERENCES BETWEEN BOYS AND GIRLS

The material in this and the next chapter is culled from fifteen years of brain, hormonal, and gender research. We have included in these chapters information that has often been corroborated by more than one source. Our role has been to collect and *apply* brain and gender research. We are most beholden to primary laboratory and field researchers, among them Laurie Allen, Ruben and Raquel Gur, and Camilla Benbow, for revealing the nature of the brain in ways that we could take into the lives of teachers, parents, and other caregivers.

The most difficult issue in doing brain and gender research comes up in this simple question, How do we *know* the difference is an accurate one? Every reader and every expert has a different standard of certainty. Some of my colleagues in psychology and education insist that there are no real differences between the minds of males and females, despite all the evidence to the contrary.

This said, we know we are presenting a theoretical approach. In the end, you the reader decide whether the research and theory are accurate. If your intuition says yes to the theories, that *yes* carries the most weight. In the fifteen years I have been helping the culture apply neurobiological research, I have made sure to check a specific researcher's finding with colleagues' findings, multicultural sources, anecdotal confirmations, personal observation, and just good common sense.

THE WIDE SPECTRUM OF GENDER IN THE BRAIN

Brain Sex, by Anne Moir and David Jessel (New York: Dell, 1990), is still the best resource I've found for understanding brain-based gender differences. This is ironic, since it is more than a decade old. Yet no other volume tells it like it is in the same way this one does.

Brain Sex was also made into a three-part television series that appeared on the Learning Channel. Also see S. Begley, "Your Child's Brain," *Newsweek,* Feb. 19, 1996; and J. M. Nash, "Fertile Minds," *Time,* Feb. 3, 1997. Quotations from experts are from these sources.

HOW THE BRAIN WORKS

A highly readable source for brain-based material is Robert Sylwester's *A Celebration of Neurons,* from which I have quoted frequently in Part One of this book (Alexandria, Va.: Association for Supervision and Curriculum Development, 1995). See also *Neuroscience: Exploring the Brain,* by Mark Bear, Barry Connors, and Michael Paradiso (Baltimore: Williams and Wilkins, 1996) and *Essentials of Neural Science and Behavior,* by Eric Kandel, James Schwartz, and Thomas Jessel (Norwalk, Conn.: Appleton and Lange, 1995).

HOW BOYS' AND GIRLS' MINDS ARE DIFFERENT

See *Brain Sex* by Moir and Jessel. Also helpful are *Sex on the Brain,* by Deborah Blum (New York: Penguin, 1997); *The Anatomy of Love,* by Helen Fisher; and *Human Sperm Competition,* by Robin Baker and Mark Bellis (London: Chapman and Hall, 1995). On the National Geography Bee, the source of the statistic is a New York Times story on May 31, 2000 (appearing in the Spokane *Spokesman Review*). The comment by Ruben Gur was taken from the Learning Channel series.

Eilene Green, of Canejo Valley Adult School in Thousand Oaks, California, puts out a worksheet, "Male Brain/Female Brain," for her gender trainings. She has collected Web pages, books, articles, and other material in a wonderful synthesis.

A special note of thanks is due to Terry Trueman and Stacie Wachholz for their diligence in helping with the tables. Thanks also to the Jossey-Bass development team.

WHY THE BRAINS ARE DIFFERENT

On women experimenting recently with testosterone, see the Harvard Men's Health Watch (Oct. 2000) and "Why Do Men Act the Way They Do?" by Andrew Sullivan, *Reader's Digest,* September 2000. On CAH studies, the source is Sheri Berenbaum, appearing in *Brain Sex.*

2   HOW BRAIN-BASED DIFFERENCES AFFECT BOYS AND GIRLS

AREAS OF LEARNING-STYLE DIFFERENCE

Paul Fochtman, formerly a Michigan school principal and now the headmaster of the American School in New Delhi, was instrumental in getting the Australian research to me. I thank him. The University of Newcastle's Family Action Centre has put out two manuals, *Improving Boys' Education* and *Improving Girls' Education,* that are very helpful. Thanks also are due Mike Norton, of the Traverse City, Michigan, *Record-Eagle,* for his articles on Paul and on the subject. Studies in Michigan on the Cadillac, Petoskey, and Traverse City School Districts were very telling.

LEARNING DIFFERENCES AND THE INTELLIGENCES

If you have not been exposed to the work of Howard Gardner and Thomas Armstrong, I hope you will discover it now. It is immensely valuable.

The Sylwester quotes are from *A Celebration of Neurons.*

THE STATE OF BOYS AND GIRLS IN OUR SCHOOLS

Readers interested in checking up on the state of boys and girls in school might enjoy checking the U.S. Department of Education's National Education Assessments.

The most recent, comprehensive sources for information on the state of boys and girls in our schools are *The War Against Boys,* by Christina Hoff Sommers (New York: Simon and Schuster, 2000), and Judith Kleinfeld's study, *The Myth That Schools Shortchange Girls* (she can be reached at the College of Liberal Arts, University of Alaska, Fairbanks). The Horatio Alger Institute has also done important recent studies, as has the Commonwealth Fund, whose *The Health of Adolescent Girls and the Health of Adolescent Boys* are seminal. Previous to these studies are two works we have already referred to: *How Schools Shortchange Girls,* by the American Association of University Women; and *Failing at Fairness: How Our Schools Cheat Girls,* by David and Myra Sadker (New York: Touchstone, 1994).

There is no doubt that from a statistical point of view boys are failed by schools more than girls; thus political advocacy for girls has suffered recent attacks. But our research constantly indicates that in the classroom itself girls are shortchanged as well, and no vigilance for the majority of the shortchanged (boys) should erase vigilance for the minority. Once statistics are moved aside, children of both genders are left yearning for our collective help.

PART TWO

CREATING THE ULTIMATE CLASSROOM
FOR BOTH BOYS AND GIRLS

3 ## THE ULTIMATE PRESCHOOL AND
KINDERGARTEN CLASSROOM

NUTRITION AND LEARNING

Robert Arnot, *The Biology of Success* (New York: Little Brown, 2000). Michael Schmidt, *Smart Fats: How Dietary Fats and Oils Affect Mental, Physical, and Emotional Intelligence* (Berkeley, Calif.: North Atlantic Books, 1997).

DEALING WITH AGGRESSIVE BEHAVIOR

Aggression Nurturance

Michael Gurian, *The Good Son: Shaping the Moral Development of Boys and Young Men* (New York: Tarcher/Putnam, 1999) provides a cradle-to-college developmental plan. It deals with such issues as discipline, bonding, and aggression at length.

DISCIPLINE TECHNIQUES

The work of Thomas Boyce was reported in *USA Today* by Marilyn Elias ("Bossier Preschool Kids Are Healthier," Mar. 8, 2000).

USE OF PSYCHOTROPIC MEDICATIONS

The work of Ken Jacobson and Paul McHugh was reported by George Will in the *Washington Post* ("Drugs Not Good for What Ails Them"), Dec. 7, 1999.

Before teachers or parents begin to discuss use of a medication, we hope they will consult the many available resources. Two that are easy to read and helpful are Lawrence Diller's *Running on Ritalin* (New York: Bantam, 1999) and David Stein's *Ritalin Is Not the Answer: A Drug-Free, Practical Program for Children Diagnosed with ADD or ADHD* (San Francisco: Jossey-Bass, 1999).

4 THE ULTIMATE ELEMENTARY SCHOOL CLASSROOM

STRUCTURAL INNOVATIONS

Class Size, Number of Teachers, and Teacher-to-Student Ratio
Deborah Meier, "Smaller Schools: More Smart Adults," *Los Angeles Times,* Aug. 1999.

Using Group Dynamics and Group Work as a Basis of Pedagogy
Anthony Alvarado, "Professional Development *Is* the Job," *American Educator,* Winter 1998.

Use of Computers and Other Media in Elementary School
Jane Healy, *Failure to Connect: How Computers Affect Our Children's Minds, and What We Can Do About It* (New York: Simon & Schuster, 1999); Gloria De Gaetano and Kathleen Bander, *Screen Smarts: A Family Guide to Media Literacy* (Boston: Houghton Mifflin, 1996).

The Outdoor Classroom
Statistics reported by Andy James, Spokane *Spokesman Review,* Mar, 5, 2000.

BONDING AND ATTACHMENT IN ELEMENTARY LEARNING

The Role of the Mentor
Daniel Goleman, *Emotional Intelligence* (New York: Bantam, 1995).

HOW TO PROVIDE DISCIPLINE IN THE ELEMENTARY CLASSROOM

Discipline Techniques to *Prevent* Undisciplined Behavior
Balboa Elementary School, in Spokane, Washington, is led by Principal Lou Haymond.

DEALING WITH CRUELTY, HAZING, AND VIOLENCE

Jesus Villahermosa is a gang expert and Pierce County, Washington, sheriff's deputy. The profile is adapted from "Facing the Threat," *Spokesman Review,* June 18, 1998.

SuEllen Fried and Mara Weyforth, *On Target to Stop Bullying,* Stop Violence Coalition, 301 E. Armour, Suite 440, Kansas City, MO 64111 (816-753-8002).

John Caputo is professor of communication arts at Gonzaga University in Spokane. He presented these statistics at the Town Forum and Workshop for the Northwest Alliance for Responsible Media in Spokane.

INNOVATIONS FOR ACADEMIC EXCELLENCE

Innovations for Teaching Language Arts, Especially Reading and Writing
Tony and Ula Manzo, *Teaching Children to Be Literate* (Orlando: Harcourt Brace, 1995).

Standardized Testing

Linda McNeil, "Creating New Inequalities," *American Educator,* June 2000.

SPECIAL EDUCATION, LEARNING DISABILITIES, AND BEHAVIORAL DISABILITIES

Fast ForWord is featured in "Educators Need to Know About the Human Brain," by Ron Brandt, *Phi Delta Kappan,* Nov. 1999.

5 THE ULTIMATE MIDDLE SCHOOL CLASSROOM

STRUCTURAL INNOVATIONS

Separate-Sex Education

Principal Michaelson appears in a story in *Education Week,* Nov. 25, 1998, by Kerry White, titled "Separate Worlds."

Rites of Passage

Rite of Passage, 1561 Highway 395, Minden, NV 89423, info@riteofpassage.com.

Another fine program is Youth Leadership Development Intensive, designed from a business leadership model, by John Scherer, Mark Yodel, and their colleagues at John Scherer and Associates in Spokane, Washington. It presents an ongoing rite of passage over a series of evenings and weekends.

In *A Fine Young Man,* my book on adolescent boys (see Additional Resources), I featured ICA Journeys, a national organization that offers rites of passage for youths of all ages. They can be reached on the Web at www.icajourneys.org.

Use of Uniforms

"New York Pupils to Need Uniforms Through Grade 6," by Randal C. Archibold, *New York Times,* Mar. 19, 1998.

Classroom Size and Other Innovations

Information regarding Menlo Park was provided by Lenora Yuen, a school psychologist in Portola Valley, California.

BONDING AND ATTACHMENT

"Sixth Grader Holds Class at Gunpoint," Associated Press, Mar. 24, 2000.

Handling Students' Emotional Stresses

REACT, Nov. 1–7, 1999.

Community Collaboration

"Student Leaders Say Parents Vital to Success," Hearst Newspapers, Jan. 28, 1999.

Barbara Ewing, the Antioch schools, and the African American Academic Achievement Committee are featured in "After-School Plan Is a Success for Antioch," by Elizabeth Bell, *San Francisco Chronicle,* Sept. 27, 1999.

BROTHERS is featured in Neal Peirce's *Washington Post* column, June 2000.

Marian Howard's work is featured in "Changing Bodies, Changing Relationships," by Lynn Slaughter, *Family Magazine,* Oct. 1999.

INNOVATIONS FOR TEACHING LANGUAGE ARTS AND MATH AND SCIENCE

Innovations for Teaching Language Arts

Carol Jago, "Don't Discard the Classics," *American Educator,* Winter 1999–2000. Her book is *With Rigor for All: Teaching the Classics to Contemporary Students* (Portland, Me.: Calendar Islands, 2000).

Innovations for Teaching Math and Science

The Department of Education offers the National Education Assessment for public review. See also Christina Hoff Sommers's *Who Stole Feminism?* (Carmichael, Calif.: Touchstone, 1995).

"Gore Goes Back to School," Sandra Sobieraj, Associated Press, Mar. 25, 2000.

"Beyond the Gender Myths," Margo Hornblower, *Time,* Oct. 19, 1998.

6 THE ULTIMATE HIGH SCHOOL CLASSROOM

BONDING AND ATTACHMENT

Chris Peck writes a Sunday column for the Spokane *Spokesman Review.* See Mar. 5, 2000.

Communication and Conflict Resolution

Frank DiLallo can be reached through Catholic Youth and School Services at 419-244-6711, or Toledopi@Impresso.com.

The Art of Mentoring

Contact John Rhymes at Flint Elementary School, in Flint, Michigan.

Leonard Pitts Jr., "A Painter of Flowers, of All Things," Knight-Ridder, Jan. 27, 2000.

H. Stephen Glenn, Ph.D., and Michael L. Brock, M.A., *7 Strategies for Developing Capable Students.* Rocklin, Calif.: Prima, 1998.

Peer Leadership, Not Peer Pressure

Adrian Raine's studies are featured in *Newsweek,* Mar. 13, 2000.

The Medical Foundation can be reached in Boston, at 617-451-0049, or ljwallace@tmfnet.org (Laurie Jo Wallace).

STRUCTURAL INNOVATIONS

Class and School Size

Christopher Burns, "Students Will Wait and See If French Reforms Work," Associated Press, Oct. 22, 1998.

Uniforms

Principal Reynolds was quoted in "High School Fashion Wears Thin," Associated Press, Nov. 17, 1999.

Pius X High School is featured in the *Lincoln Journal Star,* in an article by Shane Anthony titled "Pius Dress Code," Sept. 1999.

Time and Time-of-Day Innovations

"Sleep Researchers Look to Change School Hours," *Washington Post,* Sept. 22, 1999.

The Innovations Students Are Asking for

The Mead Summit is featured in an article by teen reporter Jake Farley, of Mead High School, in the Spokane *Spokesman Review,* Nov. 1, 1999.

Counterinnovations

Barbara Carton, "When Girls Wrestle Boys," *Wall Street Journal,* Jan. 19, 1999.

Rites of Passage

Psychotherapist Steven Johnson is director of the Men's Center of Los Angeles and a consultant for the Millennium Oaks rite of passage. He can be reached at 818-348-9302.

Improving Sex Education

The report "Involving Males in Preventing Teen Pregnancy" is filled with information about programs around the country, including *Hablando Claro.* See *Teen Pregnancy Prevention,* July 1998.

Freya Sonenstein, *Involving Males in Preventing Teen Pregnancy: A Guide for Program Planners.* Urban Institute (see www.urban.org/family/invmales.html).

Gender Education

Michael Gurian, *Understanding Guys,* and *From Boys to Men* (Los Angeles: Price Stern Sloan, 1999).

Ric Stuecker and Suze Rutherford can be reached through National Training Associates at www.nta-yes.com, or in Sebastopol, California, at 800-624-1120. Mary Pipher's work is *Reviving Ophelia: Saving the Selves of Adolescent Girls* (New York: Ballantine, 1995).

Principal Callahan is quoted in *REACT* magazine, Sept. 20–26, 1999.

INNOVATIONS TO IMPROVE ACADEMIC LEARNING

Teaching Mathematics, Science, and Technology

Jeri Buckley tells her story in *Teaching Tolerance* magazine, Spring 2000.

Teaching Reading and Literacy

Judy Greene's story is taken from a listserv operated by the University of Missouri-Kansas City's Department of Education. We thank her for sharing her story with colleagues.

On Language!, see Jane Fell Greene, *American Educator,* Summer 1998.

Standardized Testing

Statistics are taken from the 1996 UCLA study of thirty thousand college freshman, coauthored by Linda Sax. The study and associated details appeared in "Grade Inflation Rampant," by Erin Van Bronkhorst, Associated Press, Mar. 29, 1998.

Expert quotes in this section come from "Where the Boys Are," by Brendan I. Koerner, *U.S. News & World Report,* Feb. 8, 1999.

Passage cited in the Education of the Handicapped Act is from 23 Fed. Reg. 42478, 1977.

ADDITIONAL RESOURCES

Abbott, K. "Abstinence Program Stirs Controversy." *Rocky Mountain News,* July 28, 1997.

Able-Peterson, T. *Working the Streets: Issues Surrounding Teen Male Prostitution.* New York: Able-Peterson, 1991.

Able-Peterson, T., and Bucy, J. *The Streetwork Outreach Training Manual.* Washington, D.C.: CASSP Technical Assistance Center, 1993.

Active Parenting. *Successful Parenting: Self Esteem Is the Key.* Marietta, Ga.: Active Parenting.

Active Parenting. *Successful Parenting: The Single Parent Family. A Challenge for Parents.* Georgia: Active Parenting.

Alexanderson, K. "An Assessment Protocol for Gender Analysis of Medical Literature." *Women and Health,* 1999, *29*(2), 81–98.

"The American Girls Premiere Review." *School Library Journal,* 1998, *44*(5), 83.

Anderson, J. E., and others. "HIV Risk Behavior, Street Outreach, and Condom Use in Eight High-Risk Populations." *AIDS Education and Prevention,* 1996, *8*(3), 191–204.

Annotated Bibliography: Outreach Services for Homeless Mentally Ill Persons. Delmar, N.Y.: National Resource Center on Homelessness and Mental Illness, 1990.

Anti-Defamation League. www.adl.org.

Arnold, W., and Barnes, F. "Peer Education Program Reaches High Risk Adolescents with AIDS Information and Prevention." Paper presented at the Fifth International Conference on AIDS, June 1989, *5,* 702 (abstract no. TDO 26).

Aronson, J., and others. "When White Men Can't Do Math: Necessary and Sufficient Factors in Stereotype Threat." *Journal of Experimental Social Psychology,* 1999, *35*(1), 29–46.

Bagilhole, B. "The 'Gender Dimension' of Both the 'Narrow' and 'Broad' Curriculum in UK Higher Education: Do Women Lose Out in Both?" *Gender and Education,* 1998, *10*(4), 445–458.

Baru, E. "The American Girls Premiere Review." *Multimedia Schools,* 1998, *5*(5), 63–64.

Begley, S. "Your Child's Brain." *Newsweek,* Feb. 19, 1996, pp. 55–58.

Bennett, W., Finn, C., and Cribb, J. *The Educated Child: A Parent's Guide from Preschool Through Eighth Grade.* New York: Free Press, 1999.

Benning, V., and Nakashima, E. "Allen Urges Lifting Sex Ed Requirement." *Washington Post,* May 31, 1997.

Berger, A. "What Stress Can Mean to Teen-Age Girls." *New York Times,* May 25, 1999, sec. F, p. 8.

Billie, K. "What I Learned in Gym." *Psychology Today,* 1998, *31*(6), 8.

Bills, S. "Waiting on Abstinence." *Macon Telegraph,* July 17, 1997.

Blythe, T. *The Teaching for Understanding Guide.* San Francisco: Jossey-Bass, 1999.

Bodine, R., and Crawford, D. *The Handbook of Conflict Resolution Education.* San Francisco: Jossey-Bass and National Institute for Dispute Resolution, 1998.

Boellstorff, L. "Nebraska Revises Sex-Education: Application for Federal Funds Addresses Concerns of 'Abstinence-Only.' " *Midlands News,* July 20, 1997, sec. B.

Botvin, G. J. *Life Skills Training: Promoting Health and Personal Development.* New Jersey: Princeton Health Press, 1979–1996.

"Boy Bullies Are Popular; Girls Aren't." *USA Today,* Aug. 1998, pp. 5–6.

Brown, R., and Fletcher, R. (eds.). *Boys in Schools.* Sidney, Australia: Finch, 1995.

Budge, D. "Girls May Not Be So Superior." *London Times Educational Supplement,* Sept. 18, 1998, p. 2.

Caron, A. *Don't Stop Loving Me: A Reassuring Guide for Mothers of Adolescent Daughters.* New York: HarperPerennial, 1991.

Caron, A. *Strong Mothers, Strong Sons.* New York: Harper, 1994.

Catalfo, P. *Raising Spiritual Children in a Material World.* New York: Berkley, 1997.

Cooper, K. J. "Worldwide Effort Focuses on Education 'The Girl Child'—Poverty-Fighting Method Also Helps Population Control." *Seattle Times,* Feb. 21, 1999, sec. A, p. 17.

Creighton, A., with Kivel, P. *Helping Teens Stop Violence.* Emeryville, Calif.: Hunter House, 1992.

Damon, W. *Greater Expectations: Overcoming the Culture of Indulgence in Our Homes and Schools.* New York: Free Press, 1995.

Damon, W. *The Moral Child: Nurturing Children's Natural Moral Growth.* New York: Free Press, 1988.

Darling-Hammond, L. *The Right to Learn: A Blueprint for Creating Schools That Work.* San Francisco: Jossey-Bass, 1997.

Delamont, S. "Educating the Other: Gender, Power, and Schooling." *British Educational Research Journal,* 1998, *24*(5), 35.

Diamond, J. *Guns, Germs, and Steel: The Fate of Human Societies.* New York: Norton, 1997.

Diamond, J. *The Third Chimpanzee: The Evolution and Future of the Human Animal.* New York: HarperPerennial, 1992.

Dunshea, G. "Beginning Principals and the Issue of Gender in Rural and Regional Areas." *Asia-Pacific Journal of Teacher Education,* 1998, *26*(3), 203–215.

Elias, M. "Sports Means Sex for Boys, Not Girls." *USA Today,* Aug. 26, 1998, sec. Life, p. 01D.

Emerson, J. D. "Abstinence-Only Approach Ineffective in Reducing Teen Pregnancy." *South Carolina State,* Aug. 12, 1997.

Epstein, D. "Sex and Sensibilities." *London Times Educational Supplement,* July 2, 1999, Issue 4331, p. 17.

Epstein, D. "Where the Kids Are: Power Relations in Classrooms and Playgrounds." *British Educational Research Journal,* 1999, *25*(3), 401–404.

Eyre, L., and Eyre, R. *Teaching Your Children Responsibility.* New York: Simon & Schuster, 1984.

Eyre, L., and Eyre, R. *Teaching Your Children Values.* New York: Simon & Schuster, 1993.

Family Life Council of Greater Greensboro. *Wise Guys: Male Responsibility Curriculum.* Greensboro, N.C.: Family Life Council of Greater Greensboro, 1996.

Federal Bureau of Investigation Hate Crimes Report. www.fbi.gov/ucr/hatecm.htm.

Foster, M. "Race, Class, and Gender in Educational Research: Surveying the Political Terrain." *Educational Policy,* 1999, *13*(1/2), 77–85.

Francis, L. "Attitude Toward Science Among Secondary School Pupils in Northern Ireland: Relationship with Sex, Age, and Religion." *Research in Science and Technological Education,* 1999, *17*(1), 67–74.

Gatenby, B. "Exploring Gender, Management Education, and Careers: Speaking in the Silences." *Gender and Education,* 1999, *11*(3), 381–294.

Gates, A. "In Praise of the Most Unpopular Girl at Lawndale." *New York Times* (late ed., East Coast), May 16, 1999, sec. 2, p. 21.

Gazzaniga, M. "Groundbreaking Work That Began More Than a Quarter of a Century Ago Has Led to Ongoing Insights About Brain Organization and Consciousness." *Scientific American,* July 1998, pp. 51–55.

Glasser, W. "A New Look at School Failure and School Success." *Phi Delta Kappan,* 1997, *78*(8), 596–602.

Gooden, A. *Computers in the Classroom.* San Francisco: Jossey-Bass and Apple Developer Press, 1996.

Goodman, P. *Compulsory Miseducation and the Community of Scholars.* New York: Vintage, 1962.

Gurian, M. *A Fine Young Man: What Parents, Mentors, and Educators Can Do to Raise Adolescent Boys into Exceptional Men.* New York: Tarcher/Putnam, 1998.

Gurian, M. *What Stories Does My Son Need? A Guide to Books and Movies That Build Character in Boys.* New York: Tarcher/Putnam, 2000.

Gurian, M. *The Wonder of Boys: What Parents, Mentors, and Educators Can Do to Raise Boys into Exceptional Men.* New York: Tarcher/Putnam, 1996.

Gurian, M. *The Wonder of Girls: A New Approach to Raising Girls.* New York: Pocket, forthcoming.

Haase, D. "New Push for Abstinence Coming out of Washington." *Star News Online,* July 25, 1997, www.starnews.com.

Hall, S. S. "Bully in the Mirror." *New York Times Magazine,* Aug. 22, 1999, pp. 31–35.

Hammick, M. "Undergraduate Research Supervision: A Gender Analysis." *Studies in Higher Education,* 1998, *23*(3), 335–347.

Hancock, L. "Why Do Schools Flunk Biology?" *Newsweek,* Feb. 19, 1996, pp. 58–62.

Hanson, S. Letter. *Florida Times Union,* July 29, 1997.

Hayes, E., and Flannery, D. *Women as Learners: The Significance of Gender in Adult Learning.* San Francisco: Jossey-Bass, 2000.

Healy, J. "Computers, Language Development, and Literacy at the Preschool Level." *NAMTA Bulletin,* March 1999, pp. 1–5.

Heckman, J., Smith, J., and Taber, C. "Accounting for Dropouts in Evaluations of Social Programs." *Review of Economics and Statistics,* 1998, *80*(1), 1–14.

Henig, R. "Males Need to Be Taught to Treat Females with Dignity." *USA Today* (final ed.), Jan. 2, 1998, sec. News, p. 14A.

Henig, R. M. "New Fat-Acceptance Trend Troubling, Too." *USA Today,* Oct. 2, 1998, sec. News, p. 15A.

Hernandez, A. *Peace in the Streets: Breaking the Cycle of Gang Violence.* Washington, D.C.: Child Welfare League, 1998.

Heywood, D. M. "Fewer Teen Pregnancies Is News to Applaud, Mother's Day Details Not for Last Minutes." *Vancouver Columbian,* Apr. 30, 1999, sec. Editorial, A10.

Hilland, C. "Here for the Glamour." *London Times Educational Supplement,* Jan. 15, 1999, Issue 4307, p. SS31.

Hinds, D. "Don't Be Trapped by Gender Stereotypes." *London Times Educational Supplement,* Nov. 13, 1998, Issue 4298, pp. SS8A-SS9A.

Horan, P. F. Letter. *News and Observer,* Oct. 6, 1997.

Hunt, J. "Program Teaches Leadership Skills to Schoolgirls." *Seattle Post–Intelligencer,* Nov. 19, 1999, sec. C, p. 11.

Huppert, J. "Learning Microbiology with Computer Simulations: Students' Academic Achievement by Method and Gender." *Research in Science and Technological Education,* 1998, *16*(2), 231–245.

Improving America's Schools. "Creating a Better School Environment: Tying the Pieces Together." Education Reform Institute, 1998. [www.ncbe.gwu.edu/iasconferences/archives/1998/institutes/environment].

Institute on Race and Poverty: Center on Speech, Equity, and Harm. www.igc.org/an/niot/.

Ith, I. "Rant and Rave." *Seattle Times* (final ed.), Aug. 16, 1998, sec. L, p. 5.

Jameson, T. "$50 Million Teen Abstinence Program Set to Start, But Is It Doomed Already?" *Inquirer Washington Bureau,* sec. Lifestyle, 20 July 1997.

Keys, S., Bemak, F., and Lockhart, E. "Transforming School Counseling to Serve the Mental Health Needs of At-Risk Youth." *Journal of Counseling and Development,* 1998, p. 380.

Kientzler, A. "Fifth- and Seventh-Grade Girls' Decisions About Participation in Physical Activity." *Elementary School Journal,* 1999, *99*(5), 391–414.

Kipnis, A. *Angry Young Men: How Parents, Teachers, and Counselors Can Help 'Bad Boys' Become Good Men.* San Francisco: Jossey-Bass, 1999.

Kirby, D. "Reflections on Two Decades of Research on Teen Sexual Behavior and Pregnancy." *Journal of School Health,* 1999, *69*(3), 89–94.

Kohn, A. *What to Look for in a Classroom.* San Francisco: Jossey-Bass, 1998.

Ladson-Billings, G. *The Dreamkeepers: Successful Teachers of African American Children.* San Francisco: Jossey-Bass, 1994.

Learning First Alliance. "Every Child Reading: A Research Base." *American Educator,* Spring/Summer 1998, pp. 54–63.

LeBlanc, A. N. "The Outsiders." *New York Times Magazine,* Aug. 22, 1999, pp. 36–41.

Leopold, E. "Forum Backs Revised Population Policy—New Plan Shifts to Improving the Lot of Women Worldwide." *Seattle Times,* July 2, 1999, sec. A, p. 17.

"Letter." *Wall Street Journal,* Dec. 28, 1998, p. A15.

Lillard, P. P. *Montessori Today: A Comprehensive Approach to Education from Birth to Adulthood.* New York: Schocken, 1996.

Lopez, D., Little, T., Oettingen, G., and Baltes, P. "Self-Regulation and School Performance: Is There Optimal Level of Action—Control?" *Journal of Experimental Child Psychology,* 1998, *70*(1), 54–74.

Manthey, J. "Boys and Girls Are Different! Creating Gender-Friendly Schools." Kid Culture in the Schools Workshop, Petaluma, Calif., 1998.

Mather, M. A. "Gender Stats Making News." *Technology and Learning,* 1999, *19*(5), 59.

Maxym, C., and York, L. B. *Teens in Turmoil: A Path to Change for Parents, Adolescents, and Their Families.* New York: Viking, 2000.

McDonald, K. "Studies of Women's Health Produce a Wealth of Knowledge on the Biology of Gender Differences." *Chronicle of Higher Education*, 1999, *45*(42), A19–A22.

Meckler, L. "New Study Takes Closer Look at Sex and the Teenage Girls." *Associated Press*, Aug. 13, 1999, sec. A, p. 3.

Mercer, N., Wegerif, R., and Dawes, L. "Children's Talk and the Development of Reasoning in the Classroom." *British Educational Research Journal*, 1999, *25*(1), 95–111.

Montgomery County, Maryland, Committee on Hate Violence. Members.aol.com/ OneMC4All/ndx.html.

Murphy, S. *The Cheers and the Tears: A Healthy Alternative to the Dark Side of Youth Sports Today.* San Francisco: Jossey-Bass, 1999.

NAMTA Journal (North American Montessori Teachers' Association), *21*(2), *23*(1), *24*(1), and *24*(3).

Nash, J. M. "Fertile Minds." *Time*, Feb. 3, 1997, pp. 49–56.

Nash, J. M. "Is Sex Really Necessary?" *Time*, Jan. 20, 1992, pp. 47–51.

Newman, Rev. Dr. S. A., Jr. Letter. *Albany Times-Union*, July 23, 1997.

Noble, H. "Steroid Use by Teen-Age Girls Is Rising." *New York Times*, June 1, 1999, sec. F, p. 8.

O'Connor, C. "Race, Class, and Gender in America: Narratives of Opportunity Among Low-Income African American Youths." *Sociology of Education*, 1999, *72*(3), 137–157.

Office of Elementary and Secondary Education, Safe and Drug-Free Schools Program. www.ed.gov/offices/OESE/SDFS.

Paechter, C. "The Gender Politics of Educational Change." *British Educational Research Journal*, 1998, *24*(4), 485–486.

Painter, K. "Talk to Your Kids Early and Often About Facts of Sex." *USA Today* (final ed.), July 19, 1999, sec. Life, p. 08D.

Parent Institute. "25 Ways Parents Can Build Children's Self-Esteem." Fairfax Station, Va.: Parent Institute, 1991.

Parent Institute. "25 Ways Parents Can Help Children Learn and Help Them Do Better in School." Fairfax Station, Va.: Parent Institute, 1991.

Parent Institute. "25 Ways Parents Can Motivate Children and Help Them Do Better in School." Fairfax Station, Va.: Parent Institute, 1991.

Parent Institute. "25 Ways Parents Can Talk and Listen to Children and Help Them Do Better in School." Fairfax Station, Va.: Parent Institute, 1991.

Parent Institute. "Skills for School Success: Expressing Ideas in Speech and Writing." Fairfax Station, Va.: Parent Institute, 1993.

Parent Institute. "Skills for School Success: Reading for Meaning." Fairfax Station, Va.: Parent Institute, 1993.

Parent Institute. "QuickTips: How to Work With Your Child's Teacher." Fairfax Station, Va.: Parent Institute, 1995.

Parent Institute. "QuickTips: Sharing the Family Work Load Teaches Responsibility." Fairfax Station, Va.: Parent Institute, 1995.

Parent Institute. "QuickTips: Ways Busy Parents Can Help Kids Succeed in School." Fairfax Station, Va.: Parent Institute, 1995.

Parent Institute. "QuickTips: Helping Your Child Avoid Problems with Diets and Eating Disorders." Fairfax Station, Va.: Parent Institute, 1996.

Parent Institute. "QuickTips: Is Your Child Under Too Much Pressure?" Fairfax Station, Va.: Parent Institute, 1996.

Parent Institute. QuickTips: Seven Habits of Highly Responsible Students." Fairfax Station, Va.: Parent Institute, 1996.

Parent Institute. "QuickTips: Ten Ways to Help Your Child Deal with Peer Pressure." Fairfax Station, Va.: Parent Institute: Parent Institute, 1996.

Penrose, J. "Using Personal Research to Teach the Significance of Socially Constructed Categories." *Journal of Geography in Higher Education,* 1999, *23*(2), 227–239.

Peterson, K. S. "Physical Battle of the Sexes Starts Young." *USA Today,* July 26, 1999, sec. Life, p. 01D.

Peterson, K. "Teen Girls' Depression Hits Hardest away from Home." *USA Today,* June 24, 1999, sec. Life, p. 01D.

Peterson, K. "Teens Put Parental Influence First, But Some See It Fade." *USA Today,* Aug. 24, 1998, sec. Life, p. 04D.

Proweller, A. "Shifting Identities in Private Education: Reconstructing Race at/in the Cultural Center." *Teachers College Record,* 1999, *100*(4), 776–808.

Quillin, M. "Franklin Schools Slice Sex-Ed Chapters out of Health Books." *News and Observer,* Sept. 25, 1997.

Reed, L. "Troubling Boys and Disturbing Discourses on Masculinity and Schooling: A Feminist Exploration of Current Debates and Interventions Concerning Boys in School." *Gender and Education,* 1999, *11*(1), 93–110.

Rimm, S. *See Jane Win: The Rimm Report on How 1,000 Girls Became Successful Women.* New York: Three Rivers, 1999.

Roitman, J. Letter. *Knoxville News-Sentinel,* July 29, 1997.

Rosenthal, C. S. "One Experience Is Worth a Thousand Words: Engaging Under-graduates in Field Research on Gender." *PS, Political Science and Politics,* 1999, *32*(1), 63–68.

Ryan, K., and Bohlin, K. *Building Character in Schools.* San Francisco: Jossey-Bass, 1999.

Schwabsky, B. "Age of Experiments: Postcards from a Time of 'You Had to Be There.'" *New York Times,* Mar. 21, 1999, sec. 14NJ, p. 10.

She, H.-C. "Gender and Grade Level Differences in Taiwan Students' Stereotypes of Science and Scientists." *Research in Science and Technological Education,* 1998, *16*(2), 125–135.

Stoddard, M. "Teens Doubt Abstinence-Only Sex Education Program Will Succeed." *Lincoln Journal Star,* Aug. 25, 1997.

Stuecker, R., with Rutherford, S. *Reviving the Wonder: 75 Activities That Touch the Inner Spirit of outh.* Champaign, Ill.: Research Press, 2001.

Sukthankar, N. "Cultural Factors in Mathematics Education Contributing to the Shortage of Women Professionals in Papua New Guinea." *Educational Review,* 1999, *51*(2), 173–181.

Teaching Tolerance. www.splcenter.org/teachingtolerance.html.

U.S. Department of Justice. "Hateful Acts Hurt Kids." www.usdoj.gov/kidspage.

U.S. Department of Education, Office for Civil Rights. www.ed.gov/offices/OCR.

Upchurch, M. "Child's Play—Nicholson Baker Looks at the World Through the Eyes of a 9-Year-Old Girl." *Seattle Times* (final ed.), May 24, 1998, sec. M, p. 2.

Vincent, S. *The Educational Register.* Boston: Vincent/Curtis, 1997.

Waltman, M., and Burison, B. "Explaining Bias in Teacher Ratings of Behavior Alteration Techniques: An Experimental Test of the Heuristic Processing Account." *Communication Education,* 1998, *46*(2), 75–94.

Washington State Safe Schools Coalition. Members.tripod.com/~claytoly/ssp_home.

Weiner, G. "Educational Research Undone." *Gender and Education,* 1998, *10*(4), 461–462.

Weinman, Janice. "Gender Equity in Cyberspace." *Educational Leadership,* 1999, *56*(5), 44–49.

West, J. "(Not) Talking About Sex: Youth, Identity, and Sexuality." *Sociological Review,* 1999, *47*(3), 525–547.

Wetzstein, C. "Jane Fonda, Condom Manufacturer Team Up Against Abstinence-Only Ed." *Washington Times,* sec. Culture, Oct. 8, 1997.

"What You Can Do to Get Girls Involved in Technology." *Technology and Learning,* 1998, *19*(3), 20.

Whitehead, A. N. *The Aims of Education.* New York: New American Library, 1929.

Whitehouse, D. "Scientists Have Literally Seen the World Through Cat's Eyes." (Special News Bulletin). *BBC News Online,* Oct 8, 1999.

Whitmire, R. "Study Says Girls Involved in School Are Less Likely to Become Pregnant." *Seattle Times,* Aug. 5, 1998, sec. A, p. 9.

Wiske, M. S. (ed.). *Teaching for Understanding: Linking Research with Practice.* San Francisco: Jossey-Bass, 1998.

Wyon, D., Abrahamsson, L., Jartelius, M., and Fletcher, R. "An Experimental Study of the Effects of Energy Intake at Breakfast on the Test Performance of 10-Year-Old Children in School." *International Journal of Food Sciences and Nutrition,* 1997, *48*(1), 5–12.

THE MICHAEL GURIAN INSTITUTE

If you would like to bring the information and innovations in this book to your community, please contact us for more information.

The Michael Gurian Institute provides trainings internationally in how boys and girls learn differently. The Gurian Institute staff is committed not only to training teachers and parents but also to making participant school districts, corporations, and agencies self-sufficient in their ability to train their own staff in ongoing ways.

For information, visit our website: www.gurianinstitute.com.

THE AUTHORS

Michael Gurian is an educator, family therapist, and author of three national bestsellers, including *The Wonder of Boys,* which has been published in ten foreign languages. *Boys and Girls Learn Differently!* is his fourteenth book. He is cofounder, with Patricia Henley, of the Michael Gurian Institute at the University of Missouri-Kansas City, where, along with the institute staff, teachers are trained in brain-based and gender innovations. He is an international lecturer whose work has been featured in the *New York Times, Wall Street Journal, USA Today, Washington Post, Time, Newsweek,* and other major print media, as well as on the "Today Show," "Good Morning America," PBS, and CNN. He lives in Spokane, Washington, with his wife, Gail, a family therapist, and their two children, Gabrielle and Davita. He can be reached at www.michael-gurian.com.

Patricia Henley, as assistant research professor at the University of Missouri-Kansas City, is the former director of the Michael Gurian Institute and presently director of the University Academy. She is also former director of the University of Missouri-Kansas City School of Education's Missouri Center for Safe Schools. She previously served as a teacher, principal, assistant superintendent, deputy superintendent, and superintendent of schools. During her tenure as a principal, she was National Distinguished Principal and a Reader's Digest National Hero in Education; her school received the National Blue Ribbon Award and PTA Advocacy in Education Award. She has appeared on numerous media, including "Good Morning America." She and her husband, Bob, live in Independence, Missouri. They have three grown children, Laura, Kevin, and Bob Jr.

Terry Trueman has been an educator, counselor, and writer for more than thirty years. He has taught in Australia, Central America, and the United States. *Boys and Girls Learn Differently!* is his fourth book. His first novel, *Stuck in Neutral,* has won numerous awards. He lives with his wife, Patti, a veteran teacher, and their son, Jesse, a senior in high school, in Spokane, Washington.

INDEX

A

AAUW (American Association of University Women), 65, 66, 246

Abstract reasoning, 45

Academic learning (elementary age): language arts, 176–180; math/science, 180–185

Academic learning (high school): grade inflation/academic failure and, 302–304; math/science and technology, 293–297; reading and literacy, 297–301; standardized testing to assess, 301–302

Academic learning (preschool/kindergarten): language development, 110–113; math/spatials, 102–110; promoting, 100–102; special education, 113–115

Academic performance: female advantage/male disadvantage in, 56; research on gender bias in, 58–59. *See also* Learning

Accountability testing, 185–187

Acting out lessons, 192

ADD (attention deficit disorder), 56, 61, 116

ADHD (attention deficit and hyperactivity disorder), 56, 61, 89, 116, 117. *See also* Special education

Adolescence: bonding/attachment in late, 264–274; drop in self-esteem during early, 219–221; fears during late, 311–312; inadequate social skills/maturity expectations in, 224–225; individuality issues during, 277, 279; national survey on sexual activity during, 287–288; need for alpha role models, 232–233; peer humiliation during, 222–223; problems with gender type fit in, 223–224; providing gender education during, 289–292; rites of passage and, 212–214, 284–286; school time and hormonal system during, 280–281; sex/psychosocial education during, 229, 286–289. *See also* Children; Peer pressure; Ultimate middle school classroom

Aggression nurturance: described, 92–93; increasing empathy nurturance/verbalization and, 94–96

Aggression-and-withdrawal response, 32

Aggressive behavior: aggressive nurturance and, 92–96; defining elementary classroom, 172; gender differences in, 90–92; ultimate preschool/kindergarten classroom and, 90–96. *See also* Discipline techniques; School violence; Zero-tolerance policies

Alcohol/substance abuse: drug testing for, 273; gender bias in, 61

Aldrich, R., 43

Allegre, C., 275